Mike Dunn's previous book, *The Belt Boy*, was listed for both the William Hill and Cross Sports Book of the Year awards, 2016. Mike, former Head of Sport for *The Sun*, the *News of the World*, *The Independent* and the *London Evening Standard*, would like to thank his family for their help, support and patience.

I wish to dedicate this book to the American Indian Movement (AIM) and the martial art of American Kenpo. Together, they represent the beginning, and ending, of my brutal life. I fought and killed in Vietnam and Algeria, and returned to the UK an angry, disorientated alcoholic, suffering severe post-traumatic stress disorder. The military had desensitised me to death and normal emotions; miraculously, Kenpo turned me back into a human being. My background – I was born in England but raised on a Northern Cheyenne reservation – then completed the circle by teaching me how to actually be that better person.

I would like to give a special "thank you" to Senior Great Grand Master Edwin K Parker, the founder of the American Kenpo system. He saved my life – he gave me kenpo. I would also like to thank Phil Hegarty for leading me to Mr Parker; and I am eternally grateful to my wife, my soul-mate, Sheila.

— Bob Rose, AKA Grey Wolf

GREY WOLF

Written and interpreted by Mike Dunn
and based on the true story of martial
arts Grand Master Bob Rose. Some
names and events have been changed
to protect identities.

Contents

Part One

THE NORTHERN CHEYENNE

wolf [*Canis lupus*]
wʊlf/noun

1. *a wild carnivorous mammal, living and hunting in packs. In Native American Indian culture, the wolf is a spiritual pathfinder, symbolising intelligence and leadership.*

WHEN I CLOSE
MY EYES

Last night was bad, really bad, Sheila says. I was screaming and yelling, most of it incoherent, rambling – all of it anguished and tormented. Some phrases she could work out because she's heard them before: "Charlie's in the wire"; "incoming mortar". Then, an endless flow of numbers – map references, artillery and helicopter coordinates – sometimes the same ones, sometimes not.

But the worst thing about last night, she says, was the terror in my voice. It was wild and desperate; I sounded like a tortured soul. "You were shaking badly, Bob. Your legs were thrashing around like you were in a spasm or something."

Apparently, I was shivering and sweating all at once: I must have been wracked with fear. Sheila says I tumbled to the floor and – even though I was somewhere between sleep and consciousness – I tried to curl under the bed in a foetal ball, my arms tightly wrapped over my head. That would have been the mortars. I hated mortar attacks in Vietnam. I needed cover.

Sheila thinks the bombardment subsided after a while because I suddenly stood. I was awake now; I remember feeling a strange sensation of awareness – I could see my surroundings, I knew Sheila was there, and yet all my senses were functioning in another time and another place. I headed for the back door, flicking on switches so the blackness outside would be broken by the tracer-like beams of our exterior lighting. We were still in danger: the defences could have been breached. We could be surrounded. Sheila heard me mumble: "Charlie's here."

She followed softly behind and watched. Watched me dart swiftly between the areas where the exteriors lights hadn't broken the darkness. Watched me move around in a peculiar half stoop, half crouch as though my body were trying to stay as close to the ground as possible, just in case deadly pieces of shrapnel were slicing through the night air, or Charlie was unleashing his AK-47s and rocket-propelled grenades. I needed to keep my head down.

Then she watched me slowly inspect the perimeter walls, as though my life depended on their impregnability. Watched me check the fences, looking for gaps that shouldn't be there; watched my senses tense – listening acutely for the slightest out-of-place sound or movement. All the while, half stooping, half crouching.

Sheila watched this tormented solo act being played out in the grounds of our isolated bungalow on a bitterly cold December night in Cornwall, 2016. It was almost 3.30am. "The stars were beautiful, though," she told me later. "It was like the whole solar system was watching you."

Slowly I headed back; nobody had broken through. Sheila let me walk past her; my breathing was heavy, she said. Then she watched me flick the exterior lights off and return to bed. We spoke but I never heard her. I closed my eyes but I didn't sleep. I was still in another time and another place. I craved sleep but I wouldn't succumb to it. I never do: that would be too dangerous. We might come under attack again. Charlie could do that. He never went away.

"Last night was really bad," Sheila said, gently nudging me a couple of hours later. "You were at war again, Bob."

I never sleep because when I close my eyes I only see the nightmare kaleidoscope of my life. When I close my eyes, I see my friend. The one who wasn't supposed to die because we always looked out for each other, we had each other's backs. When he breathed in, I breathed out and we both knew in that moment we were alive, we'd survived another day, inseparable and impregnable. Then I see his slaughtered body, the mossy grass surrounding him still flattened from the weight of the helicopter rising to take me to safety. I must swap places with him. That was our unspoken pact.

When I close my eyes, I imagine the faces of the people who died that I never saw. The ones on the other end of a mortar attack, or napalm, or violent sweeping blasts of gunfire shot blindly into Vietnam trees because I knew there was someone out there waiting to kill me behind all the undergrowth. It's easier to kill people when you don't have to look them in the face.

When I close my eyes, I hear the screams, the tortured noises of war, the sounds that echo the atrocities. Sometimes seeing doesn't always do it; sometimes you need to hear what death sounds like, particularly when it's messy and slow and a man is trying to stop the inside of his stomach from spilling out and you're trying to inject morphine and yet he screams even more when the needle goes in. Why would an injection hurt a man whose innards are already pouring out of his body? Isn't he already in enough pain? That's when the sound of death is at its loudest.

When I close my eyes, I think about the people I have killed. There were so many. The Algerian rebel was my first. Does someone still mourn his death as much as I mourn my friend's? I'm bothered about them, yes, I'm certain they bother me – yet I know I would kill them again if I had to. At the time, killing them didn't bother me at all. That not-being-bothered bit bothers me a lot now.

When I close my eyes, I realise there is no morality in war, in killing or being killed. Am I fighting for the goodies or the baddies? Is it war crime or is it bravery? It all depends on whose side you're on, doesn't it? There's only survival, and who gets to live and who doesn't. The Blue understands this. Even when the killing stops and you're the one who gets to carry on living, life is never the same again. It's all obscene, there is nothing uplifting about war and death. I have no time for heroism. Don't tell me there are heroes. I don't want medals. It's all necessary, and yet it's all definitely fucked up.

When I close my eyes, I see the next day's battle and I see my own death. I see my own body cut in half, I see my own legs lying on the ground, I am disembodied from myself, one half looking back at the other, wondering what happens next. If one half could be saved, which one should it be: the one that held the rifle, or the one that knelt down to take aim? Do the two halves combined equal one evil? If one could be without the other, would a better whole emerge? This is also Blue stuff.

At night time, I try not to close my eyes at all. But the problem is we all need sleep, and that's when the visions come to me, just like I used to wait for a target. Nightmares patiently waiting to ambush me.

That's when I make the sounds of war, when Sheila, my wife, hears the terror in my voice. She's been listening to it now for the 40 years we've been together and she says my screams keep getting louder and louder.

My name is Bob Rose, I'm 80 years old, and I've experienced a life that isn't normal – a life that has been bloody and violent, tortured and tormented. I permanently carry the scars of that life; they can't ever heal. I let the military turn me into a cold, professional killer: one who could execute without feeling remorse, sadness or regret. Those two small words – "I let" – are important because I have to accept responsibility for the choices and decisions I made. Nobody forced me. What the military never taught me, though, was how to survive once there were no more battles to fight. They never told me about remorse or regret or loss; they never taught me how to combat the nightmares.

My story is definitely not about salvation. I haven't found redemption or peace, and deep down I don't like myself very much. The word "closure" makes me laugh, it's so utterly small and useless and incapable of righting all the wrongs and bringing back the bodies. I've tried committing suicide four times and I've tried just about every religion there is. None of that's for me. I'm trained to know 350 ways to kill with my bare hands. Scratch the surface, and the cold killer is still within me. The man who used to kill without hesitation. I was out of control when I came back from war and the only reason I'm still alive – or not in prison – is because I embraced an astonishing martial art made famous by Elvis Presley and Chuck Norris. That, and Sheila, have enabled me to share my story.

The following is simply the raw, brutal reality of my life; uncensored, unrefined, and all of it seemingly unconnected. Except there is something that links the insanity.

The most important component part of my story is one I haven't told you about yet: the Northern Cheyenne. They gave me the thread. They led me to Grey Wolf, and Grey Wolf was the only constant throughout. The military turned me into a killing machine, but they never stole my soul. That belongs to the Northern Cheyenne – as you're about to discover...

LITTLE FAWN

I am told I was a cute-looking child with jet-black hair that Mum made me keep neat and tidy, in a military sort of style. "You're going to break all the girls' hearts one day," she would say, teasing, and I'd feel myself redden awkwardly. I was naturally fit and always looking for adventures. If someone had to climb a tree, it'd be me; if someone had to carry something heavy – it was me. I was born on August 21, 1937 in Sutton Coldfield, and didn't have any brothers or sisters. I don't think I was spoilt, although heaven knows Mum smothered me with love and affection. Sometimes it was embarrassing and I'd have to say "Get off, Mum" if she tried to kiss and cuddle me in public.

My father was a regimental sergeant major in the British army; I very rarely saw him during my childhood. In fact, he wouldn't really have a major impact on my life until I was 12 years old, when he forced me to stand up to a bully. Sometimes, I wish I could blame all the bad stuff I did when I was older on the fact he was mainly absent. But I don't think that's the case. Whenever we were together, I felt love and immense respect for him, even though he rarely showed it back. That wasn't his nature.

I should say right now that I wasn't actually christened Bob – my real name was Gordon. But I hated it; I hated being teased – stuff like "Watch out, here's Gord Almighty" – it just plain annoyed me from an early age. Next began a complex genesis that gradually saw the name Bob emerge by the time I was 15: first I was called Rosey, which I also hated, then Rosebud, which I loathed, then Bud, which I detested – and then Bob, which I insisted on.

From an early age I became obsessed with collecting toy soldiers. The best times of all would be birthdays and Christmas. That's when I'd be allowed to choose some toy soldiers from Lewis's old department store in Birmingham. "Britains" were the best and I would take them home, desperate to tear open the packaging and recreate famous battles on my bedroom carpet. Whenever Dad was home, he'd join in and tell me stories about heroic colonels and armies. I loved those moments. One Christmas, I was given a box of soldiers that hadn't been painted – and a little box of oils with a thin brush. I don't think I'd ever been happier.

With Dad away so often, I lived at home with Mum – and my great-grandmother, Ada Louise, who was to have an enormous impact and influence on my early life. In 1942, I decided to tell her about the visions, because I trusted her the most. "I'm really, really scared," I told her.

I was almost five years old and sometimes I'd see things that I suspected other kids didn't see. I was too frightened to ask them because they'd think I was crazy, and maybe I was, and that thought alone frightened me even more. I'd see glimpses of people or animals – maybe on the other side of the road, or outside our house – but it would only be for a second, and then "woosh", they'd be gone. I guess it was like staring into a lightbulb, looking away, and then seeing the reflection again, still shining, on another part of the ceiling. It was driving me insane. I knew I had to tell someone, so I chose my great-grandma. I was too scared to tell Mum and Dad in case it'd get me into trouble.

"I'm telling you, I really, really see things. I do, Great-gran. Why are they there? Are they going to kill me?"

I waited in trepidation for her explanation, tears ready to burst from my eyes. I was terrified what she might say, how she'd react. She might be annoyed – worse, she might tell my parents. Incredibly, she believed me; more, she knew and understood. She took both my hands softly and blanketed them so all I could see was her old, crinkled skin, and she explained everything so I'd no longer be scared. This is what she said: "You have nothing to fear, I promise you. I know what it is you see and I see it, too. You're like me, you have Northern Cheyenne blood; we are blessed with a special gift – the ability to see into the next world."

I remember staring at her so hard I thought my eyes would pop out of their sockets. I doubt I understood a word she'd said – what on earth was "the next world" or "Northern Cheyenne"? – but the relief I felt when she said it was overwhelming. I wasn't going mad, I wasn't in trouble, and I wasn't going to be killed. She must have sensed my confusion, though; without me saying a word, she explained that another world existed alongside the one we lived in. "The things you see are the people – we call them spirits – from that world." And she added: "They will never, ever, harm you. You have absolutely nothing to fear. You are special, my child. You have a special gift."

I have never forgotten those words. I didn't even try to remember them. They just stuck, like a big sticking plaster inside my brain that would never peel off.

My great-gran shuffled her chair next to me as we sat at the kitchen table, and for probably the first time ever, I looked at her and saw little things that I've remembered clearly ever since. I saw how old she looked close up: her skin was darker than mine and her face was creased with thick, heavy lines, like I'd seen a tractor leave in a muddy field near our house. Her face looked worn and lived-in; maybe she'd seen a lot of bad things and each one of those things had left a mark. Her eyes were black, like space, I couldn't see where they ended. I could fall into those eyes and never stop falling. I was pretty sure those eyes had special powers.

She had long, tightly woven grey plaits that framed her weathered face and she wore a long, thin, canvas-style necktie that had tassels on each end. It dangled deep on to her chest and was decorated with mysterious, brightly coloured symbols. There we were, just the two of us sat on the wooden chairs Mum tucked under the kitchen table, the one with the shiny surface that could be wiped clean and would always be shiny. The two of us in our little semi-detached house in Birmingham. Mum was out at work in Woolworths; Dad was away with the army somewhere. In fact, I barely knew him, and whenever I did see him he looked tall and strong and a little bit scary. I didn't want to upset him one little bit.

Looking back now, I realise this was an extremely tricky moment for my great-grandma. She'd sparked my imagination, but I was only a child and not really capable of taking everything in that she needed to tell me. How did she know all this stuff? Maybe she'd been in this position before, though, with her own children, because she started telling me all about her life – and my family history – in a way that I could grasp. I had never felt so enthralled. We sat for hours; all I did was listen and let it all sink in.

She told me about the Northern Cheyenne, who they were, how they lived, and the battles they fought against the Americans. She told me my great-great-grandfather had been a fearsome warrior, who'd fought in a very famous battle. When I was a bit older, when I could better understand stuff, I was amazed to discover she'd been referring to the defeat of General Custer at the Battle of the Little Bighorn. I have since read books on the subject – and, specifically, the role played by "Little Hawk". That was my great-great-grandfather. For now, though, she simply said: "He was an extremely brave man, and I can see you have his spirit in your soul."

Next, she told me about her life, how she lived on a reservation in Montana, but left after falling in love with my great-grandfather. He was a Scottish engineer, working in America on the great Yellowstone River project. Some years later, when she was reminiscing again about her life, she told me: "He took me back to Scotland to meet his Mum and Dad, but they hated me; they'd never met a Native American before, and they didn't like the colour of my skin. I wasn't good enough for their son."

So, the pair fled and came down to the Midlands, where they worked on the canals for many years, living on a narrowboat. They had a son – my father – which is why I was born and raised in Birmingham.

Great-gran saved the best bit for last, though. Leaning towards me as if she was about to impart some incredible secret, she whispered: "My Northern Cheyenne name isn't Ada Louise. It's Little Fawn. That's my true name. That is the spirit within my soul." *Little Fawn*. I adored that name, it conjured so many exciting images in my young mind. It made me want to have a Native American name as well, so I could feel different, so I could be more attached to the Northern Cheyenne.

I always called her "Great-gran" out of respect, because I learned that was the Native American way. But Little Fawn and I became increasingly close after our chat, and I constantly begged her to tell me more and more Cheyenne tales, especially ones about warriors and battles. It all sounded so brave and mystical and exciting – another world, and I loved the fact I was connected to it. It set me apart. It took my mind to a magical place many thousands of miles away from humdrum Birmingham.

Little did I realise I would soon be living there myself.

Everything changed when World War Two began. All I can vaguely remember is the bombing. I can picture Mum and Great-gran grabbing each of my hands and rushing down to the bottom of the garden, where we had a little air-raid shelter. That's when I registered what panic sounded like: their short, rapid breaths, their hushed-yet-urgent "come on, come on, quickly Gordon" and then the immediate silence when we squeezed inside the shelter, the door closing shut, the darkness, the intimacy, Mum holding me tight in a space under her arms, I guess to add another layer of protection. The silence between us was terrible. It was a conversation of its own, but without words. Terror and dread, in that confined space, sounded just as loud as the bombs outside.

With no end in sight, Mum decided the three of us – her, me and Great-gran – should leave Birmingham and live out in America, on the same reservation where Little Fawn had lived in Montana. My imagination ran wild: it would be an incredible adventure. "You're going to love it, and you'll make lots and lots of new friends," Great-gran promised. I dimly remember walking on board a massive ship, at Liverpool I think, clutching a box of my favourite toy soldiers that I'd demanded to take. There must have been a huge train journey across America, too, because I remember changing stations a lot and trying to sleep on our seats in the carriage.

By the time we arrived, I was fully prepared for a new life in the great outdoors, probably poorer, but happy and fun, with lots of laughter and running around. Instead I came face to face with racism, bullying, and the sort of poverty that is just plain ugly and brutal.

I'll never forget my first glimpse of the reservation. One of Great-gran's cousins met us in a battered old pick-up van, and I couldn't understand a word of what he said as he greeted her in a language I'd never heard before. They hugged and then she turned to me and said: "Say hallo to Uncle Mike." Then she crouched down and whispered: "His Cheyenne name is Michael Blackhawk. You're going to hear a lot of strange names from now on." Uncle Mike had big, broad shoulders and there were all sorts of symbols and strange scribbles running down his bare, muscular arms. He was chewing heavily on something and I was a bit scared until he patted me on the head, smiled, and then hurled all our bags on to the back of his van, which had no roof, just low sides to keep everything in. We all squashed on to one long seat at the front and sat in stony silence as we started to take in our new world.

I'd expected to see tepees. Instead I saw dilapidated wooden shacks, some huddled together in ramshackle clusters, others on their own on small plots of scruffy land. The road wasn't like roads back home; it was a big, wide dusty track, with lots of holes which Blackhawk kept swerving round until I began to feel sick. Somewhere in the distance I sensed there were huge mountains surrounded by giant trees. I didn't notice the Blue, then. Here and there, I'd see rusted old cars, burnt out and abandoned by the side of the road, and as we drove along, I'm sure I spotted old fridges that had been dumped in ditches, with their rust-speckled white edges sticking out at crazy angles. It looked like a giant rubbish tip in the wilderness.

I fell very, very quiet until Uncle Mike stopped his car outside one of the wooden shacks. "This is it – everyone out," he announced, still chewing intensely. He leapt down to sort the bags, leaving Mum, me and Great-gran to inspect our new home. As soon as Mum pushed open the front door, I wanted to leave. I wanted to cry. It was dark and it stank. Stank of damp and decay and rot. The floor was thick with dust, and as we turned into the main sitting room I saw a pile of jumbled furniture stacked higgledy-piggledy in the middle of the floor, like someone was starting to build a bonfire of it all. The kitchen area was small and barren – it had a gigantic fridge – and there was a rickety old table in the middle with a bowl on it. But there was no sink, and no sign of any taps. There was a toilet, but the lid was down and I didn't dare lift it. Uncle Mike appeared and dropped the bags in the sitting room. "Where do we get our water from?" my mum asked. "Just across the road there," he said, pointing to some place outside the open front door. "There's a hand pump and you'll need to fill up some buckets. Take as many as you can, it saves time."

I knew I wanted to cry but I knew Mum wouldn't want me to, so I didn't. I just stayed silent as Mum said: "Cheer up, everyone – we'll soon have this place looking like home, won't we?"

In the end she did. But there was a lot of hardship ahead.

RACISM

His blotchy-red face bulged with hatred. Pure, undiluted hatred. If it was liquid, it would be bile because when he talked it felt like that horrible, acidic feeling you get when you've eaten something rancid and you want to vomit. I'd never seen or heard such venom before and when he really started yelling, top-of-the-voice kind of yelling, he made me tremble with fear.

I'd made the mistake of walking into a shop on my own because I'd seen some toy soldiers in the window and they looked interesting, possibly US cavalry. I think I was about seven, maybe younger. We'd gone to the nearest town outside the reservation, where Mum would often buy stuff the Cheyenne couldn't get. She was next door getting groceries with Great-gran, so I innocently wandered off to the toy shop and strolled in, anxious to inspect those miniature soldiers. I was quite tall for my age, and probably looked a little older than I actually was then.

He started the second I walked in. "What the fuck do you think you're doing in here, boy?" I'd heard the "fuck" word a lot on the reservation. "Can't you read that sign over there – or are you just too plain fuckin' dumb to read? Have a good look at it, the one in the other window." I turned slightly to my left. "Yes – that's the one. The one that says 'No Indians in Here'."

He was stood right in front of me now, and bent down until his fat face was leaning straight into mine – so close, I could smell his stale sweat, and see his rotten, brownish-yellow teeth as he opened his mouth to release another torrent of the bile stuff. "Do you know what that means, boy? Do you know what it fuckin' means? It means no fuckin' Indians in here. So what you doing here, boy? You're a fuckin' Indian, ain't you? Tell me: Are you a fuckin' Indian? Because I know you are, I can smell you are." When he said the word "smell" his nose twitched, like it'd just picked up a foul sewage odour. Then, in an evil, low, hushed tone, he whispered: "I know where you're from and you're not welcome here. So get the fuck out of my store right now – or else the police will drag you away. For ever."

At that point, the shop door opened as someone else came in and I darted out, running as fast as I could until I reached my mum and great-gran, who were loading groceries on to the back of Blackhawk's van. Gasping for air, I told them what had happened; I was still trembling, and this time I let Mum hug me in public. They both calmed me down and sat me in the front of the van. But they didn't go back. They didn't have it out with the man. They didn't say "How dare you talk to our child like that?" That taught me a lot about America and the Northern Cheyenne.

Back on the reservation, there was a similar problem. Like all the other kids, I went to the Cheyenne school, which was also in a battered old shack. We had one teacher, an American called Mrs Patterson, who looked quite old and stern, with little round-framed spectacles and short, grey hair, almost like a man's. She was OK, I suppose; she was kind, but she didn't notice how I'd get excluded by the other kids. My skin wasn't dark enough for them. Sometimes I'd ask to join in a game and they'd push me back, saying: "Go away. You're not one of us. You're not Cheyenne, you're an outsider." I'd often spend playtime on my own in the classroom until lessons started again. Eventually I told my mum, and a few days later she took me round to Billy Buffalo's home after school. "He wants to see your toy soldiers, so bring them with you," she said. That was the beginning of our friendship; then I met Jimmy Redcloud and the three of us rapidly became a little gang, hunting and exploring together.

Living on the reservation was about learning how to survive, in so many different ways – whether it was making friends, or whether it was using the God-damned water pump, with its great big heavy lever that only let out a trickle, no matter how hard you pushed down on it. The environment wasn't pretty, and for many, alcohol was the only way to get through the day. I'd regularly see drunks staggering and swaying and cursing. There really wasn't much sign of happiness on the streets. People were just existing. Nobody cared about them. But beyond the shacks and the poverty was the great outdoors, and that was where I slowly learned the skills that, in the end, probably kept me alive.

When I was eight years old, I held a rifle in my hands for the first time and felt very grown-up indeed. Blackhawk had a Winchester, which I had seen slung, hanging on a nail in his living room. It looked beautiful to me, especially its glossy American walnut handle – the stock – which tapered to almost halfway along the length of the rifle itself. "Would you show me how that works so I can go hunting, Uncle Mike?" I asked one day. He didn't even flinch. To him, it was perfectly normal to teach a small boy how to fire a gun.

The following weekend he drove me out to a makeshift firing range – or rather, a field with some fence posts stuck side by side in a line. Battered old tin cans were perched on the tops of some of the posts and I could clearly see where the wood below had been splintered by bullets, shot way off target.

I was desperate to take aim and fire but first he gave me a lecture about the Winchester. "The Winchester is America's most famous rifle," he said sombrely, like a school master giving a very serious lecture. "But it was also used by many, many bad men to slaughter our brothers and sisters, so – in the wrong hands – it's a very dangerous weapon." I didn't really have a clue what he was talking about but I was itching to give it a go.

"First you must learn about the gun and how it works." I sighed with impatience, but I was also captivated as he talked to me about the muzzle and, in an extremely serious voice, said: "Never, ever, point this at something unless you plan to kill it." It was all I could do not to smirk, given that we would be firing at tin cans.

Then he showed me how to open the action, how the safety worked, and where and how the bullets were loaded and reloaded. "Always make sure the barrel is clean and empty," he said. At this point he picked up a thin rod, which he pumped up and down the barrel vigorously. Then he picked up an old oil can and let one or two drops fall on to the surface of the rifle, around the hammer. "Ok, I haven't put the bullets in yet, so just pick up the gun and press the end of the wooden stock into your shoulder. That's it." Then he showed me where to wrap my hand under the wooden forearm, and where and how to place my right hand so my finger could curl round the trigger. "Now, lean your face into the side of the stock and look along the top surface of the gun for the two little bits that stick up – one is near to you, and one right at the end. Those are the sights. They have to line up when you fire at the target."

Once he was happy I'd got the general idea, he loaded the gun with two big, shiny bullets. I remember thinking how perfect and smooth they looked. It was hard to imagine they could rip something to shreds. Then, standing close behind so his body was actually pressed into mine, Uncle Mike let me take aim. The rifle was heavier than I expected and I found it hard to keep steady, but he helped support it by putting his hands over mine. I tried my hardest to get the sights level with the tin cans, pressing my head right against the wooden handle like he'd said. Just when I thought everything was lined up, I squeezed the trigger. The gun let out an almighty bang that ricocheted with deafening ferocity around my eardrums; I would have flown backwards with the force had Uncle Mike not been pressing his weight against me. Shaken, my ears still buzzing violently, I looked past the sights to the fence post – and there it was. The tin can hadn't moved.

"Don't worry," he chuckled. "This takes a lot of practice." But I was hooked, and I persuaded Uncle Mike to keep taking me to the range every week from then on – sometimes even two or three times a week until, eventually, the tin cans started to fly off the fence posts. I told Billy and Jimmy what I'd been doing and they started to come along, too. "Wait till the other kids hear about this," said Billy.

Holding that Winchester made me feel extremely grown-up; it felt comfortable, and although it took a while before I became really accurate, I wasn't clumsy with it and I wasn't the least bit afraid. In fact, I earned a reputation for being a good shot. Rifles simply made sense. They held no fear for me, and killing tin cans was great fun.

SUN DANCING

It was illegal then – and it's still illegal now. I was nine years old, and I was about to witness a ceremony that was beyond my wildest imagination, something that was both mesmerising and shocking in equal measure, something that made me wince and look away, and yet something I couldn't avert my eyes from. Above all, even though I was still a child, I knew I was watching something I would be connected to for life, something it would be impossible to forget. I can see it as clearly today, 71 years later, as I did at the time. With the benefit of hindsight, I know it never left me. More, it rooted deep within – into my soul and psyche and spirituality – and, as my life plummeted towards death and violence, it even found ways to keep me alive.

I want to describe it as I saw it. In other words, through the eyes of a child. I didn't understand the full significance at the time. For example, I remember seeing dolls; much later I realised they were effigies. I also know now that the ceremony only took place – and continues to – because America hasn't found a way of holding back the power of history. All the laws, all the courtrooms, all the prisons, all the might at the United

States' disposal has been rendered useless by an unconquerable spiritual belief. They made it illegal, but they haven't stopped it.

The following is what I witnessed when I was nine.

First there was dancing, and the dancers wore traditional Native American robes and head-dresses. It felt like a carnival; everybody was there, everyone was excited and happy. Elders with weathered skin and faces that were criss-crossed with lines that looked as deep and permanent as the ravines and valleys carved into the surrounding Montana mountains. Women, old and young, with long, black plaits and complicated necklaces and bracelets, children running around, laughing, playing; girls with elaborate puppets and boys with miniature bows and arrows. They were all in a loose circle around a clearing in the woods where bonfires were usually lit. This time, instead of firewood and broken bits of furniture, there was a table in the centre – and on top of that was a brightly-painted buffalo skull. I was standing next to my great-grandma and held her hand when I first saw the skull. It looked menacing. "Don't worry. That is our offering to the Great Spirit," she whispered, sensing my uncertainty. Next to the skull stood three huge poles that had been cut from mighty trees, painted with mystical symbols and adorned with strange-looking dolls that dangled from nails and hooks. Shortened stumps stuck out from the sides of the poles, no doubt the remains of sawn-back branches.

Eventually, the dancing stopped and a respectful silence descended. Everyone stood still and we children stopped fidgeting and playing. Something important was about to happen and we all tried not to breathe for fear it would get us into trouble.

Three young men – I was later told they were 18 years old – approached, each bare-chested. I knew only one, Whitehawk, and I remember how proud and fearless he seemed as he walked into the clearing. By the time they reached the buffalo skull our silence was broken and there was an eruption of cheering and applause. Men, women, children started chanting their names and I joined in, yelling "Whitehawk, Whitehawk, Whitehawk!" as loudly as I could. I didn't really know why, it just seemed the right thing to do. I had no idea what was coming.

I never once took my eyes off Whitehawk. He was wearing beat-up jeans and his feet were bare, just like his chest. I could see he wasn't powerfully built: his muscles hadn't fully developed yet. He didn't look like a warrior, but he was about to become one in a way I could have never imagined.

It was mid-afternoon and the Blue way up high struggled for attention above the tops of the cathedral-high firs surrounding us. The chanting and excitement started to die down and a group of elders emerged, talking in hushed, solemn tones. I couldn't tell what they were saying but it felt like something holy was about to happen. I didn't know. Whitehawk's chest was falling and rising heavily, like the bellows we used to start a fire. My own breathing seemed to get tangled up with his as a spreading sense of tension mounted.

The three young men separated, each standing by one of the upright poles. Whitehawk stood perfectly still, his body as vertical as the pole he was next to, his eyes perfectly horizontal to the horizon, like he was staring at some far-off point. I tried to follow his gaze but couldn't see past the tangled branches and bushes that surrounded the clearing. Two elders gathered alongside his left-hand shoulder; I recognised Medicine Bull and Rising Sun among them, their faces like my great-grandmother's – aged, weathered and creased. They all looked deeply serious and preoccupied; suddenly a little murmur arose and Rising Sun stepped clear of the group and stood directly in front of

Whitehawk. He had a hunting knife in his hand, its blade – maybe five inches in length – still low-down by his left leg. Occasionally it would catch the sun and a blinding flash of light would explode into life – then flicker out, lamely, moments later. The atmosphere was like nothing I'd ever experienced: everyone was silent and yet there was a deafening explosion of expectancy and anticipation. Of what, though? I inched forward for a better view – just in time to see Rising Sun raise his knife to the left of Whitehawk's chest.

That's when I heard the first whimper – Rising Sun pressed the point of his knife on to Whitehawk's skin and cut a short vertical line, maybe three inches long, into his chest. Blood seeped out from the sides instantly. Then he did exactly the same again, so there were now two vertical and blooded parallel slits in Whitehawk's chest, maybe an inch apart. I had barely blinked in disbelief when Rising Sun turned slightly – and did exactly the same thing, leaving another pair of slits, this time on the right side of Whitehawk's chest. I glanced quickly towards the other two poles, where exactly the same ritual was being performed.

By now, another one of the elders had moved in front of Whitehawk. In his hands were two short-yet-sturdy wooden skewers, stripped bare of bark, and he began to push one of them through the slits in his chest. My gaze shot to Whitehawk's face and that's when I saw his top row of front teeth biting down ferociously hard into the skin below his lower lip. It was like he was silently screaming but trying to smother his wail by pushing it back into his own chin. My own teeth mirrored what he was doing, as though I needed to feel pain myself to actually believe I was witnessing this. Once the stick was threaded through, so both ends were protruding equally out of his skin, another skewer was pushed through the open slits on the other side of his chest.

I think I saw him stagger as the second skewer went in, but that might be unfair. That might have been my head shaking from side to side. But he never yelled, not then. He must have wanted to; I know I wanted to, that was for sure. But the ritual wasn't yet complete. Once the skewers were in, Medicine Bull stepped forward carrying pieces of cord, which he quickly tied on to the four ends sticking out of Whitehawk's chest. Then he draped the rest of the cord round the stumps protruding from the pole and slowly pulled it back until Whitehawk – still standing but leaning back at an angle – was left suspended.

His pain must have been unbearable as his weight pressed against the sticks wedged into his skin; I stood there, mouth open wide, eyes bulging, trying to make sense of what I'd just seen, expecting his skin to burst open in a shower of flesh and blood at any moment. As I took it all in, the elders began circling him, and I could hear them chanting faintly in their own language. At that point, Great-grandma turned to me and said: "Come on, we must leave now. Your friend Whitehawk, and the others, are extremely brave."

I bombarded my great-grandma with questions. "Why did they do that, it must hurt so much, what will happen to them?" She explained that I'd witnessed a sun dance; that the three of them would stay suspended for at least two days and two nights – with nothing to eat and just sips of water – until their bodies fell into stupor. "They will be in great pain, but they are warriors, and proud to be Northern Cheyenne. When they fall into stupor, they will connect with the spirit world and see visions of the spirits that will guide them in the next life. That is their destiny; that is why they are there, that is what they want to do."

Then she added: "It will only finish when the skin on their chests tears open and we can offer their flesh as a sacrifice to the Great Spirit."

That night I could think of nothing else; even with my eyes closed, I could clearly see the image of Whitehawk hanging only by a rope connected to the sticks in his chest. The image was so acute, so real, I felt my own chest burning with what I imagined the pain must have been like.

I was still a child, but my young imagination was captivated. I even believed I was old enough and brave enough to do a sun dance myself. I felt it was my Northern Cheyenne duty: the ritual hadn't frightened me, and in many ways I already felt linked to it. But I knew it would never be allowed, I was still too young; in fact, I didn't get personally involved in a sun dance again for another 22 years, when life seemed black and meaningless and I was facing death and annihilation in Vietnam.

Instead, I found another way of connecting with the spirit world.

MY FIRST KILL

The Blue had always been there, of course, but I only truly *saw* it when I killed for the first time.

It was a glorious, sun-drenched day, not a cloud in the sky; I was with Billy Buffalo and Jimmy Redcloud, just the three of us searching for tracks. We'd been hunting for hours, our eyes feverishly scanning the undergrowth for the slightest clues. We'd never killed anything before and I remember thinking how calm life felt as we trudged through a field of servile wheatgrass that bowed down under our footsteps, then sprang back up as we walked past.

We'd almost reached a line of trees when I spotted the target for the first time. A female deer, standing alone, unaware. Her strong, brown body was almost lost against a giant brown backcloth of barks and woodland. It never occurred to me she might be beautiful. Swivelling, I frantically signalled at the others to hit the deck. Half whispering, half commanding: "Quick, lie flat, don't make a sound. We've got one."

I saw them collapse limply out of view into the springy grass, turned, and knelt down low myself. The target was still there. She hadn't moved. I felt in control but I sensed expectancy in the air: everyone – everything – was waiting to see what my next move would be.

For a few moments all that filled my world was the thump, thump, thump of my heart against the wall of my chest, like someone rap, rap, rapping on a front door – ceaselessly, loudly. I lay flat out on the grass, clutching and arranging my weapons, trying hard not to make a sound. I knew this was an important moment in my life: Billy and Jimmy were watching and would report back my every move. My reputation was at stake.

I listened intently to the stillness and stared manically at the target, desperately trying to hypnotise her into not moving. Suddenly, my precious silence – my advantage – was shattered by the dramatic swoop of a bald eagle, dive-bombing towards us, its huge wings spread menacingly wide. Damn it. My eyes shot upwards and followed the flight path of this unwelcome intruder until, mercifully, it arched off to the right and quickly transformed into a dot, disappearing into the distance. And that was when I noticed, when I truly saw for the first time, the Blue. The Blue in Big Sky country.

Suddenly the Blue felt infinite and crushing and just plain massive. So big it had just swallowed up a giant bald eagle. The Blue was the colour of the world. It was the sum of all life, the universe. Unblemished, unflinching, vast. It was much more powerful than me and my weapons.

Here I was, lying in the long grass, about to cross the divide between the life I could see above – and the death I was plotting back on earth. The Blue of Big Sky country would witness my first kill. I wondered whether it would be judgemental. I decided no: I was too insignificant for the Blue to care. I couldn't upset the Blue, I was just a small dot among far weightier rocks and boulders. I could be brilliant, or I could be bad. The Blue wouldn't flinch.

It would let me do what I wanted. It would let everyone do what they wanted because it would always be there, and our actions – the good, the bad and the evil – would always be small and insignificant, just like me. None of it mattered, the Blue was the only constant, so really the stuff we did would be neither right nor wrong.

"You killin' it or what?" An impatient rustle from behind abruptly shattered my crude introspection. I returned sharply to the real world.

"For Christ's sake – shut the hell up," I half whispered, half implored, furiously. I knew who the culprit was – Billy. His nickname was Buffalo Big Head. On account of his gigantic forehead. My focus returned to the target and I realised I was not in the right position. I needed to readjust my angle of attack so I could get a clearer shot.

I tried to remember everything I'd been taught for this moment. "Always check the direction of the wind. If you have to move, don't let the target sense your own scent." I slowly tugged out some blades of grass and threw them into the breeze, half watching their flight, half watching the target. I was still in this.

Then I slithered, painfully slowly, towards the target. Without me realising, my T-shirt had crumpled up towards my chest, exposing my bare stomach. As I wriggled forward my body upset an ants' nest and suddenly I felt them invading my skin. They'd got me: if I jumped up, it would all be over. I slid on, squirming as the ants crawled beneath my trouser belt, until my target was side-on and I had an uninterrupted view of the entry point. Her heart.

I knew I would only have one shot; there'd be no second chance if I missed. But I couldn't shoot while I was lying down: I had to stand and shoot almost in one complete, uninterrupted moment. It had to flow: it needed balance, accuracy, temperament, speed, determination. I had been taught there is artistry in killing, and now I understood what that meant. There couldn't be hesitancy, or self-doubt either. No second thoughts.

My left hand was already clutching the bow, one I'd made six months earlier from an old stick that I'd held under the steam of a kettle, until my hands and wrists were red-raw and the stick's bark had peeled away to expose clean, white wood underneath.

I pulled my right hand at a sharp angle over my neck and reached back to pull out one of my home-made arrows hiding in my home-made quiver. I'd made the arrows just like I'd made the bow – steaming and stripping sticks of wood, then sticking on goose feathers for the flights.

Now I was ready: with the bow and arrow in position in my hands, I slowly rose until I was fully standing. This was my moment of greatest vulnerability: there was now a much greater chance the deer would see me. I didn't shake, I didn't drop the arrow and, as soon as I stood, I pushed forward on the bow and pulled back on the string – like I'd been taught – and released the arrow.

I watched it slice through the innocent air, blinking only at the moment it tore straight into the target's heart and stayed buried in her body, the goose-feathered end protruding horizontally but vibrating as the doe reeled. It was a perfect shot; an adrenalin-fuelled surge of excitement suddenly shot through my body and for some reason I looked up at the Blue and yelled: "Yes!"

I instinctively ran forward and could hear the others doing the same, yelling and hollering, and all of us feeling like warriors. My deer was strong, though, and she wasn't finished. Even with the arrow buried in her heart, she began to turn and stagger away into the trees. But her legs were like a rag doll's now and, exhausted, she soon slumped, almost dead – but not quite. I grabbed my knife, pressed my knees into her twitching body and – instinctively and without flinching – cut her throat, her warm blood spurting out over my hands. Then I remembered to do something that felt important and necessary, although I didn't fully understand why. I looked at her motionless body and whispered: "Thank you." And for a few seconds I fell quiet and still and I definitely felt something eerie, a strange sensation that made me feel I was, somehow, connected to the creature I'd just killed.

Maybe she was beautiful. Maybe her eyes took a final glance at me. I don't know. That was Blue stuff.

My deer was big close up, and the three of us struggled to lift her carcass and hang it over a branch so the blood would drain off. Next, I began cutting her up – first down the middle to release the entrails, then into lumps of meat we could take back. It was a big deal for me – Billy Bighead and Jimmy were amazed by what I'd done. My reputation would soar when we got back.

Killing her hadn't bothered me in the slightest. My only sensation had been the strange sense of connection – and the elation. My only regret was that I couldn't walk back triumphantly carrying the whole carcass intact. Looking back now, I realise this moment defined me – and the soldier I was to become. The physical act of taking life was functional, a task, a means to an end. I could do it and feel no need to analyse or fret about what I'd done. I just did it. There was no remorse because nothing inside me questioned my action. It just seemed entirely natural and normal.

We walked out of the woods into the bright sunlight, carrying our clumps of raw, red, bloodied meat, and there it was again. The Blue. It hadn't changed. I knew it wouldn't. I could do what I wanted in this world.

I was nine and a half years old.

GREY WOLF

I was never really frightened until the mountains faded from view and night fell. All that remained in the darkness were the spooky outlines of distant shapes that seemed to become increasingly sinister and ominously closer the more I tried to fathom out what they were. That's when I started hearing sounds and sensed there were animals and creatures in front of me – and behind me – in the woods: wild beasts that, to my young mind, were growing bigger and bigger and more ferocious by the second.

Their ceaseless scurrying soon became a cacophony boring into my brain; I imagined them preparing to circle me, getting ready to pounce and eat me alive. My senses became tuned in to the tiniest sound, sounds I never knew I could hear, little creatures all part of the great conspiracy to devour me.

If only I'd realised then what a chilling portent this was of the terrors that were waiting for me in the future – 22 years away.

For now I was still a child; a 10-year-old who had persuaded Great-grandma and the elders to let me go on a vision quest. I hadn't been able to get the image of the sun dance out of my mind. Why was Whitehawk willing to go through so much torture, just to connect with the spirit world? Hadn't my great-gran told me

I had a special gift that would let me see into that world as well? Why did I sense there was a secret that weighed heavy round the reservation, like giant dew drops clinging to the morning undergrowth? Why did Little Fawn always seem to be whispering to the elders, and why did they always look so conspiratorial? I would lie awake at night reliving the sun dance until I became utterly convinced there was something missing deep within me. Like Whitehawk, it was my destiny, my duty, to find out what.

"I've heard talk, Great-gran," I said to her very seriously one afternoon. She looked at me like she instantly knew what I was about to say. She looked much older now, like there wasn't much time for her left on this earth and she understood there was still work to be done first. "I've heard people talk about the spirit that is within them – and how they have seen that spirit themselves. Why haven't I seen mine, Great-gran? I want to, I'm old enough, show me how."

The following night she took me to see Medicine Bull – one of the elders I had spied at the sun dance. I was nervous meeting someone so important and respected but he smiled, revealing two missing front teeth, shook my hand, and said "Hallo" warmly. He still lived in a tepee, made from animal skins that had been decorated inside and out with brightly coloured Cheyenne symbols and beads. The three of us sat cross-legged round a blazing stove in the centre, a giant chimney pipe carrying the smoke out through a slit in the apex of the roof. Around us, Medicine Bull had split up the inside of his tepee into little rooms, hanging skins to create dividing walls. I spotted lots of other stuff hanging, too: rifles, bows, axes, utensils.

I felt very grown-up, sat there gravely, as the two of them explained how a vision quest worked. "You must sit on your own in the wilderness," said Medicine Bull. He paused, lifted up a glass by his knee, and took a hefty gulp. The unmistakeable, sweet-yet-pungent smell of firewater filled the air. I looked at him squarely and noticed he had deep, black pools for eyes – just like Little Fawn. I wondered if they could be brother and sister. There was something serious about his face, something believable, wise and immensely experienced. "You'll have no food with you, and very little water, but you must sit still and resist sleep for as long as you can," he continued. "After many hours, perhaps days, your body will slump, exhausted, and you will start to hallucinate. That is when your spirit will come to you."

A week later I was sat, alone, on the remains of a rotting log, its damp bark making my jeans increasingly wet and uncomfortable. Behind me were the sprawling woods where I had shot the deer. In front of me were rolling fields that ran all the way up to the foothills of the Montana mountains – great, gigantic pyramids of rock that were either unblemished granite grey, or sprinkled here and there with little white blankets of snow. They looked so powerful and indestructible against the Blue, with just occasional balls of cotton wool clouds frozen still around the mountainous peaks.

But the novelty and majesty didn't take long to wear off. I had a small rucksack on my back with three plastic bottles filled with water inside. It was soon time to take my first sip but it did little to quench either my thirst, or my hunger. Medicine Bull had drilled into me that I must stay as static as possible so the spirits would approach me. I wondered if the elders were hiding in the woods behind, checking I was obeying orders, so I sat still – as much frozen by fear as anything else.

As the day dragged on, and the Blue around the mountains slowly turned, first, into a warm red glow but then increasingly black and menacing, I felt my eyes become heavier and heavier as sleep tried to worm its way into my brain. Then I'd suddenly jolt back to my senses, certain I'd heard Medicine Bull's voice – or was it his spirit? – saying "You must resist sleep for as long as you can." So I'd talk to myself, or I'd talk to my mother and to Little Fawn, as if they were next to me, and I'd tell them what I was doing and what I was thinking, or who I liked and didn't like at school. I even told them secrets I'd never told them before – safe in the knowledge they'd never hear.

Then there was the hunger, oh God, the hunger. It started almost immediately, but once my brain succumbed, all I could think about was the deer or rabbit that would have been hunted that day. Then I'd imagine my favourite chocolate bars and sweets and I'd begin another insidious slide towards sleep as I conjured giant platefuls of food in my mind. This time, the unexpected squawk of a bald eagle overhead snapped me back to reality.

Next came the biting cold and my body began to shiver, at first gently, then more and more violently as it succumbed to the plummeting temperature – and a spreading sense of fear. That's when I started to hear the animals that were getting ready to eat me, and suddenly I was no longer a fearless spirit hunter. I was simply a child who was alone, frightened and vulnerable in the dark, a child increasingly succumbing to sleep. But I had begged to be here; I wasn't going to face the humiliation of giving up and facing Great-gran and Medicine Bull looking like a quitter. So I didn't cry and I didn't call out for help, even though I craved the warmth and security of my family deep inside. I simply endured – until my body, through sheer exhaustion and famine, fell inextricably into stupor.

That was when I saw it: when my mind and body were reduced to a state of near-deathliness, when the whole of my world was blurred and indefinable, I clearly saw the beguiling face of a wolf. My wolf... Grey Wolf.

Everything fell into focus around the contours of his sharp face. There was nothing else but this clear vision, and in that mesmeric moment, I felt an instantaneous and overwhelming connection, as though a part that had always been missing within me had surfaced. I didn't flinch, I didn't turn away; Grey Wolf had hypnotic, impenetrable black eyes that were powerful, fearless and majestic. But there was comfort, security and familiarity in those eyes as well; I could see protection, I could see home. It was then that I understood: I was now complete.

I was Grey Wolf.

I am absolutely certain that everything I saw when I was that nine-year-old boy was exactly as I've just told it. I still see Grey Wolf today. He has never left my side and I am certain his presence has kept me alive in the face of intense human atrocity, depravity, misery and pain. I have experienced violent extremes – slaughter and torture – that underline the hideous cruelty humans are capable of. Make no mistake, I have been to hell. I have seen and touched death and there is no logical reason why I'm still alive. Only Grey Wolf knows why.

SCHOOL OF
HARD KNOCKS

He never saw the punches coming. He never stood a chance. It was the unexpectedness of it, the shock, the insolence, the audacity, the "what the fuck" of it all that felled him. They were good punches, too, one to each side of his pit-bull face. As he toppled backwards, his eyeballs seemed to pop out of their sockets as if they were trying to have another look at what had just happened. It was like his eyeballs were standing up to ask: "What the fuck was that?"

I was 12 years old and I was in desperate trouble. I had just struck my schoolmaster on each side of the face in front of a packed classroom.

We'd left Montana a year earlier. Great-gran had stayed behind – I didn't know it then, but her health was fading. I'd begged Mum to let me stay; I had a sinking feeling about going home. "I like it here, my friends are here, I want to be with Great-gran. I don't want to go back."

On the day we left, I held Little Fawn tightly, thinking if I didn't let go, they couldn't make me leave. Tears rolled down her cheeks and she gave me a traditional Cheyenne neck tie with feathers, which I wore all the way back to England. I still have it today, and I carried it with me through two wars. I'll never forget her final words as we let go of each other: "We will be together again in the next world, I promise. The spirit of Grey Wolf will never leave you, my child." I'd held my tears back until that point, but then the first trickle crept from my eye and I sobbed all the way to the railway station. I never saw her again.

There was another reason why going back worried me: my father. I no longer knew who he was. I hadn't seen him for the past seven years – practically my entire childhood, or certainly the most formative years. I could barely remember what he looked like. On the ship back, I started grilling my mother. "What do I say to him when I see him? What do I call him – Dad, or Sir? Does he really want to see me? What did he do while we were away? Did he kill anyone in the war? Is he strict?

"Does he love me?"

My mum, of course, gave me hugs and reassurances because that's how she was – a great softie. She tried to thrash me once on the reservation with a belt in the kitchen. I'd upset her over something and she was furious. She grabbed the belt in a right temper and lashed it across the back of my legs with all her might. The problem was, the more she struck, the more I laughed – uncontrollably. She was using the thin cotton belt she'd tugged off her cotton dress; it was completely soft and harmless. No matter how hard she tried to thrash me, the more comical it became. In the end, I picked her up, sat her on top of the washing machine and said: "Mum, what on earth do you think you're doing?" We fell apart laughing. We loved each other to bits. But I was still extremely nervous when we walked down the path of my grandad's old house in Erdington for the first time.

I looked up to the heavens hoping to see the Blue, thinking of Little Fawn, but all I saw was eternal grey. I walked solemnly behind Mum, and glanced in amazement at the neat and tidy front garden. I hadn't seen one of those on the reservation. I was scared.

Suddenly the front door opened, and my dad stood commandingly in the void, so big I couldn't see beyond his frame. In a flash he seemed powerful and strong. He looked exceptionally smart, with an immaculate starched white collar, black tie and dark suit, and his shoes were so polished they practically sparkled on the doorstep. I noticed a short, neat moustache, course dark hair, and darkish skin. My heart raced.

I watched as Mum put down her suitcases and hugged him tightly. Then, turning, she smiled. "Gordon – say hallo to your father." He grinned, but there was no rushing to pick me up; no man hug. That wasn't his style. Instead we shook hands, and I can still feel the force behind his crushing grip. There was a declaration of the terms of our relationship in that handshake. I instinctively knew that if I respected him, if I obeyed his rules and regulations while I was living under his roof, then I'd be OK. I absolutely knew, with great certainty, that it wouldn't be good to cross him.

I was quickly enrolled into the local secondary school and straightaway struggled to fit in. I knew how to survive in the wilderness; I didn't know how to survive in the classroom.

Everything was new: I'd never seen such a huge school before, I'd never seen so many boys all in one place. On the reservation, there were about 20 of us in a wooden shack, and that's where we sat all day. There was no moving between different classes. Now I was in a cluster of cold, Victorian, brick-built buildings with metal-framed desks and chairs all in rigid rows and battered, wide corridors that smelt of secret cigarettes and farting. It wasn't a cosy or familiar space. I'd never lined up in a playground before, and never marched military-style into a class. I thought that was silly, so deliberately hung back or pretended not to hear the teacher's instructions. That led to detention – something else I wasn't used to.

Then I got into big "what-the-fuck" trouble. I was in a maths class and the teacher was Mr Griffiths, who looked and sounded like a snapping, snarling pit bull. Short, bulky and ferocious. His nose seemed to be slightly higher up his face than most people's. When you stood in front of Mr Griffiths, he appeared to be looking down at you disdainfully, as though you might be a nasty smell.

When he talked, he talked about pi and obtuse angles and circumferences and nonsense that was incomprehensible to me. I plain didn't understand maths, and nobody had worked out yet that I was dyslexic. Halfway through one of his classes, bored and fidgety, I started doodling his face on a scrap of paper. Just like a proper pit bull, he sniffed it out – and hit the roof.

"Rose, come to the front immediately!" he barked. I genuinely had no idea what was coming. "Face the class and hold out both of your hands, palms upright. Do it now, boy."

I did as I was told, half smirking. He walked to my side, agitated, mumbling under his breath: "You'll be sorry for this, boy." Without any warning, his left arm shot high into the air. I vaguely saw the whites of his straining knuckles as they flashed down in front of me and the wooden ruler he was gripping ferociously in his own hand smashed, hard, on to my open palms; two rapid strikes – smack, smack. The blows stung, really stung. I'd never experienced anything like it on the reservation.

I jumped, an electric-shock kind of jump, and without thinking I turned and smashed two heavy punches into either side of his squashy face. First a right, fist clenched, then a left: smash, smash. I will never forget the look of shock that flashed across his face as he toppled backwards to the floor. I vaguely sensed a giant intake of breath as the class gasped and then, like Mr Griffiths had, fell deathly quiet.

It would be no exaggeration to say that landed me in a lot of trouble. Mr Griffiths pushed himself back up, roared "Silence!" to the entire class – although nobody had dared make a sound – then grabbed me by the hair and dragged me straight out of the room to the headmaster, who demanded an explanation. "He hit me," I said. "So I fought back." I was shaking now, but I wasn't going to cry. I'd never seen a teacher hit a child before, and I was simply defending myself. My reaction seemed normal to me; I didn't know or understand any different.

Thank God, my dad was away yet again, but someone must have phoned home because Mum turned up soon after. I explained what had happened and she tried to calm the head by explaining that corporal punishment was not something I'd encountered in Montana and that I'd always been taught to fight back if I was attacked. To some extent, that was true. I had reacted by instinct. I had no experience or understanding of why the teacher was hitting me. I'd never upset a teacher enough in the past to be hit by one. I didn't know it was allowed. The head listened, nodded, and then told her I'd be expelled instantly if it happened again.

For a while, the kids thought I was a hero for daring to do it. But I wasn't up to speed academically, and it showed. I grew increasingly frustrated, then angry, and the bile bubbled increasingly away within me. I knew I was miles behind all my classmates; it didn't feel good.

Inevitably, I started to be singled out and made fun of. I became a target for bigger and stronger bullies. Word got round that I'd come from an Indian reservation, so pretty soon I was labelled "paki". I was about 13, and desperately needed to find a way of making friends. I turned to drink, and hanging around with the wrong sort of kids after school. We'd take it in turns to nick cans from corner shops while the rest of the group distracted whoever was serving. I started smoking Woodbines as well, which I'm annoyed with myself about now, but we didn't know any better in those days.

I know my dad would have gone berserk if he'd found out. I'm not saying he was cruel or indifferent to me, he absolutely wasn't. He just wasn't around most of the time, and when he was, it simply wasn't his style to show his emotions publicly. It was his job – his life – to bark out orders and keep a stiff upper lip. It didn't mean he loved me any less, he just didn't know how to show it.

When I did see him, however, he'd often surprise me. I started to get into fights, one a particularly ugly clash with a boy called Denis Burton over a game of marbles. We were hitting each other pretty hard, and blood was smudged across our faces. We got dragged apart and hauled in front of the head, who was furious to see me in trouble yet again. "You could be expelled for this, Rose," he barked. I never told Dad.

About a week later, the same kid wanted to have another go and started chasing me down the street as I headed home. I thought I'd better stay out of trouble and was almost at our garden gate when Dad, who must have been watching the chase, suddenly appeared and demanded to know why I was running away. "He wants to fight me, but I'll get into trouble at school if I do," I explained.

"Well, I'll tell you this, lad," he boomed. "You'll get into even more trouble if you don't. Take that kid out – right now." I looked at my father's eyes: he was serious, so I turned round and laid into Dennis with everything I had, although he was stronger than me. Dad eventually parted us, took me back home, and when we sat down at the kitchen table he said: "You took a hammering there, didn't you? But you didn't give in, and that's good enough for me."

That was the first time I began to understand my dad. Not long after, Dad came out of the army, and I saw far more of him. He never really glorified his military life, or told me heroic stories, but there was something about his stature and the way he controlled the house – and how we spoke and behaved within it – that continued to command respect and obedience.

He only hit me twice in his life – and I was already an adult by then. The first came after I'd joined the British army myself, and returned for my first weekend home. Sundays in our house were very traditional; we all sat together at the dinner table, and everything was laid out neat and proper. Without thinking, I leaned over and said: "Pass the fuckin' salt, would you, Mum."

Next thing I knew, a fist came hurtling across the table and knocked me straight off my chair on to the floor. Dad looked down over me and said: "Language like that is for the barrack rooms, lad, and not for your mother."

The second and last time came when he refused to give me a key to the door when I was 25. His rule was unequivocal: I had to be back in the house by 11pm. That night I showed up at two o'clock in the morning with my cousin, rolling drunk. I told my cousin "That bugger's not going to carry on treating me like this." I knocked on the door – and kept on knocking until the lights came on upstairs.

I could hear my father coming down the stairs, the door opened, and "whack": he struck me straight between the eyes. As I hit the floor, I remember seeing the door slam shut and all the lights went back off upstairs. Next morning, he simply said "Morning lad, everything all right?" And that was it.

Even after he'd died, he still found a way of surprising me. We kept an old army knife he cherished, but one day I noticed it had inexplicably disappeared. We looked for it everywhere without success. Then, one Sunday morning, I went downstairs to make a cup of tea for my wife Sheila, and found the back door was wide open. "Shit, someone's broken in," I thought.

I had a good look round, but couldn't see anything wrong at all. I went back upstairs with her tea, then sat on the end of the bed, puzzling. Suddenly, I became aware of a silvery glint in the room. There, on top of the dressing table, in plain view, was Dad's knife. "You found Dad's knife," I said to Sheila.

"That's impossible, what you talking about, Bob?" she replied. "You know I can't find it anywhere."

I hurried back downstairs to find the front door was open again, even though I'd shut it.

I instantly knew what I had to do. Dad's ashes were still in a jar in our house, so I got dressed quickly and drove off with them, heading for the spiritual Dewerstone rock, out on the wilds of Dartmoor. It was bleak and isolated out there that day – a murky drizzle hung in the air and it was bitterly cold. With nobody around, I dug a hole and stuck his knife and some of his ashes in it. Next, I cast his remaining ashes to the four corners, uttering a Northern Cheyenne chant as I did so.

I have absolutely no doubt he had found a way of telling me to perform this final ritual, which I'd forgotten all about. He never talked to me about his background, but I suspect he shared Great-gran's deep spiritual beliefs. One of the few things I knew about his war service was that two of his toes had to be amputated after gangrene had set in. His unit had been attacked in North Africa and he'd trudged for miles and miles on his own across the desert. But it wasn't the physical injury that worried him – it was the fact he would no longer be whole when he entered the next life. According to the Northern Cheyenne, that would not be good. Six months before he died, he'd said: "When I go, lad, you must dispose of my ashes the Native American way."

"Yeah, ok, Dad." Then I forgot all about it – until the front door episode reminded me.

DRUMMER BOY

I left school with no qualifications when I was 15 and a half. You could in those days, it was normal. I even knew what I wanted to do: to join the army and become a bandsman. I loved playing the drums. On the reservation I would join the tribal drummers; I loved it – the beat came naturally to me. "OK," said Dad, and he got me a position as a junior bandsman in the Royal Scots Dragoon Guards. I'd be based at the Stirling barracks in Edinburgh.

I took to it like a duck to water. Maybe it was in my blood because of my dad and all our family history. My grandfather on Dad's side, Harry Rose, served in the military police during the First World War; during the second he became a reserve policeman and ambulance driver. His wife, Louisa, was an air-raid warden and got a commendation for bravery and a Bakelite medal from the king. Her medal is currently in a museum on Dartmoor.

Some of the kids I was living with in the barracks really struggled; it was their first time away from home and they couldn't handle it. Not me. I shared a dormitory within the thick, old stone walls of Stirling Castle with 20 other recruits, our beds and lockers lined up in two rows of 10, facing each other. I even persuaded everyone to call me Bob, and that name stuck for life.

I took to all the orders, commands, cleaning, marching like it was all I'd ever been waiting for. I absolutely loved it. I especially loved my drummer's uniform: scarlet red jacket with white sash and belt, black trousers with two thin golden yellow stripes down the side – all topped by the famous bearskin. I felt fantastic wearing all that. Proud. At home.

We'd get up at 6am, when the duty piper and drummer would go round the barracks waking everyone up. After breakfast, we'd go to the band room and start practising regimental marching music until lunch. The afternoons were reserved for marching drills.

Once a week we'd go to a rifle range, learn about handling, cleaning and loading guns, then do target practice. It came so naturally to me; my life then couldn't have been any better. It was all fantastic, except there was a problem back home: Mum couldn't stand me being away. She'd never been parted from me, and my absence started to make her ill – a depressed kind of ill – and she begged Dad to buy me out.

I had no idea about this until he unexpectedly arrived at the barracks one weekend and took me aside for a quiet chat. "You're going to have to come out, it's as simple as that, lad," he said. I was heartbroken. I couldn't argue, and I was worried about my mum. I didn't want to leave, but 18 months after joining, I was back in Birmingham.

MURDER

You're certain you've murdered someone when you see the blood. When the blood forms a pool round a gaping wound in the side of the head, a pool so disproportionately large to the scale of the head that you think the entire body is leaking out on to the floor.

You're certain you've murdered someone when you see the axe you plunged into the side of the head now lying in the middle of the blood, submerged in the oily mass. Strangely, the mass looks blacker than you expect. You expected to see red. Maybe the drab, grey concreted ground is discolouring the red.

You're certain you've murdered someone when a panic-stricken voice yells "Run!" and everyone scarpers as another trickle of blood seeps out. You run with them, certain you've murdered someone.

You're certain you've murdered someone when the cold sweat starts and won't stop and you can't sleep because at any moment there'll be a knock on the door and it'll be the police and you'll hear a voice telling your father: "We have reason to believe your son may have information about a murder yesterday."

I was certain I'd murdered someone. That's why I ran – and didn't come back for another five years.

I loved my mother, truly, but I resented her deeply for what she'd done. I was 17 years old and seriously pissed off. She thought I'd get used to civilian life – but I didn't. I couldn't. I'd tasted the military – and loved it.

By now, my parents had moved to Castle Bromwich and Dad got me a job in a local garage to learn how to be a paint sprayer. I detested it, and to break the boredom got involved with a gang of bikers in the area. I didn't even have a bike of my own, but they were tough and they let me hang around with them. We'd go off for rides – me on pillion – and inevitably those outings would turn into chases and clashes with rival gangs. Then, one weekend, word was passed round that we needed to "tool up" because we were going to take on a bike club in Shard End. We had history with them.

I was pumped up on adrenalin as I left the house and grabbed a fireman's axe from our garage, which I stuffed into my belt. Tooled up. "I'll show 'em." We all gathered, me on the back of someone's bike again, and rode off to a car park at a local café, where the other club was outside, waiting for us.

Some of them had weapons in their hands – coshes, batons, that sort of stuff – and as soon as we got off our bikes, everyone waded in. It was mayhem, bodies clashing into each other in a giant brawl. I started laying into one particular guy, who was bigger than me, and at some point he managed to knock me to the ground.

As I scrambled up, furious and totally out of control, I grabbed the axe inside my belt, raised it high in the air, and plunged the blade wildly towards the side of his head. He fell instantly, blood spurting out on to the ground. I let go of the axe and watched, frozen, as the blood formed a pool around its handle and blade. It looked strangely cocooned, a piece of evidence that the blood was now forming a protective shield around the head.

It was another "what-the-fuck" moment, just like with Mr Griffiths, and everybody fell silent. Only this time nobody got up, and we all stared at a lifeless body, an inky, bloody pool, and an axe. Someone yelled "Run!" and that broke the silence. Everyone scarpered; black leather-clad limbs dashing off in all directions. Some part of my brain was still functioning: I dipped my hand into the blood, picked up the axe, and ditched it over a hedge as we sped off.

I got home, convinced I'd killed him. His body hadn't moved from the moment it hit the ground, and I'd never seen so much blood come out of someone's head. Some of it was on my hands, which I scrubbed ferociously as soon as I got into the kitchen. Mercifully, none of it had splashed on to my clothes.

I couldn't bear to tell anyone: I didn't want to shame my parents. I was terrified, and there was only one option: I had to get away before the police got to me. I knew a pal in Liverpool, who I trusted, so I phoned him and explained what had happened. "You've got to get out of the country," he said. "I might be able to get you a job on a cargo ship. Just get over here as quick as you can."

I barely slept that night, convinced there'd be a knock on the door at any second. The next morning, I stuffed some clothes into a bag and darted down the stairs, shouting to my parents: "I'm just nipping into town. See you later." They wouldn't hear or see me again for a very long time.

I managed to hitch my way to Liverpool, and headed straight for my mate's flat. "A couple of my pals can get you on a ship tonight," he said. "But you need to get over to the docks right now." Sure enough, there was a job for me on a cargo ship carrying coal to mainland France. The first stop was Marseilles, and I spent the entire crossing thinking about what I'd done. The body hadn't moved. There wasn't even a twitch or a scream or a cry or a breath. It was lifeless. Then I cursed myself for hurling the axe over a hedge. "Fuckin' idiot, the cops'll find that," I said to myself.

At some point in the middle of the night I went up on deck alone and leant against a rail, staring bleakly out to a cold, black sea that increasingly turned into a vast pool of blood the more and more I gazed out. I even thought I saw, bobbing between the waves, an axe that was refusing to sink. The more I stared, the bigger and bigger the axe became. "A passing ship will pick that up," I thought. "I'm finished."

An icy shiver shot through me and I went back down into the hull, where I tried to grab some sleep; instead I spent the rest of the night eavesdropping on two other deckhands, who were talking about the French Foreign Legion and a place called Fort Saint Nicolas.

Part Two

THE FRENCH FOREIGN LEGION

The wolf rarely attacks prey that is standing still, and has the patience to surround it for many hours or days before pouncing.

THE END
OF BOB ROSE

I first caught a glimpse of Fort Saint Nicolas as the cargo ship inched into Marseilles harbour. The sun hadn't fully risen, one or two lights were stubbornly resisting dawn – the city looked half awake, half asleep. The fort's ancient stone walls seemed to rise forbiddingly out of the water: they looked stern and impenetrable. If someone had told me it was a brutal prison, full of dark chambers and torture, I'd have believed them.

I finished my mopping duties, grabbed my passport and bag and disembarked, eyes firmly set on the fort's ancient walls, looking for a gate or a sign. "They'll take anyone," I'd overheard the deckhands say. "You can enlist at the fort. It's that simple."

By now, I was convinced every police force in the world was hunting me. I didn't know much about the French Foreign Legion, although I suspected it would be hard and tough. I also had this vague idea it took people who were on the run, who could use a false identity. It wouldn't ask too many questions. As it turned out, I was pretty much right.

It was around 11am by now and, as I walked round the fort's sprawling perimeter, I noticed two massive entrance gates, a sentry box, and a legionnaire standing bolt upright. There was a café nearby, so I sat at an outside table and ordered a beer. I needed one, and the barman was willing to accept my English shillings.

I couldn't take my stare off the legionnaire. He wore khaki, with a blue cummerbund around his waist and bright red epaulettes on his shoulders. He had a rifle by his side and was wearing a distinctive white hat, which I later realised was the famous Legion kepi. He looked like he belonged in a photograph for a tourist postcard – immaculate, strong, a perfect symbol of the Legion's public façade. I was clearly in the right place: on the wall, I could see a sign that read "Bureau d'Engagement".

It took me another two beers to summon up the courage. I picked up my bag, walked over to the legionnaire, looked up to his face, and said: "*Parlez-vous Anglais*? I want to join the Legion."

He probably wasn't meant to flinch, but I'm pretty sure he smirked. Moments later, somebody came out from a guardroom behind the gates and led me into a small office where old, faded black and white photographs of Legion parades hung lopsidedly on the stone walls. There then began a series of long waits, punctuated only by different people walking hurriedly in and out, occasionally casting stern glances at me – but saying nothing. What if they were on to me? Was I about to be turned in? I was starting to panic heavily when a French-Canadian officer marched in. "I'm a sergeant from the Deuxieme Bureau," he proclaimed. "It is my job to find out who you are, and why you want to join the Legion. Are you running away?"

I didn't see any sense in lying; I clung to the belief they'd accept me come what may because maybe they needed the bodies. "Yes," I replied. "I've murdered someone back in England, where my parents live. But it was a gang fight and everyone had weapons."

He sat down and started asking more questions about my background, taking notes all the time. I told him I'd served in the Dragoon Guards. "I also know how to handle a rifle," I added, trying to impress. He gave nothing away, and once he'd finished writing, he left – leaving me alone again with the lopsided photographs.

About an hour later he returned and said: "How do you want to enlist – in your real name, or under a name we give you?"

He then explained how anonymity worked in the Legion. "If you choose to take a new identity, the only person who will ever know your real name will be me. But you must never tell anyone your real name. Understand?" I nodded ferociously.

I could have walked off at any point, but they were promising me shelter and anonymity and protection. My new name was to be Italian for some reason – Gian Falconie – although I was quickly nicknamed "Chicco" because I was so young. I was also called "Johnny" because it didn't take long for everyone to realise I was English.

The whole process for me to cease being Bob Rose, to effectively disappear off the face of the earth, took about three hours from the moment I walked into the fort. But there was more of my past to be erased before I could begin my new life. I was led to a barrack room, where I suddenly met other recruits – there were maybe around 100 in there, lying or sitting on triple-tier bunk beds.

Language was an instant barrier; so many were being spoken all at once. I could hear Spanish and Italian, but there were harder Eastern European languages as well. There were no other English voices in there although I did latch on to two French-Canadians, Ed and Chris, who became mates. I'd no real idea what I was getting in to. I'd done 18 months in Scotland, banging a military drum; I'd no concept at all of the wars the Legion was fighting.

It wasn't like today, when you can find out everything on your mobile phone.

At least I had some idea what barrack room life was really like. I looked around and saw kids who I could tell would never last, who'd become easy targets, who wouldn't know how to stand their ground. As the night wore on, I was approached by other recruits asking first for cigarettes – and then, more menacingly, for my English currency. I kept saying no, but one lad, a tall, tough-looking Czech, kept persisting, and tried to pin me back against the bunkbed. "I've got no fuckin' money," I yelled, pressing my forehead hard into his, ready to lock horns with him if he pushed any further. "Do you fuckin' want some?" Dad would have been proud. Nobody asked me for money after that.

We were woken abruptly the following morning when a ferocious senior sergeant burst into the barrack room in full khaki drill uniform, clutching a stick under his armpit and roaring: "*Raus, raus!*" The Legion may have been French, but I was constantly amazed how many NCOs were German – most of them leftovers from the Second World War.

We were all still in civvies, we hadn't eaten or washed, but the sergeant herded us outside into a huge parade ring where he made it clear we had to strip off – underwear, socks, boots, the lot – until we all stood, shivering, stark naked. Bundles of threadbare, green overalls were chucked in a pile in front of us and we were told to each grab a pair. They stank and they were filthy. It felt like thousands of recruits had worn them before us, and they'd never been washed. Then we were thrown plimsolls and a T-shirt. It was like wearing rags, and it was all we wore for the next couple of days.

Next came medical tests and admin. That was our chance to say: "Sorry, it's all been a massive mistake. I want to go home." Some did. I didn't. I dutifully handed over my passport and absolutely anything that was in my pockets or still in my bag. Which was pretty much nothing. There really was nothing left of Bob Rose.

I was ushered into an office, where a heavyweight contract was ready in my new name. I couldn't understand a word of it, but the Deuxieme Bureau sergeant was on hand again. "Sign this and you remain in the Legion for the next five years. There will be no turning back. This is your last chance."

I looked at the thick document, flicked through its incomprehensible pages written entirely in French, and thought, "What the hell!" I signed – writing Gian Falconie for the first time – knowing I couldn't go back, couldn't phone Mum and Dad. I was pretty sure I'd be heading for a battle zone, as well.

Any evidence of my previous life disappeared once and for all when I was given a Legion haircut later that afternoon. My hair had never been particularly long, but it was scraggy by now, and flirting with the top of my overall collar at the back. I queued up like everyone else – and came out scalped within seconds. I'd never seen so much of my head. All that was left of my hair was a faint black shadow: staring back at me in the mirror was a raw, untrained thug. The sort you wouldn't want to meet.

I was starting to get on well with the French-Canadian recruits, Edouard and Christophe, who sounded more American than French when they talked. I still think those were their real names, but I shortened them to Ed and Chris in any case.

Ed was similar to me in many ways: he was up for an adventure and actually liked the tough, cropped-hair look. It sort of summed him up. He was built like a man-mountain; his legs and arms must have been twice the width of mine, and bulged like they were ready to explode at any moment. His neck was so dense it was hard to tell where his head started. "One day they're going to tip you lengthways and use you to batter open the fort gates, head first," I cracked. "Yeah, and you know what," he replied. "I won't even feel it."

Chris, however, was more considered and less likely to wade in. He was at least three inches shorter than me – about five foot eight – stocky, with a sharp, keen nose and alert eyes that could sense trouble from afar. He didn't look as yobbish as Ed or me; there was intelligence in his face, and heaven knows I couldn't see much of that around me. He was like a human satellite: he missed nothing. "It's about to kick off over there," he said as we ate lunch one day. I turned, and sure enough, some of the Italians started pushing over chairs and shoving each other about.

The following morning we were wakened at 6am again by the German and shovelled on to the fort's battlements, where we were given basic chores – mainly sweeping and cleaning. An hour or so later, we were herded down for breakfast, which – like all our meals – was served on a buffet basis. But it was survival of the fittest: if you didn't grab what you wanted quickly then "woosh", it'd be gone, and nobody came round with refills. Sometimes scuffles would break out, but I'd already laid down my marker. Nobody got in my way.

Two days later we were marched down to the docks and pushed on board a battered, rusted-up freighter, an older version really of the cargo ship I'd come over on. We were being sent to Algeria for training. We looked more like a rabble than soldiers; we were packed like sardines into a dark, filthy hold, with just tattered and torn deckchairs to lie on for the next couple of days. "Where the hell's Algeria?" I asked Chris. "What we being sent there for?" I couldn't have pointed to it on a map back then. But Chris knew more about the Legion's history. "We'll be going to the Legion HQ at Sidi-bel-Abbes," he said assuredly. "It's been there for years; it's where everything's based, and where all the training goes on.

"It's where they'll try to turn us into fuckin' legionnaires."

TORTURED TRAINING

The French Foreign Legion turned me into a killer. They saw in me all they needed. They dismantled me piece by piece – like one of their Mauser rifles – and then reassembled all the parts until they produced the perfect killing machine.

I was someone who would kill on command. I never questioned orders and I never broke down. The act of killing became a cold, calculated operation. I pulled a trigger, I threw a grenade, I killed. I never prayed for redemption the next night. I just waited for the next order – and the next target. Targets weren't humans with sensitivities, or loved ones, or children. I was desensitised to such introspection. They were just targets, like the tin cans on the reservation were targets when I was learning to fire my first rifle as an eight-year-old. Like the deer was a target. Killing a man was no different.

I can say this now because I'm older and wiser and I've had a long time to think about what happened to me while I was still a teenager. Don't get me wrong, I'm not against the Legion. I truly believe it remains the most professional military unit in the world. It instils comradeship and brotherhood like no other unit. "*Legio Patria Nostra*". The Legion is our homeland. That isn't simply a motto to me, it actually runs through my veins, it actually means something. I get goosebumps just saying it. I was – and still am – part of that homeland. Yes, the Legion took everything off me: my name, my passport, my history, even my country. But when I left, it gave me back a new nationality. Legionnaire.

That's what I remain and, if I had to, I'd parcel the 17-year-old I used to be right back there and do it all again.

There is a "but", though. The Legion is vicious, cruel, bloody and brutal. Extreme discipline is based on a culture of extreme bullying, whereby the commanders bully the NCOs who want to be commanders, who – in turn – bully the Legionnaires who want to be NCOs. They bully the recruits, who want to be Legionnaires – and the recruits bully each other. There is no immunity within this chain; it's a constant.

If you screw up, you get hit. Not a gentle clout-round-the-ears kind of hit. No: Legion punishments are full-on remorseless blows to the head, into the stomach, into ribs, legs, balls – anywhere a man doesn't want to be struck. Sometimes you'll be struck with clenched fists. Sometimes with boots. Sometimes with rifle butts. They're the worst.

Nobody flinches during the beatings, either. Nobody jumps in to stop them. Everyone looks the other way, certain their turn will come, sooner or later. If you really fuck up – a spectacular "what-the-fuck" fuck-up – like I did – you'll be dragged off to a penal battalion, where you'll wish you'd never been born. Where, among other treats, you'll be forced to dig a coffin-shaped grave out of hard, gravelly earth and then lie in it overnight with a guard making sure you stay there. That happened to me. It's what I had to accept to stay a Legionnaire.

No matter what level of seniority you're at, there's no reprieve from the kickings, the punishments, the brutality, the yellings, the humiliating, the training, the parading, the marching, the hiking, the cleaning and the scrubbing.

Our introduction to this life only started when we reached Sidi-bel-Abbes. Our first sight of the base was one of those rare take-your-breath-away moments. "Fuckin' hell!" said Chris. "What the fuck!" added Ed. Poetic.

It was awesome, though. Without even entering, it felt huge and domineering, a formidable desert colossus with ancient sandstone walls defying both invaders and centuries. We entered through a mighty gateway and walked into a huge parade ground which, despite its size, was utterly dominated at the far end by a monument to the dead in the form of a gigantic globe. I noticed gravel and stone paths running in parallel lines along the middle of the parade ground and wondered what they were for. I'd soon find out – that's where we'd be dragged for punishment. That's where we'd be forced to crawl on bare hands and knees, the jagged rocks tearing at our skin until we were coated in a clotted mash of blood and sand dust. That's where we'd duck-walk in intense, relentless heat, wearing heavy steel helmets with no inner padding. That's where we'd be forced to jump, run, crawl – and jump, run, crawl again, then again and then again.

The parade ground also gave us our first glimpse of real Legionnaires; scattered around were guards wearing white kepis carrying machine guns, or units marching in full kit. They looked strong and big and immaculately drilled and they were proudly singing in unison "La Legion Marche" like it was their national anthem. It was. It was an impressive and inspirational sight. We had a long way to go to reach their level.

We were checked in, shown to dormitories with more triple-tier bunk beds, and given basic medical checks. Then it was off to the mess hall, where the food was substantially better than we'd had in Fort Saint Nicolas. There was even steaks and mugs of wine at dinner – and as much beer as I could sink.

The next two weeks were spent doing basic chores – cleaning, sweeping – until we were all interviewed once again by the Deuxieme Bureau. "They're giving us another chance to get out," said Chris. But nothing had put me off – yet.

Then it got serious: we were re-issued kit and went into proper training. Two sets of khaki drill uniforms, including boots – but no kepi, we had to earn that first. Just a head cover from the sun; webbing equipment and belts and bullet pouches. We were handed denims, though, which meant we could finally dump the god-damned overalls we were still wearing. But our denims had to be washed and ironed every day, and our boots kept immaculately black and waterproofed – always with Dubbin.

Our accommodation went up a gear: we were moved into smaller barrack rooms – about 20 of us in each one – with a single bed and locker to store kit. Ed and Chris were with me, along with a Czech, a couple of Poles and three Germans. The rest were French and Swiss. It was a good unit, we got on – but none of us ever dared ask about each other's backgrounds.

There was a price for such relative comfort, though. Three NCOs watched over us microscopically, inspecting anything and everything – even our teeth and ears. If any one of them suspected the slightest fuck-up, the room could be turned upside down, lockers and beds overturned and possessions flung out of windows. One night Chris came back pissed, still clutching cans of beer, which he stupidly stuffed under his bed. One of the sergeants must have been tipped off: he stormed in the following morning, about 15 minutes earlier than usual, and woke Chris up by ramming the butt of his rifle straight into his stomach. Chris doubled up and puked all over his bed blanket. I won't repeat the torrent of abuse he got for that. He spent the afternoon trying to crawl on his bare stomach through rolls of barbed wire. It was as though he was the enemy.

Most days kicked off with a five-mile run into the surrounding hills. If you threw up – and most did – you'd be forced to run again in the afternoons, this time with a sack of sand or stones strapped on your back. Then it was basic army training, which covered everything from dismantling and reassembling weapons, scrambling up and down trenches and through assault courses, to French classes, and even singing.

I saw plenty of beatings during weapons training. To be honest, if it was ever justified, I suppose it was then. You were expected to take a rifle apart and then reassemble it in seconds, which was fair enough. A second could be the difference between life and death. But some of the recruits were all fingers and thumbs at first – so they were regularly struck in the face, the stomach and the testicles with whatever rifle it was they'd failed to put together correctly. They soon improved.

Singing and marching were taken extremely seriously, and some evenings we'd be paraded through the streets of the local town, like we were a Welsh male voice choir. Those parades gave us a rare chance to see our surroundings; we were truly in a desert wilderness. Everything was coated in layers of thick, sandy dust: the people, the animals, the children, the cars, the windows of the dishevelled bars and cafés.

It felt like we'd gone back centuries in time: goats and sheep were being ushered down the main street by dusty boys in dusty shorts; women, covered from head to toe in draped, white haiks – with only their eyes exposed – giggled as we marched past; men with long beards and dusty jeans loitered in little conspiratorial groups looking alarmingly suspicious. When we eventually returned to town on patrol duty, those clusters seemed to look even more menacing, especially at night.

The hub of the town was the market, where the dust even managed to take the shine off a kaleidoscopic array of fruits and vegetables piled high on rickety wooden tables. The market was where the action was: it was loud and bustling, and clearly the heartbeat of this dusty outpost.

God only knows what the locals made of us as we marched past in full uniform and full voice, although they'd probably seen and heard it countless times before. Nevertheless, it was hard not to feel proud in those moments.

Training intensified as each day passed: the morning runs into the hills soon became 10-mile marches in full kit. That was no fun. The sun and the heat were remorseless, especially when you were wearing a heavy steel helmet, and carrying heavy ammunition and weapons. Each week the route got a bit longer... then a bit longer.

There was no let-up, either, when you returned knackered, bruised and aching all over. That's when the endless inspections, cleaning kit, cleaning toilets, cleaning floors really pushed your tolerance levels. It was only the fear of more punishment that persuaded you to comply. The punishments never went away, and it was usually the Italian NCOs who dished it out the most. They'd hit you for any tiny reason: I got kicked in the balls for climbing a rope too slowly. The NCO came up to me while I was still dangling and launched himself into a karate-style kick. His body was in mid-air as his boot landed straight in my crotch. I let go of the rope and slumped to the floor, where I threw up almost immediately.

The regime was cruel, and it broke some of the kids. One day a rumour went round that a Swiss recruit had died after he was beaten to a pulp in training by two NCOs. Ed claimed he knew the kid and swore the rumour was true. "I'm fuckin' tellin' you, they fuckin' killed him," he said. "And you know what? The Legion doesn't give a fuck. As far as they're concerned, the NCOs were *entitled* to kill him."

The best bit of training for me was learning how to use different weapons. We were shown how to handle grenades and sub-machine guns, and three 7.5-millimetre rifles – a bolt-action repeater, a lightweight semi-automatic, and one that could actually fire grenades through a special attachment. It was the closest I came to being back on the reservation; the accuracy I'd mastered there didn't desert me. Chris, Ed and I would gamble packets of cigarettes on who'd be the best shot. I won so many times, I introduced a line of credit. "This is how it'll work," I explained. "We'll shoot for next month's rations, and then the month after that – and so on." There were barely enough months left in the end.

Training also included basic judo skills. We'd be shown how to fall and roll, and where the most vulnerable points on the body are to kill an attacker. I'd no idea then just how crucial those introductory lessons would prove to be for me in later life.

We were pushed to our limits each and every day, and I slowly began to realise an awful truth: I loved it. All of it. The marching, the hiking, the assault courses, the inspections, the singing, the cleaning, the scrubbing, the crawling, the scrambling in and out of trenches, the sweating, the repetitiveness. Even the cruelty. Sometimes seeing someone getting punished made me feel good – I wasn't being punished, so therefore I must be doing something right. I wanted to do it right. Someone died in training? I'm not surprised. I'm not even bothered. Just bring it on, because I can handle this. How tough am I? Here, let me show you. My name is Gian Falconie, and I'm going to be a fuckin' Legionnaire.

We were doing French classes and I was starting to pick up the language. We were also being taught about the history of the

Legion, and I was captivated. I was learning about famous battles – crushing victories, hideous defeats, Camerone Day. I came to realise how that day, in particular, embodied everything the Legion stood for. We celebrated it each year on April 30 with an immaculate parade and show, like a giant village fete. Afterwards, we'd get severely pissed. Bob Rose loved it. He didn't know, then, that his drinking was already starting to spiral dangerously out of control.

No, I was too unbelievably fit to worry about being pissed. I felt I could walk through walls. I would silently watch the serving Legionnaires, the way they walked around – proud and confident – and I'd say to myself: "That'll be me soon." And it was: a month or so later we made the grade. That's when we were each presented with the white kepi; that's when we officially became Legionnaires.

They made a big deal of it, too. The presenting of the kepi was extremely special. The ceremony was held in one of the old barracks, where everyone paraded in full uniform, with all our instructors present, along with all the NCOs who had beaten and battered us along the way. We were each handed a kepi, then everyone joined in a booming rendition of the Legion's marching song, "Kepi Blanc" – to the same tune once used by the German Panzer divisions. Once the final chorus was over, we were finally allowed to place the kepi on our heads.

I felt like a million dollars in that moment, like I'd achieved something special. It was my equivalent of passing all the school exams I'd flunked with A-star grades in every one of them. I'm not saying a tear rolled down my cheek – that would have been one of Ed's rumours – but I absolutely thought about my parents. Especially my dad. I knew he would have understood, and he would have been incredibly proud. But I didn't even dare phone him.

JUMP TO IT

I remember never feeling so alive. I remember the green light, the shout "*Allez*", then I remember the fall. The eternal, rapid descending, the instant realisation you're hurtling through nothingness. The struggle with your brain to remember the training as you dive through the emptiness. The vague awareness time is running out. I remember never feeling so utterly helpless in my entire life – yet never feeling so exhilarated, either. The adrenalin rush was more powerful than killing, and I'm well qualified to know that. It was better than sex and, after four wives and countless prostitutes, I'm well qualified to know that, too.

I felt closer to the Blue, that's for sure. It was engulfing me, surrounding me, I was breathing it in, and I felt its unconquerable power as I plunged. I was just a tiny micro-dot, too small for the eye to see, maybe too small for a microscope even, impudently passing through its infinite expanse. How dare I trespass into its domain like this? How dare I get this close?

I understood in a flash how tiny the planet is, how miniscule our lives are. I sensed it on the reservation when I killed the deer. Now I could see it; when you get that close you see the evidence, the proof that nothing about my life mattered. The Blue wouldn't blink if my parachute failed to open and I smashed helplessly to the ground. I was simply an irrelevance in its long-term plan.

Then came the relief. When you're watching yourself hurtle towards certain death, when there's nothing to catch you or break your fall, the survival instinct kicks in. The "I-don't-want-to-die" feeling. The elation you feel when your body is suddenly jerked upwards, defying the very laws of gravity, and you look up to see a great white umbrella billowing above your head, is as infinite as the Blue. "Ha! I'm going to live!" Then, you naively think you've actually conquered the skies. You've sussed them out, you know how to trespass and get away with it – you'll even chance it again. You forget the Blue doesn't give a damn.

I was proud, though. Proud all my training had kicked in when it needed to. Proud I'd completed it. Proud I was on my way to joining the French Foreign Legion's elite regiment: the "1er Regiment Entranger De Parachutistes". The revered Premier REP.

I volunteered for parachute training after first learning to become a truck driver with the Third Foreign Infantry Regiment. Remember, I was barely 18 years old and had never driven a vehicle in my life before. It was a way of learning. I started on old Jeeps at base, but quickly moved up to troop-carrying army trucks. We'd drive up high into the surrounding mountains, along narrow, twisting roads – dust tracks really, often scattered with heavy fallen debris and rocks that made steering even more challenging. Sometimes the tracks were so steep, and narrow, you didn't dare look down. My foot would be pressed constantly to the floor, the gearbox grinding in agony each time I changed down, the engine wheezing and spluttering so much it was barely alive. Like everything in the Legion, it struggled between life and death.

I craved something else, though, something more exciting. Being a driver was OK, but when I was encouraged to be a parachutist, well, I jumped at the chance. I was transferred to another old, fortified base at nearby Saida, slightly more inland from the coast, for pre-parachute training. Chris and Ed were no longer with me and, like everything in the Legion, the training started with more bullying and punishment – only this time it was even more brutal and unforgiving than before. It was like we had to prove ourselves all over again. Our days were spent marching and hiking in intense, blistering heat; then more weapons training; then more cleaning, more polishing and more scrubbing; then guard duty patrols and close combat sessions – when it seemed the only purpose was to hurt us as much as possible. There were ceaseless inspections and ceaseless punishments for tiny indiscretions. I lost count of how many times we were forced to crawl on our stomachs through a trench filled with raw sewage. Or stand perfectly still, arms stretched out horizontally to hold a rifle perfectly flat and still as the sun drilled down.

One hike across the mountains was particularly evil – we clambered up and down peaks and valleys carrying full kit: rifles, ammunition, food, water, shovels, the works. It was a ceaseless, back-breaking slog. We returned bruised and battered and barely alive from exhaustion – in a worse state than the lorries I'd driven up those mountain roads.

That seemed to be the final hurdle – after that we were transferred to a French army base at Blida, which felt like a holiday camp by comparison with modern, spacious quarters and real food. That's where we actually caught sight of a parachute for the first time. First, we practised jumping and landing by strapping on a harness and clambering on to an elevated platform – sufficiently high up to break an ankle if you fell. From there, you jumped, and just when you were about to hit the floor, the harness would yank you back up violently, until you were left dangling above the floor.

Then the harness would be released and you'd try to land without breaking any bones.

Next, we were shown how to fold our own parachute and what to do if it didn't open. I'll never forget the instructor saying: "Always fold and check your own 'chute. Never let someone else do it. That way you've only yourself to blame if it doesn't open." We all grinned nervously at one another when he said that.

We also spent time dangling from a pulley on a wire strung high across the camp, so we could learn how to navigate in mid-air. Suddenly, it felt like I was in a boys' adventure camp; life then could hardly have been any better. Suddenly, we weren't being pushed into relentless chores, and at night we'd drown ourselves in beer and wine and sing ferociously.

The first time we went up in a plane was simply to see how it was done, to watch Legionnaires shuffle forwards to an open door until they disappeared one by one. It didn't put me off, but then I wasn't stepping out into the abyss.

After about three months, the big day came. I think there were about 30 of us in the sort of plane you'd actually beg to jump out of, it looked so antiquated. We put on our packs, and sat in two long rows facing each other. Once the plane levelled, everybody's eyes switched nervously to the red light, and we waited anxiously for it to flicker on. When it did, we stood in unison and hooked our chutes to the overhead wires running down the length of the plane.

I was nervous, of course, but I had confidence in the parachute and the way I'd been trained, even how to land without breaking any bones. Inevitably, red switched to green, the first man disappeared, and we all shuffled nearer our destinies. I didn't hesitate when I reached the door, and I didn't look down once. Once I heard "*Allez*" I leapt as far out of the plane as I possibly could. As I looked down on the world below, I yelled out: "One thousand, two thousand, three thousand, four thousand" and then – on cue – a sharp tug pulled me back, the chute opened, and I floated sedately through the Blue. Training kicked in: I looked all around to check nobody was in trouble or about to crash into me from above; I checked and adjusted my drift, and then simply enjoyed the freedom of falling.

All too rapidly the ground loomed closer and closer and I gripped the shoulder straps more tightly. Just before landing, I released my rucksack, which was attached to a rope around my waist, so it arrived before me. Then, with knees bent, I landed firmly back on earth. I did five jumps altogether, making the grade only when I'd completed the final one. Christ, I got drunk that night, and another grand ceremony followed when I was presented with a parachutist's silver wings and a certificate, which has somehow survived all the ensuing violent years, and is now framed at my home in Cornwall.

COUNTDOWN TO
AN ASSASSINATION

It's amazing what you learn about a man when you watch him through a rifle's telescopic lens for six consecutive days. Before you decide to pull the trigger and end his life.

You get to know all the really *personal* stuff, the tiny details of his life. What side of the face he scratches himself on first thing in the morning; how he shaves; how little he washes; and yet how vain he is when he thinks nobody's watching. It's amazing how many times a man combs his hair when there's nobody else around.

His life plays out uncensored within the perfect circumference of the lens: its flawless sphere completely encircles everything that happens in his small world. Once he's within that tiny globe, he can't get out.

It's also alarming – and a little bit sad – how ordinary, how repetitive, a man's life can be when you're studying it this closely. You really notice the patterns in his life.

The man I watched always woke around 7am; always crawled, head first, out of his foxhole, still wearing a tatty vest and jeans he'd slept in overnight to combat the biting cold. Next, he'd straighten himself, fling his arms out high and wide in a dramatic stretch, yawn expansively, and fiddle with the zip of his trousers before turning to piss against some rocks that were increasingly stained from the same early-morning ritual. Then he headed to a wash area where he splashed his hands and face and cleaned his teeth. Mundane, isn't it?

He'd stroll over to a communal kitchen and dining area, underneath a large canvas roof held in place by cord wrapped round obliging tree branches. There he'd sit, usually in the same seat, ladle black coffee into an old battered tin can, and wrap his fingers round the outside for warmth. He had a rifle, sometimes slung over his right shoulder, sometimes casually propped by his side. I'd noticed a knife, too, a five-inch blade in a sheath hanging from his belt. The top of the sheath was always open and I noticed the knife's bone handle had a pattern etched over its surface. I wondered if he'd cut anyone's throat with it.

Sometimes others joined him: they'd nod reverentially, and they'd carry weapons too. Their common bleariness subsided as they started to chat. Sometimes, though, he'd be on his own. That was a weakness, I noted. That made him vulnerable – open, perhaps, to a sniper's bullet.

Around 11.00am he'd disappear to the latrine and afterwards slink back to his foxhole for a while. Around 1pm he'd return to the canteen area, where he'd dunk chunky pieces of bread into soup or stew.

There'd usually be more variety to his life in the afternoons – sometimes he'd be on the radio, talking incessantly and passionately. I couldn't hear his words, I couldn't speak his language, but his body language was often melodramatic, there'd be lots of animation to accompany the silent words. Then, he might rush off and tell someone else all about the conversation he'd just had over the radio.

I got to recognise the people he spoke to the most. They must have been the ones he trusted. Sometimes, he'd spread a giant map on to a table top, like it was a tablecloth, and flatten its creases and folds. There'd usually be lots of excitable pointing after that, bodies huddled together, clearly deep in conversation and thought.

Other times, he'd fiddle with rifles and ammunition. It's a wonder where he got them from: I'd see US Browning automatics, German sub-machine guns, even British grenades. That's the sort of detail I could pick up through my telescopic lens, that's how close I could get. He'd lay them out all around him, dismantling and re-assembling, cleaning, oiling, and chatting to anyone who wandered over. He'd leave ammunition scattered around, too; this would not be a wise moment to shoot him.

Sometimes, he wandered off to the camels, huddled in a far corner. I hated these creatures; they're ill-mannered, they spit, they stink, there's violence in them. I'd watch him tug out scraggy clumps of mountain shrub and hold it to their chomping mouths.

Sometimes he'd sit alone, on an upended log near the military vehicles. He'd seem lost in thought and suddenly he'd no longer look like a terrorist, or a soldier, or a rebel. There was no uniform on him in those moments, he didn't fit any role model. I never considered whether he was human; I never pondered whether he was a family man; I never wondered if he had a wife or children. His eyes were brown but they were usually set fierce and fiery under heavy, black eyebrows. They didn't usually betray softness. But I'd spotted him when his mind was somewhere else. My lens had seen weakness. This might be a good moment to pull the trigger.

His evenings were spent round an outdoor fire, in front of the eating area. He'd carry a plate of food from the kitchen and sit on scattered logs that circled the blaze. He'd talk, smile, scratch his face, run his hand through thinning strands of black hair, stand, kick dust around, curse, wipe dust off his legs, laugh convulsively, like a whole-body spasm, piss against the rocks, sit again, drink some more, eat some more. Talk some more.

Sometimes he'd hear something and leap up, alert, senses radar-sharp. Everyone would watch, everyone would look and listen, everyone would be edgy. There were 50 of them altogether; I'd counted them all through my viewfinder. Then he'd sit down again and the chatter would slowly return.

Inevitably, weariness set in, the night sky would be at its darkest, the flames would die and sleep would beckon. He'd get up, stretch like he did in the morning, go to the latrine again and crawl back into his foxhole. Alone. The others shared. But he was always alone. That confirmed his rank.

The next time I'd see him, it'd be 7am again, and his day would start all over. His was a life that fitted easily inside a telescopic lens. A lens that was perched on top of my German-built bolt-action Mauser rifle.

It was a life that would be easy to end. The only question was: When?

The answer came soon after I qualified to be a sniper. My shooting skills hadn't gone unnoticed, even when we were training to be parachutists we still did plenty of target practice. I was bloody good at it; learning how to be a sniper seemed a natural progression. I was transferred once again, this time to Zeralda by the coast. It was an opportunity to handle the best rifles and sights; to learn how to slither unseen over sand dunes, or scale the surrounding mountains to stalk an enemy target, wearing camouflage that blended into the terrain.

It wasn't much different from what I did on the reservation: it was an adventure, and I would be revered and respected at every level of the Legion if I was successful. I didn't stop to consider consequences or meaning-of-life stuff. Blue stuff. I knew I was training to kill – otherwise what was the point of doing it? I was in the bloody Legion, it was part of what I'd signed up for.

My first target was always going to be the most important, not because it would prove I had the nerve to kill a human but because it would prove I could be relied on, I could be trusted to execute an order professionally – and return without calamity. I wasn't doing it because it felt like sport; I wasn't going round telling everyone "I can't wait to kill someone". Or at least I wasn't then. I was simply aching to be a good Legionnaire, and being a sniper seemed a step closer to achieving that.

First, I had to learn about concealment. How to make myself invisible by stuffing branches and shrubs into my mesh gillie suit, so I'd vanish into the surroundings. Again, this was easy for me. It was all about reading the land, and it went straight back to my childhood in Montana and the Northern Cheyenne. There, I was hunting for food – but it was still an act of killing. The deer had no idea I was so close. The Cheyenne had taught me about laying low into the ground, to the point where my contours were lost in the lumps and bumps of the surrounding terrain. They taught me about scent, and how to manage wind direction so even the mildest breeze couldn't betray my whereabouts. The trick, then, was to get as near to a target unnoticed as possible. It was exactly the same now.

I became increasingly familiar with the vast Aures mountains, further inland, where many terrorist camps were hidden. Scaling those peaks – some of them snow-capped at their highest points – was a leg-aching, lung-bursting ordeal, especially climbing with kit, ammunition, shovels, sleeping bag, food, water and medical kit. The sheer weight of what soldiers carry, not just Legionnaires, is so often taken for granted. Guns and ammunition are not light. Then, on top, you have all the stuff you need just to survive for a few days.

Sometimes it was hard to imagine there was even a war going on. Small groups of us – usually four or five – would climb those barren, inhospitable peaks and live unnoticed among the rocks and scorpions for two- or three-day stretches, learning how to survive. We were in the north, where the mountains were fronted by rugged cliffs; in the south, they looked down to the Sahara's sweeping, sandy expanse. All we'd hear was the sound of our own lungs gasping for oxygen; all we'd see would be more and more roller-coaster peaks stacking far off into the distance, like waves spread endlessly across an ocean. The test was to simply exist up there: to build a camp without being detected, to do all the normal stuff – communicate, sleep, eat, drink, go to the toilet – as though we were invisible. To leave no sight or scent of our existence.

The days would be stiflingly hot under a relentless sun; the nights bone-numbingly cold. That's when we understood why we could see snow. But there was Montana beauty up there, especially during daylight, when the mountains seemed tall enough to actually touch the roof of the Blue. In the evenings, we'd build a small fire and practically sit on top of it to stave off the biting, icy wind, our hands wrapped round tin cans filled with soup or baked beans. I realise now how peaceful those moments were, looking up to myriad constellations illuminating the blackness, all impossibly intertwined with each other. "Where's the fuckin' Plough gone?" I mumbled to myself, utterly unable to detect it among the chaos of a million stars.

It was living on nerve ends, though; these were days and nights with a deadly purpose and we were flirting with death; we could have been ambushed at any moment. As the camp fire died, we'd crawl into sleeping bags and sleep fitfully behind low stone walls we'd built during the day, hoping they might offer some protection if we were attacked. We never were. Not then.

We'd return to Zeralda, where another exercise would be lined up: this time, finding a target and getting as near to it as possible, without being detected. We'd be handed coordinates – usually a location in the mountains again – but this time instructors would be strategically placed with binoculars watching for any sign of movement as we approached. It didn't pay to be spotted: if they saw you, punishment was usually severe. But I was good. It all made such sense to me, maybe it was even in my blood; after all, my forefathers had either been Native American scouts or in military reconnaissance. Like them, I could read the land.

I managed once to get so close to the target, I was able to tap him on the shoulder and say: "You're fucked." After three months, I was presented with a sniper badge; a week later I was transferred to a reconnaissance unit and sent on my first mission. To kill.

The French were fighting the Algerian National Liberation Front (FLN) in what, during the 1950s, was the equivalent of a terrorist-style war. So far, I hadn't even seen a dead body: I'd been on patrols of the local town, and up into the mountains, but these were mainly acclimatisation exercises to get us used to the terrain. I'd seen injured troops returning to base but I'd never been close enough to hear their cries or see the extent of their wounds.

All this was about to change, drastically, although I wouldn't see a war in the sense of vast armies lining up against each other. I saw French planes dropping bombs, and I went in afterwards to see the carnage left in their wake, but I rarely endured bombardment myself. Instead, we were at the mercy of land mines and snipers; we relied on intelligence to hunt out terrorist cells. Sometimes we purged villages and communities and dragged in women and children to be interrogated. They knew where the enemy was hiding and they knew where the weapons were stashed. I grew to hate children in that war.

My first mission was to identify – and then execute – a senior rebel leader. Intelligence believed he was based in a camp in the Aures mountains, near where we'd trained. I was called into an office and scattered across the table were black and white photographs of my target. "We want this man taken out before we attack the camp," said my commanding officer. "We have to be sure he doesn't escape during the raid. Take your time, study his face, keep the pictures. First go on a recon patrol, then report back. You must be sure we've found the right man. Then you must be completely sure he's dead before we go in."

The photos were black and white, grainy, and clearly taken from a distance, in what looked like a kasbah. Some were close-ups of his face that had been enlarged too much and were pixelating; others were full-length and sharper. There were people in the background, or to the sides, hints of market traders and ancient stone walls. In one, he was stood by the entrance to a dark alley that no doubt teemed with stalls and snake charmers and scents and spices.

I was surprised by what he was wearing: he looked more like a businessman than a rebel, like he was trying to supply a line of pots and pans to one of the traders. He wore a dark suit, white shirt and thin, black tie and was well groomed and clean-shaven. I was told he was middle-aged, mid-40s. He was tall, about six feet I'd say, broad-shouldered, with only the faintest hint of a straying stomach. He looked fit and healthy, like he ate the right stuff and didn't waste his nights with alcohol.

His face betrayed his age, though. There were patches of jet-back hair above his ears but only a faint layer remained across the top; his receding hairline exposed his temples, revealing a broad, olive-skinned expanse of forehead. His eyebrows redressed the balance a little. They were jet-black and heavy and made his eyes appear dark, fierce and threatening. His nose was sharp and prominent; he looked like a man who squared up to the world, who didn't hide, who could sense trouble, and who wasn't afraid to be decisive. He looked dangerous.

"These pictures were taken about five months ago in Algiers," I was told. "He may have changed his image by now, we don't know. That's why we need to be sure we have the right man first."

I was never told his name. Instead I was given coordinates and a spotter, and two nights later the pair of us were helicoptered into the mountains to the closest point possible, about five miles from our destination. We carried with us basic rations: tinned food, water, medical kit, sleeping bags, rifles, ammunition and knives. Plus the photographs, although by now I had the target's face practically imprinted on my brain. I had barely looked at anything else for the previous 48 hours, and had reached a point where I was imagining what he might look like now if he had a beard, no hair at all – or wore a head cover that he never removed. I felt I knew this man.

We climbed to a spot roughly a mile from our target and spent the first night in sleeping bags behind giant rocks that must have crashed down the mountainside and permanently settled on a wide ledge. It was a good, sheltered spot and we felt reasonably safe. The spotter was Spanish, his name Felipe, and he told me all about a girl he was madly in love with back home.

Even in pidgin English he described her beautifully, almost poetically, like she was an untouchable goddess not worthy of a man's sleazy stare. He wafted his hands around in the shape of an hour glass then, with a big, wide cheesy grin, he stood up and added: "But in the bed, she's a filthy whore." Then he thrust the lower half of his body backwards and forwards furiously, like he was having a convulsion. How I didn't burst out laughing and give away our position was beyond me. I wasn't even 19 years old and still a virgin, although that situation would soon be resolved. To this day, I have absolutely no idea if he was telling the truth. I don't even know if Felipe was his real name, and I didn't even care. It was a great story. It broke the tension.

Early the next morning, we moved towards a plateau that gently arched upwards, hoping it might overlook the rebels' camp. We were wearing khaki and sand-coloured gillie suits, covered with clumps of sparse shrub. I didn't have a helmet, just a sandy Arab-style headdress to keep the sun away. The ground was thick with sandy dust and gravel; it was hard, rocky and barren, and not an easy place to find convincing camouflage. We sprawled flat out on the ground and slithered, painfully slowly, towards the overhang – increasingly sure we could hear voices.

Sure enough, the camp was sprawled out below, close enough to be in range, close enough for us to recognise faces through a telescopic lens. I really liked the fact we were on a plateau with a slight slope up to the edge, so we could lie flat out and peer over without our bodies breaking the skyline looking up from below. The slight overhang gave us protection; we had a good direct escape route that nobody could readily cut across or outflank. It was a spot where we could survive – and get away from, quickly.

I didn't need to peer through my sights to get a sharp picture of the camp's layout. It was clearly well established; foxholes were well concealed and camouflaged with foliage; dining and communal areas had sturdy wooden supports, with canvas roofs that in turn had branches and shrubs scattered over their tops to help reduce their visibility from a French plane.

I spotted camels and goats in one corner, sheltering under some scruffy trees, and there were six or seven jeeps parked close to what looked like a mountain track, although it was so rocky and narrow it was hard to be sure from a distance.

There was plenty of activity below as well. I estimated around 50 rebels, either clustered around makeshift tables, studying maps or drinking coffee, or just talking in small groups. They were armed, but there was a complacency about the way they stood. Rifles were casually slung over shoulders, or propped up against trees. They looked like they felt safe there.

I studied the position of the sun, and wind direction, and Felipe and I readjusted ourselves so our scent wouldn't be a giveaway – and the sunlight wouldn't reflect off our sight lenses. We lay static, side by side. Somewhere down there was our target, but we had to find him first. I waved my hand towards the right of the camp and muttered: "You check out those groups over there, I'll have a look at that lot drinking coffee."

It was the eyes that were the giveaway, although I needed to go back a second day to be absolutely sure. The face had changed – there was a moustache and the beginnings of a beard now. He continuously ran his fingers through its wispy black hairs, as though he were trying to tug it into becoming longer. He had a cloth headdress, with a black headband holding it in place; it was hard to see the exposed temples that were so prominent in the photographs. But there's something about a man's eyes that are permanent and unique, like an unusual trademark on a rare artefact. The eyes are the stamp of a man's individuality. They are the giveaway when you can't see much else of the face. His eyes were fierce, piercing, confrontational, commanding. They were the eyes of the man in my photographs.

He was in the dining area, and I spotted him the moment he stood up to greet someone who had just sauntered over. He wasn't wearing a suit anymore; his trousers were khaki and loose-fitting, his shirt was off-white, with two big bold pockets on the chest. He kept the sleeves long, buttoned down tightly around his wrists, with an ammunition belt slung over his left shoulder and falling diagonally down to his right hip. He looked alert; he still looked dangerous.

"That's him," I mumbled, just loud enough for Felipe to hear. He inched himself closer to my line of sight, so he could give a second opinion. The pair of us lay there, barely daring to breathe, conscious of each other's heartbeats. It felt like we lay there for an eternity; as the sun beat down, beads of sweat would squeeze into the miniscule gap between our straining eyes and the lenses until our vision would blur and we'd have to wipe the perspiration off with our shirtsleeves. Then Felipe said the three words I didn't want to hear. "I'm not sure."

He added: "I need to see him without the headdress. We need to wait." I was dismayed, but I knew it was imperative we had the right man. There must be no doubt. So we waited and waited and waited and the sun beat down and our clothes grew wet with sweat and we tried to drink from water bottles – lying down – and we used plastic bags to pee in – lying down – so the smell of urine wouldn't betray us. We watched him eat, talk, stretch, tug his beard, move around, go to the latrine area, sit round a camp fire. Around midnight he disappeared into his foxhole. He never once removed his headdress. "We'll have to return first thing tomorrow morning, before the sun rises," I said.

We returned to our sheltered rocks but barely slept that night. I didn't need to study the photographs again, I was so sure. I'd close my eyes and see his dark, piercing eyes staring back at me.

Sometimes I'd look at this image in my mind and see it slowly turn into the hypnotic face of Grey Wolf. Grey Wolf knew. Grey Wolf was my confirmation. I had the right man.

We made our way back before sunrise, and stretched into position, our sights firmly glued on the entrance to the target's foxhole. About an hour later, as the camp awoke to a new day, we saw movement and out came our man. He stood almost directly in front of us, stretched, then headed towards some rocks, where he urinated. He had no headdress and his temples practically bulged out of his head, pushing back a diminishing hairline. "OK, OK, it's him. I'm satisfied," whispered Felipe.

"I could take him out right now, there's nobody around yet," I replied. But Felipe shook his head decisively. "No, we're under orders to report back first. Let's leave now."

Two days later we were back on the same plateau, with fresh provisions and clothing and orders to "take out the target", then radio an all-clear for the regiment to move in. Felipe would be with me; we were also joined this time by two scouts who'd identified the camp coordinates originally. They stayed at our makeshift base by the rocks while we observed from the plateau.

SQUEEZING
THE TRIGGER

Six days to create the world; six days to end a human life. The irony isn't lost on me. That's how long I needed to squeeze the trigger and shoot my target, first in the brain, then in the heart. I needed to be sure he was dead.

I had many clear moments to take him out before then, but I had to take into account the other 49 rebels in the camp, what they were doing, and how quickly they could grab weapons and respond. Would any one of them be able to work out where my bullets had been fired from? Would they be close enough to scramble up and reach us before we could escape? The mission wasn't just about killing a target, it was about getting away safely.

I didn't just have one target to consider. I needed to become familiar with how the camp operated as a unit, where people tended to congregate, whether anyone had a habit of walking a bit too close to where we were lying, where they would prop up weapons, when they'd get up, when they'd eat, relax, use a radio, leave the camp and return with provisions; when they'd sleep, shave and shit. I needed to know precisely when the sun would rise, where it would cast shadows at what time of the day, when it would blaze down uninterrupted and be potentially blinding to either me – or the rebels below – and when it would start to fade. Then, there were the moon and stars to consider. How much could they illuminate the camp, would they be like floodlights giving us away as we retreated?

I didn't expect it would take six days for the right moment to arrive. That's a long time to follow a man you're planning to kill. By the end, you're as close to knowing him as a person as you might be if you'd chatted to him all the time. You get to see everything in his life: his mannerisms, habits, insecurities, facial expressions. When he's happy, angry, moody, reflective, hungry, thirsty. "He'll be going for a piss any moment now," I'd whisper to Felipe, and sure enough, off he'd go. A man's life is incredibly predictable when you watch it through a viewfinder.

There were moments when his masks would subside and I'd see him uncensored. He wouldn't look like a rebel then, he'd look vaguely human, his mind lost in another world. Maybe he was thinking about family, or children, or a woman, who knows? But his vulnerability in those moments was wasted on me: for six days he remained a target, nothing more, nothing less. An average soldier rarely gets this close to a target; doesn't breath in unison with him, doesn't connect as intimately with its humanity, its ordinariness, its life. At the end, I understood how my target conducted himself, how he physically went about the act of living. It was the little stuff I noticed: which hand he held a knife and fork in, which he picked up first, how often he tugged that silly little beard, how many cups of coffee he'd go through, what he liked to eat, how he'd desperately try to make his thinning hair look fuller than it was when he thought nobody was watching.

It was extremely personal stuff, but it didn't make him any more or less a target. At least, not then. I was there to be a sniper, and I'd permanently switched off any worries about taking a life. I was in a detached place, completely devoid of any emotion, any feeling of pity for this person. He was a terrorist, he was responsible for killing my colleagues, so he had to be stopped. If I had any thoughts at all about this man, it wasn't for his humanity, it was for the killer he had also chosen to become.

No, the hardest part wasn't shooting him. The hardest part was working out when. There were moments when he was alone, in the clear, a good, clean target. But there would always be a snag. Someone else would be too close, a group would be cleaning guns a little nearer to us than I liked, the sunlight was working against me. I'd hoped to get the job over quickly but the minutes dragged into hours and then dusk would descend and slowly men with distinct faces and characteristics became indistinct shadows and shapes flitting around in the impenetrable dark.

On day three, I thought a moment had come. It was around 4pm, the sun wasn't in my line of sight, he was within range, alone, close to the entrance of his foxhole, and my fingers were beginning to flirt with the trigger. Then I started to hear a slow, distant rumble and before I knew it, three jeeps suddenly appeared along the mountain track and parked up, and about 15 rebels jumped out excitedly, whooping and waving rifles high in the air. "Shit," I mumbled. My target ran over to greet them and the camp exploded into a flurry of bear hugs and embraces and laughter all round. "This is the last thing we needed." Felipe nodded anxiously.

The practicalities of life get in the way when you're stalking someone for so long on a mountain plateau in searing heat. There are moments when you have to shit into a plastic bag and then find a way of burying it quickly to erase the foul scent. There are moments when you've run out of water because you simply can't take the heat any longer and you've drunk too much, too soon. Then there are moments when your eyes grow weary from the sheer exhaustion of staring for so long through the small circumference of a telescopic lens.

I've no doubt the fact I'd already experienced a vision quest helped me as I lay there; indeed, my mind would slip back to being a nine-year-old boy, sat alone in the Montana mountains, fighting sleep, hunger and thirst. Now, just nine years later, I was experiencing similar sensations, fighting my own mind and body, fighting the deprivations I was enduring. I was able to see it out because I'd waited before. As each day dragged into another night, Felipe and I would slide back to where the two scouts were camped on our rocky ledge, and radio back to base that the mission was still not completed. By day five, frustration had set in. All of us were getting tetchy, bored, irritable. There was little humour.

We slithered back into position before dawn on day six and once again watched the camp slowly awaken. There was still no awareness, no sign of suspicion below; their behaviour was relaxed, confident – even sloppy. They didn't have any cover times or watches.

Around 10am, we suddenly saw unexpected activity around the jeeps; rebels were hurling bundles of kit and ammunition into the backs of vehicles. There was another outburst of embraces and hugs, and then around 30 of them clambered into six jeeps and headed off. My target stayed behind, only this time there were fewer rebels in the camp – I estimated around 35. It felt significant and I whispered to Felipe: "I'm going to take him out today, this is my chance."

The moment came around 1pm. He was sat at a table in the dining area, eating bread and soup, with two others. He was side-on to me, I had a good, clear uninterrupted view. The conditions were perfect, the sun was shining into his eyes and he was constantly lifting his left arm so his angled palm could shield against the dazzling glare. His colleagues were both sat to his right, face-on to me. Their rifles were casually propped against the end of the table. There were no obstacles in the way, and no people in the immediate area. No threat.

I held my rifle firmly in position, and pinpointed the left-hand side of his brain with my telescopic sight. For the first time my finger pulled back on the trigger to the point of no return and I fired, smoothly, efficiently and calmly. It was a clean execution, a perfect shot, a good kill in the midday sun. I saw him jolt to his right on impact; his body twisted towards me but still remained propped in the chair he was on. I now had a good view of his chest so I fired another bullet into his heart. Just like the arrow I'd shot into the deer. A bullet, an arrow, piercing the innocent air. Again, his body jumped with the impact of the second bullet, but I already knew he was gone. I was just making sure. For an instant, I noticed his eyes – his identity, his power, his humanity – were still open inside his closed body.

Instant panic broke out in the camp. The two people he'd been chatting to hit the deck and took cover under the table. Two machine guns were in position but nobody rushed to them – everyone scrambled instead for hiding places. I stayed in position, observing the chaos; nobody broke cover. Many of them hadn't even grabbed their own weapons before scurrying for shelter.

As I carried on watching, Felipe radioed the waiting regiment. "Target down. Move in." My adrenalin levels were off the scale. I was elated, I was high on success, I was dangerous, but I was also straining. Straining to get down there and see my target close-up. Straining to see where the bullets had gone in. I knew it was a good, clean kill but I wanted to see it close-up, to hold it in my hands, to feel the professionalism. "It", not "him". So Felipe and I waited and watched as our regiment moved in and annihilated everything that was still alive in the camp. There was hardly any resistance.

Once the ambush was over, I clambered down and went straight to my target's lifeless body. I didn't see them at first. I was so consumed, so obsessed with wanting to see my work that I immediately examined the bullets' entry points; one in the brain, one in the heart. Perfect. Clinical. A good, clean execution; a job well done. I felt enormous pride: I'd proved I was a shot. Everything had worked perfectly. I was a fuckin' Legionnaire sniper. The elite.

I inhaled deeply and took one more look – and that's when I saw them. The eyes. His eyes. His eyes were open, and they were looking right into me.

I shuddered. How could he do that, how was it possible? His eyes had me trapped in a hypnotic vice-like grip, and they were saying: "How could you do this? How could you kill me after you'd watched me so closely? What kind of animal are you? Do you have no limits, no humanity, no shame?"

I broke free from his stare, turned and walked away. No part of me was prepared to *think* about what I'd just done. We eventually jumped into waiting helicopters and, as we lifted off the ground and looked down on the rocky dustbowl below, I let out an animal scream. It was like some brewing force erupting out of me; a volcano that had waited 79 years – since the Battle of the Little Bighorn – to unleash its power and fury. "I am Grey Wolf. Great-great-fuckin'-grandson to Little Hawk, Northern Cheyenne warrior, sworn ally of Sitting Bull and Crazy Horse, fearless conquerors of General Custer and the 7th Cavalry." In my naïve mind, my words ricocheted around the mighty Aures mountains, sent shivers across the sweeping Sahara plains, and reverberated around Montana's mighty rocks and boulders: Gian Falconie, Premier Fuckin' Elite.

I hit the bottle the second our helicopter landed back at base. I got pissed beyond any normal level; I drank as though I was clearing out the entire supply of alcohol in that God-forsaken country. It started with Kronenbourg, it switched to any coloured wine I could gulp and it ended with spirits, mainly brandy. It was probably the moment I became an alcoholic. Eighteen years old. Dependent.

I wasn't winding down from having killed, either; I was winding down from the tension of wanting to prove how well I could kill. That was the bigger strain. The strain of showing the Legion what I was really capable of, now they'd trained me. No matter how much I drank, I never really got drunk, I just got rid of the edge. It was the only way I could deal with the aftermath. Drink also helped blur the memory of his eyes; drink pushed away retribution, guilt, blame, self-recrimination, religion, God, the Great Spirit, my soul, my morality. Doubt. Drink stopped me thinking about why I wasn't bothered. Deep down – really, really deep – I feared I was bothered. That was an abyss I didn't wish to peer into. If I drank, I wouldn't reflect – and if I didn't reflect, I could carry on killing.

I didn't know it then, but I know it now. If I was ordered to execute that target all over again, in that way, I couldn't do it. I know way too much now. I know that, in the end, the recrimination catches up with you. The guilt, the remorse, it seeps into your body one day and it doesn't leave. Who was I deluding? It was never the bloody deer, it wasn't the same sort of target. It was human, it had children, love, hopes, dreams, anxieties, fears, insecurities. It had life, and I took that life by pretending it was just a target. That is no way to kill. That target and I – we became too close. We became connected during those six days; killing became too personal.

In the end, the eyes had the final say. They never fuckin' close.

VIRGIN SOLDIER

Two massive events brought 1956 to a climactic ending for me –
and neither lasted very long. The first, was the small role I played
in the Suez Crisis. The second? I lost my virginity.

My battalion was temporarily transferred from Algeria to a base
just outside Nicosia in Cyprus as tensions over Suez mounted. I
was still a driver in the company. None of us really understood
why we'd been sent there, and none of us cared very much about
the politics. But we were quickly thrown into the action, and on
November 6 parachuted into Port Fuad.

It was a miracle we even made it on to the battle zone below. We
were flying in an old British Valetta aircraft, a great lumbering pig
of a thing, and had just stood to begin our jumps. As we shuffled
towards the exit, there was suddenly a massive thump and a
violent gush of air; the plane shuddered and rocked violently.
We'd been hit – but the shell had burst through the undercarriage
and then rocketed straight back out through the top of the plane,
without exploding, leaving two gigantic holes in its wake. Freezing
air blasted into the cabin, and although it felt like we were caught
in a tornado, the plane was still functional and we could continue
with the drop.

I landed on an old airfield and hit the deck immediately. Some Legionnaires never made it and were shot in mid-air. Our equipment was dropped in separate containers. I had no rifle with me, so my priority was to get myself armed quickly. I crawled behind a giant oil drum, crouched, and peered through holes that had pierced through its metal skin. Only then did it dawn on me that I was looking through bullet holes: the drum provided about as much cover as a piece of paper.

Next, I felt a hefty kick up my backside and a voice yelling "*Achtung!*" One of our sergeants pointed towards a container that must have burst open on landing: guns and ammunition were spewed out along the ground. He gave me cover as I raced over, grabbed kit, and joined up with the rest of my unit, now sheltering in the skeletal remains of an aircraft hangar. It was a strange war zone: there already seemed to be less Egyptian resistance and by the time we'd pushed on into Sinai, and joined up with Israeli forces a few hours later, word spread that our role was already over. It had lasted barely a day. I don't think I killed anyone.

We returned to Cyprus shortly afterwards, where all we wanted to do was get pissed, and get laid. There was plenty of opportunities for both: the old citadel was teeming with late-night bars and brothels. It was also teeming with British and French military police, who were desperately trying to keep us away from the local prostitutes. Needless to say they failed, and I lost my virginity to a French girl in the back room of a dark, downstairs bar built into the cellar of some ancient, stone-walled building.

I was completely pissed when I first saw her, sitting alone at a table. I couldn't understand why she seemed to be smiling at me; next, she was beckoning me over with a curled finger. "Lads, lads – look, I've pulled – that bird at the table," I slurred. They egged me on, so I stumbled over and started telling her how pretty she was. She had short, boyish black hair, and even though I could barely focus properly, her brown eyes were soft and inviting. I vaguely remember her holding my right hand, standing up and whispering: "Follow me." She led me through a bedraggled curtain into a small corridor, with two doors facing each other. She opened the one on the right and we entered a tiny, dark space with the vague outline of a bed almost filling the entire room. With her back pressing against me, she said "Unbutton my blouse, Monsieur Legionnaire" as though she was issuing an order. I nervously complied; about 10 minutes later I was back in the bar. I can't remember how much I paid her, but my mission was complete. My mates took the piss remorselessly; any hint of romance quickly vanished when one of them went off into the same room with her shortly afterwards.

THE DAY I DIED

I died in Algeria. I was blown up and my heart stopped beating, I was unconscious and unaware. Apparently, medics pummelled my prostrate body with electric shocks and pressed the skin above my heart, up and down, furiously. How strange; they wanted to keep me alive.

Not then, but sometime later, I felt the sensation of death. I was floating down a long, dazzlingly bright, white corridor. Above me shone millions of tiny spotlights, like a planetarium of stars, and everywhere felt overwhelmingly warm and comforting and safe. Perhaps in the way a baby feels inside the womb. It felt like I was being drawn into something divine, heavenly, somewhere not as ugly as this world.

My weightless body was drifting towards the end of the corridor, where a galactic-sized explosion of more light seemed to be waiting for me. I lifted my head to peer into this impenetrable whiteness and stared, hypnotically, as a dark outline started to form in the epicentre. I heard a voice, my voice, yet it didn't seem to be coming from me, and it was repeating – over and over – the same three words: "Take the pain." I knew I had to obey and tried moving on to my side: the sudden surge of agony was excruciating.

It was unbearable, it came in great crashing waves that were so powerful, so relentless, so mighty, they shattered the whiteness and the corridor and the warmth and the comfort. Everything bright disappeared, like someone had switched off an electric light. All that remained was infinite torture.

I was coming back from death. I was choosing to face up to living instead. The dark outline in the middle of the brightness had saved me. The outline had told me to "take the pain". Grey Wolf had spoken.

We returned to Algeria from Cyprus, and I carried on working as a sniper, based in Zeralda again. If units were moving in to ambush an enemy camp, I'd go with them, this time targeting rebel snipers who would be trying to pick off Legionnaires as they advanced. Again, I was good at it: there was something intuitive within me that could sense where a rebel might be hiding. If a shot went off, I knew rapidly where it was coming from; over the next few months I successfully killed eight or nine enemy snipers. I even became known as "The Hawk Who Watches".

I saw a lot of death during this period, or certainly much more than I'd been used to. I never experienced an enemy air bombardment in Algeria, but I certainly witnessed the carnage they left behind. Intelligence would give the coordinates of a suspected rebel camp or town, planes would be sent in, bombs dropped, and then we would follow up behind. I would frequently see severed limbs, dismembered torsos, bits of arms and legs, and fragments of flesh scattered on the ground, or over trees and bushes. Men, women and children – the bombs never discriminated. The only thing that shocked me was that I wasn't shocked by such gore. I was immune. I never blinked. In fact, I made jokes of it. Sometimes, we'd have a laugh with the dead bodies. I remember approaching the remnants of a village one day when one of the Legionnaires turned to me and said: "Oi, Chicco, give us a ciggie will you?" I handed one over, and watched as he perched a dead body, an older-looking guy, upright onto a tree trump that was still smouldering from the bombardment. Half his head was missing: it had been severed off almost horizontally, so all that remained was the left-hand side and an open gap where his mangled brain and skull were exposed. His neck and shirt were splattered with blood and bits of flesh. "There you go, mate," said the Legionnaire. "You have a nice ciggie," and he actually lit the cigarette before putting it in what remained of the victim's mouth. That was considered hilarious.

Such macabre humour didn't repulse me, any more than seeing a man with half his head missing did. It was part of a survival mechanism, it was what the living did. It was a way of underlining our superiority and reminding ourselves that we still breathed: we'd won another skirmish, we'd lived to fight another day, we were cleverer and smarter. We had no boundaries. Maybe the ludicrous machismo made us feel safer. Nobody would be sticking cigarettes in our severed heads.

The laughter stopped abruptly when my own death got in the way. I never saw the humour in that. Most of what I am about to explain was told to me by the Legionnaires and medics who helped save my life. I have absolutely no memory at all of the build-up to my death, or what happened in the immediate aftermath.

I know I'd joined another unit that was about to ambush a camp up in the mountains. I even remember working on one of their vehicles the day before. Something was wrong with the handbrake on a truck; I replaced the cable so it'd be safe to use on the steep roads and tracks that lay ahead.

We set off the following morning in a convoy, although I've no memory of even this. I was in a jeep with three others, sat directly behind the driver. That much is definite. So was the land mine we hit, the land mine that blew the jeep to smithereens, vaporising the driver and front passenger. "All that was left of them was their feet, which were still inside their boots," I was later informed. The Legionnaire sat next to me was blown apart. Apparently, his body was reduced to jigsaw-sized fragments, some pieces bigger than others, each bit severed and separated. All that remained of the jeep, all that was substantial and recognisable, was a rear wheel arch, the one behind the driver. The one I'd been sat above.

Legionnaires in the truck behind found my body propped against the jeep's last remaining tyre. I was unconscious and my skull had caved in on the left-hand side, so my head looked like a football that had some air left on one side but was completely deflated on the other. Blood was pouring out of a wound that began on the deflated side of my collapsed skull, ran down my forehead, straight through my left eye, over my cheekbone, across my lips and down to my chin. Medics realised my spine was also broken – but they also detected a faint pulse and lifted me into a makeshift ambulance. We turned around and headed back for base. That was when I died.

I knew nothing about being resuscitated. I came out of a coma three weeks later. As I woke, I instinctively tried to move; then I screamed, without embarrassment or shame, as a jolt of raw pain shuddered through my body. In a way, the pain was a relief. I was alive and I was connected. I remember a distant voice. I think it said: "Take the pain."

I didn't dare move again so I looked up at a ceiling, and wondered why it seemed so far away and why there were so many cracks and lines swirling all over its peeling, off-white surface. I convinced myself the scrawls looked familiar; I was certain I was looking at a giant, upside-down map – the same one I'd studied when I was sent into the mountains to kill.

Suddenly, a blurred shape interrupted my stupor and my eyes struggled to refocus. A woman in a bold, white apron was leaning over me. I thought she was wearing a kepi, so she had to be Legion, but I'd never seen a woman Legionnaire, so that didn't make sense. "I heard you cry out," she whispered, and then she asked me if I could remember my name, my unit – and what had happened to me. "Gian Falconie, Premier Rep," I mouthed. But why did no sound seem to be coming from my mouth? "Gian Falconie," I repeated. "Gian Falconie... Gian Falconie." The effort made me breathless and I gave up. She smiled and I felt her fingers softly touching my left hand. "Lie there, Legionnaire. We will look after you now."

I didn't know what had happened to me, or where I was, for a few more days. I slowly became familiar with my surroundings: a huge, cavernous hall that might, once, have been a grand ballroom, with an impossibly out-of-reach ceiling, propped up by huge, chunky columns that were peeling and cracked just like the ceiling. Huge fans dangled down, clattering and croaking as they tried to battle the stifling heat. The more they whirled, the more the ceiling trembled. Surely it would crash down at any moment.

I was the last bed in a long row; to my left was an entrance corridor flanked by small offices, where nurses in long, white aprons silently drifted in and out, usually carrying bottles and pans. Immediately to my right was another bed, metal-framed like mine, and all that separated us was a small, rickety cabinet and what looked like a mosquito net, drawn back. Opposite stood the columns and beyond them another row of beds, facing towards me. Every bed seemed occupied and each told its own story. Over some, Legionnaires were sat upright, on top of the covers, laughing with visitors or flirting with nurses. Over others, there was stillness; not even the giant, rattling fans could disturb the pallor of death that hung over those beds.

The bombshell came a few days later, when an elderly doctor, maybe 60 years old, sat on the side of my bed. He had a thin, angular face and harsh, chiselled features; he looked like he'd spent a lifetime delivering bad news. In his hand was a clipboard; he wore round, thin, black-framed glasses, perched low across the crown of his nose, and his eyes flitted between the reports on his board and looking at me. He spoke with a strong German accent and told me exactly what had happened.

"You were in a jeep that hit a land mine," he explained. "You were the only survivor. Your heart stopped on the way back to base. You're only alive because the medics used electric shock treatment and massaged your heart back into life. But you also sustained many life-threatening injuries that required complex surgery."

He then told me I had fractured my spine in five places, and two of my lower discs were mashed beyond repair. My skull had collapsed; to push it back, he explained, holes had been drilled into the top of my cranium. A surgeon had then inserted a small plunger, like he was unblocking a sink, and sucked my head back into shape. The holes were then filled with a compound, something like grout, that I've subsequently learned can be used in the manufacture of Astroturf. As far as I know, it's still in there.

I also came incredibly close to losing my left eye altogether, added the doctor. Two surgeons had argued over whether it could be saved: one had said no, the other wanted to try. "I was the surgeon who said no," he confessed, without any hint of remorse. "Luckily for you, I lost. The other surgeon managed to stitch your eye together and save your sight. He did an excellent job."

The doctor then told me the diagonal scar that ran from the top of my head, through my eye, and down to my chin, would never fully disappear. He was right.

He was saving the worst for last, however. His eyes looked up from his clipboard and for a second I thought I saw his fingers grip its sides a bit more intensely. "I have to inform you, Mr Falconie, that you are very lucky to still be alive. But it is also my professional opinion that you will never walk again. Your days as a Legionnaire are over, although, in time, you may be able to perform office duties."

I remember telling him to "fuck off". I remember trying to kick him, but was left grimacing wildly as another bolt of pain tore down my spine. "Fuck off, you bastard. Just fuck off. I'm not fuckin' finished."

I walked out of that hospital six months later. Six months of unrelenting torture, tears and torment. Without the spirit of Grey Wolf, without those three words "take the pain" – that doctor would have been right. Only sheer bloody mindedness got me through. First the nurses helped me sit up in bed, then they got me on to crutches, which I used day after day after day to drag myself up and down the ward, stopping to chat now and then with wounded Legionnaires. The pain was always at its worst when the entire weight of my body seemed to funnel into the bottom of my back, where my mangled vertebrae couldn't handle the shock.

Some days I'd lie in bed, push my legs together and try to lift them slowly. That's when the tears would come, when I'd almost bite straight through my lips to strangle the screams that were pressing, desperately, to erupt out of me. Like Whitehawk had at the sun dance. Nurses would try to inject me with painkillers; sometimes I'd accept, unable to suffer the torture any longer. More often, I'd refuse. Grey Wolf wanted me to "take the pain".

If I was feeling pain, I was still alive. I started to be called The Crazy Legionnaire.

Slowly, impossibly, some of the exercises became easier until I abandoned the sticks and walked up and down the ward unaided. The doctor said I'd never walk again. Fuck him. A nurse stood at one end and I walked towards her, until she was so close I reached out and fell into her embrace. "Crazy Legionnaire," she whispered and we both stood there, holding on to each other, sobbing. I don't know who she was, but her sweet-scented body, pressed against mine, was all the reward I needed for having taken those first, independent steps.

I was discharged shortly afterwards, determined to go on another parachute jump to prove I was fit enough to return to full duty. I was paraded in front of a medical board, senior officers looking stern in full kit, kepis, gloves, the works. "I was told I would never walk again but I've defied the doctors. Now I'm ready to complete a parachute jump and return to the Legion," I proclaimed. I was wasting my breath; permission was refused. Instead, I was despatched to an audio room, where I was expected to plough through piles of tape recordings and paperwork. I wasn't going to settle for that.

I spent the following six months back in the main base at Sidi Bel Abbes, dragging my body back to somewhere near full fitness. I was still in pain but the crutches were gone for good. Each morning, before heading off to the office job, I'd go for a jog, which gradually got faster and longer. Sometimes I'd break into sprints, sometimes I'd carry a rucksack. Three months after that, I was climbing over obstacles, fences, anything that needed scaling – then jumping down to see if I could land on the other side without collapsing. I even returned to the surrounding hills where I'd originally trained to be a Legionnaire, increasing the distances I'd run until I was covering five miles a day with relative ease.

I knew I'd have to complete a parachute jump if I was to return, but could I really handle it? To find out, I enrolled with a civilian school and didn't tell them about my injuries. I was terrified going up, terrified jumping out – and terrified coming down. Everything depended on whether my spine would handle the landing. The relief when my feet landed squarely on the ground and I fell into a textbook roll, knees and ankles locked close together, was euphoric. I felt a jab of pain but it vanished as quickly as it arrived. I stood up smiling, not grimacing.

One year after being told I was finished I was truly ready to prove I could be a Legionnaire. I badgered an adjutant I trusted to let me go on a Legion parachute jump. "I've already done a civilian jump," I confessed. "I'm ready." He relented, I jumped successfully, and was granted a second medical board. I walked in, knowing this would be my last chance, and straightaway noticed everyone present was dressed differently: they were wearing berets, not kepis. They were paratroopers, and this was a shoo-in. They listened to my pleas and after some low-level muttering, pronounced: "We have found you fit for service, you can return to a company." I was fuckin' back!

CRIME AND PUNISHMENT

The children were the worst. The men, well, they *looked* suspicious; it was easy to believe they were terrorists as they grouped together on street corners and whispered furtively under heavy, dark beards. It was the same with the women, their femininity buried under flowing, white haiks, only their eyes on view. It's amazing how sinister a woman's eyes can be when you can't see any other part of her face.

No, the children were the worst. Even when they were running away, they looked innocent. How can you look at a child, often desperately impoverished, malnourished and trapped in a war beyond its comprehension, and suspect it of terrorism? We did. I did. I looked at boys and girls, barely eight or nine years old, often dressed in rags and plagued by armies of flies constantly circling scabs and sores around their mouths, and saw the enemy.

Children would lead you into an ambush. We chased a group through winding passages one evening until the alleyway broke into a small market square, where suddenly we came under rifle fire. Seconds earlier, I'd heard them laughing, like children do, then they simply disappeared. There was no such thing as a sweet, innocent child for us.

That's what a terrorist-style war does. It makes you suspect everything. Even the surroundings. You couldn't believe what you saw. Women hunched under the weight of bulging bags, stuffed with pots and pans. Or maybe they were carrying weapons? Bombs? Even the emaciated cows and donkeys barely standing under the strain of leather satchels slung around their midriffs. Were they the enemy, too?

After passing the second medical board, I was attached to the 11th Parachute Brigade and sent to Algiers town, where the Legion was arresting suspected terrorists and interrogating them until they broke – often under intense torture – to reveal the location of enemy cells. My job was to round up the suspects.

In many respects, it was worse than being on an ambush. I never knew who the enemy was: it was nobody, it was everybody. The heaving kasbahs were a labyrinth of tightly packed alleyways that provided endless shelter and darkened corners for an enemy; tiny, narrow windows, as thin as skin lesions, were barely visible slits where a rifle could be propped. In such surroundings, you were constantly battling your own sanity; my grip on the rifle had an edge of paranoia. Fear was around every corner; the tension of staying aware, alert, alive was all-consuming. By the end of the day, only alcohol temporarily lifted the strain. I drank more during this period than ever before, simply to calm my fraying nerves. I started supplementing beer to get more bite, mixing stuff in – spirits, whisky, rum, ouzo.

We'd either go on patrols, or head for specific addresses provided by intelligence. Anybody without an identity card was automatically taken away. We searched every cranny, using knives to pick at walls that might be covering some secret hiding place, or caches of hidden guns and ammunition.

There'd already been 200 plastic bomb explosions in Algiers town; sometimes a car would be driven Mafia-style down a narrow street, the windows open, machine guns sticking out ready to mow down anyone looking vaguely European. I came to see it all as one giant terrorist conspiracy, even the evil mosquitos that whirled incessantly in front of me, always agonisingly out of reach. If recon said a man, woman, child – even a fuckin' donkey – was a terrorist, I'd believe them, and round them up.

There may have been rules, but I really wasn't very bothered about them. We'd go into an area, push, drag or carry suspects on to wagons, and take them to the interrogation centres – cold, isolated concrete buildings on the edge of town. Far enough away so nobody could hear the screams. If the prisoners got stroppy, we'd slam a rifle butt into their stomachs. Or thump them with a sock filled with sand; that way, there'd be no marks. Or force them into stress positions – maybe standing perfectly still against a wall, or sitting down, legs crossed, upper body erect. If they relaxed, they'd be kicked back into position.

It was standard to see suspects have their heads covered, so they had no awareness of the world around them. Torture was standard, too: I know electric wires were attached to men's testicles, because I'd hear their tormented cries.

Very few went home after a night in an interrogation centre. In the mornings, I'd watch as bodies would be dragged into helicopters, concrete blocks strapped to their feet, and then pushed out into the Bay of Algiers. Nobody checked if they were dead or alive. From the Legion's perspective, the interrogation policy worked. The idea was to drive the FLN out of Algiers town, and that's what happened. Rebels fled to the mountains, where their camps and hiding places were hunted out and bombed.

Something within me was worried, however. I'd seen and heard stuff I didn't like – stuff I didn't want to face up to, or question.

Maybe it was the children.

If I thought about the insanity too much, I might weaken. So I drowned the doubt in drink, but that led to a problem I hadn't anticipated at all. I wasn't a happy drunk; the worse I got, the angrier and more violent I became, until I got into fights – and not with the enemy. One corporal, in particular, had been getting on my nerves: he knew he had the power of his rank, it aroused him, and he couldn't resist abusing it with unnecessary punishments for trivial offences. I lost count of how many times he'd kick me on the shins because he thought my kit wasn't immaculate enough. I got sick of his sarcastic asides and insults, always loud enough for everyone to hear, just like a tap – drip, drip, dripping.

I returned to base one night severely pissed and spotted him, alone, in a guards' room. I remember mumbling to myself "I'm going to have that bastard" and I remember storming in and yelling: "Do you want some?" Everything after that is a blur. I know I smashed my boot repeatedly into his face and ribs as he lay battered and bleeding on the floor; I know he never fully recovered and eventually needed a medical discharge. It took 15 guards to subdue me; the room was trashed beyond all recognition. "It was like a tornado had hit it, only you were the tornado," one of the guards told me the next morning.

It was a court-martial offence but I was first sent for a psychiatric evaluation. My brain was X-rayed and I was hauled in front of a doctor, a crazed-professor type with the most insane black hair. Every strand seemed to be standing bolt upright, as though it was being pulled up by a powerful magnetic field. He was slightly built, fresh-faced and disarmingly young – 28 years old perhaps – and I remember thinking "How the fuck can you possibly know what it's like when children want to kill you?" He tried to sound experienced but I knew he was bullshitting. He asked me about the drinking: "How much do you drink, what do you drink, what time do you start, when do you finish, when does the anger start, do you actually feel drunk, why has it become excessive, are you out of control? Do you know what you're doing?"

Next, he moved into intelligence-test-type questions. "What shape do you see in this picture?" Then he thrust a page full of tiny black and white dots at me and asked: "Can you see the words hidden among the dots?" Bull-fuckin'-shit.

About a week later, I was hauled in front of a disciplinary committee and stood, stock still in full kit, as they solemnly read out the report's findings. Apparently, the cortex of my brain entirely lost its ability to define the difference between right and wrong when drowned in alcohol. "In effect," said the report, "he is reduced to the basic state of a wild animal, with no normal brain function whatsoever and strong homicidal tendencies." I have never forgotten those last three words.

It wasn't strictly a court martial but I was sentenced to spend three months at the Legion's notorious penal battalion at Colomb-Bechar. It wasn't run like a prison; more like a training camp – the most vicious, brutal and God-damned evil training camp I'd ever encountered.

I was thrown into a padded cell on my own as soon as I arrived and forced into detox, something I'd never experienced before largely because I'd always been able to pour myself another drink. I was abandoned, with no medication and only basic food and drink occasionally pushed through a slit in the cell door.

My body caved in rapidly: first I started to tremble and shake, my heart-rate accelerating until it felt like my chest was about to explode. Then I vomited until there was nothing left to come out, other than my own intestines. My body temperature swung erratically between excessive sweating and violent shivering. Then came the hallucinations. Gigantic reptiles, hideously repulsive with cavernous mouths and teeth the size of rock faces, were tearing me apart for food. I yelled and screamed uncontrollably as they pulled and gnawed on my flesh. My body thrashed wildly from side to side as these creatures tore into me, their evil eyes mocking me as they reduced me to lumps of flesh. It felt so real and so terrifying. Only when the nightmare subsided did I realise I was heavily soiled.

I lost count of how many days I was there but, eventually, I was allowed out and joined the rest of the battalion in a regular barracks, although we slept in bunks, not individual beds. The daily regime was an exaggerated form of what we'd experienced in training, only the assault courses and the runs were more brutal – probably because of the burning heat – and the punishments for not being fit enough or quick enough were even more severe.

We'd be woken around 5am every morning to face a full kit inspection an hour later. God help you if there was the slightest crease or mark out of place. Then came an unremitting physical regime of hard labour and exercise. We were in an old desert fort, at the mercy of the most severe Sahara sun, yet we'd be forced to toil endlessly – breaking and smashing stones, climbing over walls with heavy bags, running, sprinting, crawling, duck-walking. I remember one day being so exhausted I was physically incapable of lifting myself over a wall I had to scale.

"Falconie!" roared the commander, kicking me hard in the back of my legs as I dangled on the wall. "Let's see if 24 hours in a *tombeau* will strengthen you." I was then marched over to a barren, exposed area of the base, thrown a pick axe, and ordered to dig a grave. The lumpy ground was a cloggy mash of rocks and gravelly sand, and sweat poured out of me as I tried to smash through its stubborn layers. Eventually, I dug my grave; I was then ordered to strip to my underwear and forced to lie in it, with no protection at all from the ferocious sun. A guard watched over me as I lay there, my back pressed into the jagged rocks and stones along the grave's floor, the front of my body reddening, blistering and boiling under the intense heat. I begged for water until my lips became so cracked and dry, I could no longer hear any sound coming from my mouth. I could feel my eyelids swelling up as the minutes turned into hours, my sight becoming increasingly distorted.

At night time, when the temperature plummeted and became icy cold, a flimsy sheet was flung begrudgingly over my shivering wreck of a body. The following morning, I was dragged out and carried to my bunk bed, incapable of walking, my skin red-raw and covered in particles of harsh, grainy sand dust, deeply imbedded into my raw, engorged pores. It took me five days to recover but when I gave the wall another go, I got over it.

I was discharged after three months and allowed to return to my unit, the slate clean. My punishment had been severe but I wasn't resentful; part of me accepted I had it coming. But I also knew my five years with the Legion were almost up, so I decided to enrol on an NCO cadre course – hoping to earn a promotion. I guess I was a glutton for punishment: the training was intensely physical all over again; if you didn't move quickly enough, you got kicked – all over again. "We want you to experience how recruits will feel when you have to punish them," was how it was explained, although – heaven knows – I already knew. I stuck at it for eight weeks and rose to the rank of junior corporal, just in time to be told I could either commit to another five years with the Legion, or leave.

Maybe it was coming so close to death myself; maybe it was feeling what it was like to lie in my own grave; maybe it was the alcoholism and detox. Maybe it was the children.

Or maybe it had been the moment I was presented with my kepi and thought how proud my dad would have been. Whatever the reason, I found myself thinking increasingly about home. It was make or break – sign up for another five years, or face the music. I returned to Sidi Bel Abbes and explained how I was feeling. "If you go home, but return to the Legion within six months, you will keep your rank," I was told.

I decided to leave. Then came a strange moment: I was handed back my identity by the same Deuxieme Bureau sergeant who'd interrogated me originally when I first enrolled. The only person who knew who Bob Rose was. He gave a brief smile of recognition as he handed over the clothes I'd arrived in. Then my passport. I looked at the faded blue cover and was suddenly reminded I was a British citizen. I then flicked to my grainy black and white photograph and stared at the face of a man called Bob Rose. He looked a bit like me but I hadn't seen those two words for five years. I hadn't used them on any official paperwork or secretly scribbled them on to pieces of paper as a reminder.

What on earth happened to Bob Rose?

I remained open to the idea of returning to the Legion. I might need to; it might be my only means of escape. I was handed a certificate that confirmed I'd served for five years and noticed the words "honneur et fidelite". I felt immense pride. Yes, my passport proved I was a British citizen, but the certificate proved I was a Legionnaire. I could salute the Queen – but I might put my hand on my heart for the President, too.

I returned to England by ferry and made my way by train to Birmingham. I badly wanted to see my parents but I knew I had to give myself up first, so I headed straight for Digbeth police station in the city centre. I nervously paced up and down the pavement opposite for a while: the building looked austere, in a way Victorian buildings do, with an ornamental clock tower at one end that I'm sure was chiming: "Time's up, Bob Rose".

I switched my stare to the stone arch over the entrance door, where an old-fashioned police lamp was hanging, and thought "sod it". Without any further hesitation, I marched across the road, entered, stood squarely in front of a desk sergeant and said, as though I was addressing a commanding officer on a Legion parade: "My name is Bob Rose. Five years ago, I murdered someone in Birmingham and I've come to hand myself in." His jaw practically collapsed onto the old wooden counter he'd been leaning against and he stared at me like I was taking the piss. "Oh really," he replied. "I'm afraid we'll need a few more details than that," and he instructed me to sit on one of the chairs lined up in a row opposite.

I was eventually ushered into a small room with just a table and two or three chairs and a window. I was surprised the window didn't have bars; it was probably big enough for me to squeeze through. A couple of detectives introduced themselves and took a statement. "We need your full name and date of birth, your address here in Birmingham, where and when the offence happened – and the name of the person you murdered." They scribbled notes as I answered, but their impassive reactions alarmed me. They seemed cold and indifferent to my story, and I even added: "It's probably odd for someone to give themselves up like this, but I am telling the truth, you know." There was hardly any eye contact.

I was left alone and pondered the cold, grey walls – and the unbarred window – until they returned about an hour later.

Without even sitting down, one of them straightaway said: "Please don't take this personally, Mr Rose, but we've got absolutely nothing on you. No reports of anything. You didn't kill him, in fact we know who he is – and he's still very much alive. You're completely free to leave."

Now it was my jaw plunging to the table. "That's impossible," I insisted. "I stuck an axe into the side of his head, there was blood everywhere, and we all fled." Then, as though I was pleading with them, I added: "I'm *telling* you, I murdered him." The smirks on their faces told its own story, and they started to usher me out. "Mr Rose, if any more information comes our way, we'll let you know." With that, they broke into unrestrained laughter.

I walked out not knowing whether to laugh or cry. If I hadn't murdered that biker, then I had no reason to have fled the country, and no reason to have abandoned my parents. The last five years – the tortured training, the killing, my own death, all of it – had been for absolutely nothing. I gripped the Legion certificate still folded inside my jacket pocket and decided to smirk. There was no other option. I then headed for a telephone box and called home, the number still embedded in my brain. A man's voice answered and I said, apprehensively: "Alright, Dad?"

There was a brief, stunned silence and he replied: "Oh – you've surfaced, have you lad?"

"Yeah."

"Where are you?"

"In the city centre."

"Just tell me one thing. Are you bringing trouble home?"

"No, Dad."

He didn't question where I'd been, but added: "Ok, let me tell your mother first. Give me an hour before you show up." I waited a couple of hours, even popping into Lewis's store to check out the toy soldiers for a while. Then I headed back to the house and once again noticed how neat and tidy the front garden looked as I walked down the path and knocked on the door. Mum answered – she was already in floods of tears. "I thought you were dead, where've you been, Dad says you're not in trouble – but are you OK?"

Dad was stood behind her, we shook hands and went into the kitchen where Mum had her best china and plates laid out ready for a cup of tea. I stood by the table and before another word was spoken, Dad said: "You been soldiering then, boy?"

"How on earth do you know that?" I replied.

"Your stance. Where you been?"

"The Legionnaire Etranger, Dad."

"Thought so. Done the full time? You're not doing a runner are you?"

"No, definitely not." I pulled out the discharge papers so he could study my certificate. "I'm pretty sure his gaze paused over the words *honneur et fidelite* and then he said: "Well done, lad." He shook my hand, and there was pride in his grip. I'm certain there was, even though he was a man who never showed emotion. Mum was crying all over again; I'm pretty sure I managed to stop a tear rolling slowly down my right cheek.

"So, what you going to do now then, lad?"

Part Three

THE ROYAL MILITARY POLICE

The alpha wolf cares for the general safety of the pack; he is constantly on alert and unceasingly watches over the others.

KING KONG

The irony, the hypocrisy – the absurdity. There I was, a Royal Military Policeman, full of seniority, self-importance and morality. There I was, lecturing and arresting squaddies for getting fall-down drunk, or for heading into the wrong parts of town, or for using whores and prostitutes and frequenting brothels that were strictly out of bounds.

I'd cruise slowly along the Nathan Road in Kowloon, a notorious Hong Kong hotspot where tawdry neon lights, tawdry bars and tawdry women offered tawdry temptations to British Army personnel. What a seething mass of humanity it was; an impoverished, ugly, concrete jungle of densely populated, cheaply built high-rise apartments squashed together over bars and takeaways that could never attract enough customers to make a decent turnover. Cash was king; it got you anything you wanted, especially the illegal stuff.

Everything appealed to the lowest urges and desires – most of them below the belt. With my arm hanging out of the Land Rover window, I'd drive slowly down the heaving main street that cut right into the heart of this urban cesspit. One eye was looking for soldiers who'd wandered into the out-of-bounds areas; the other was weighing up the "working" girls, often in tight, figure-hugging silk cheongsam dresses – their choker necklines oozing elegance, the splits down their skirts suggesting something entirely different. I was looking for their regular customers, the ones who couldn't stop themselves returning, the ones who never learnt their lessons. The pissheads, the low-lifes, the ones who left their wives abandoned at home, the ones who forgot their rank and responsibilities in a bid to satisfy their alcoholic and sexual cravings.

The only place I needed to look was the rear-view mirror.

I'd genuinely planned to re-join the Legion after coming home, but Dad told me my National Service call-up had arrived while I'd been away. I instinctively applied for the British Army Parachute Regiment, but while I was waiting for the paperwork to be sorted I took a job as a bus conductor with a local bus company. I hated it. To relieve the boredom, I'd pretend I was back on a Legion parade ground and bark orders at the stunned passengers. "Move down this bus – *right now!*" I'd holler. It was funny to see them jump in alarm and then nervously glance at each other as I pushed down the aisle, demanding fares and issuing tickets.

I also met a girl, Brenda, and fell properly in love for the first time. We met in a café through mutual friends; she was full of life and laughter, bright and bubbly, with blonde hair and radiant blue eyes. She was cleverer than me – university-educated – but I found her easy to talk to. We went off on holiday together, to a small bed and breakfast outside Barmouth, in Wales, and she came back pregnant. In those days, there was only one decent thing to do. We got married. We barely knew each other, it had truly been a whirlwind romance, we were way too young, but we didn't know any better. She gave birth to my first child – a beautiful daughter we named Julie.

My call-up papers still hadn't come through and I absolutely didn't want a life on the buses. I felt out of place without an army or a parade ground. In fact, I was so impatient to be back, I joined the

Territorial Army and was posted to the Royal Military Police's Two Ports Task Force in Birmingham.

I needed to at least feel I belonged to a regiment – any regiment. Then, with still no sign of my national service paperwork, Dad said to me: "Why don't you join the Military Police full- time, lad." So that's what I did. I went straight to the nearest army recruitment office and signed up for 22 years, which everyone does, with a six-year get-out option.

The Inkerman barracks in Woking was where the Military Police's main depot was based, and they accepted me on a four-month training programme while Brenda and Julie stayed behind in Birmingham. The entrance was through a grand ceremonial arch with a tall, ornate clock tower perched imposingly above. Inside was a vast parade ground, flanked by a rectangle of imperious Victorian blocks and buildings, some with stately rows of arches along the ground floor. It looked like a giant asylum – and in some respects it was.

I'll never forget some of the characters I encountered – especially Sergeant Major Fletcher. He was the ultimate caricature of every sergeant major that ever breathed. In fact, I reckon he came out of the womb in full military uniform. Chest pumped high, unwavering stare, stickler for the smallest detail, barking voice, nose permanently sniffing the vaguest scent of trouble, immaculately attired – he had the lot. Every morning would start with a parade, nearly 200 of us, and he'd march out with his stick tucked vigorously under his arm, and come to a theatrical halt in front of the flagpole. At this point, he'd roar "Stand still!" – never realising it looked like he was addressing the pole, instead of us. Then he'd turn dramatically and pick two people out of the parade – quite randomly – and order them into the guard room, where they'd be handed extra chores for some trumped-up offence. It was all we could do not to giggle; each day we'd place bets with one another on who'd be singled out next.

He spent the rest of the day marching round the camp, hunting for someone to pick on. The trick was to always look busy, so we'd carry note pads around and if he appeared, suddenly start scribbling away as if we were on a project. He was clearly incapable of separating his professional life from his personal. I'll never forget one incident: I'd already completed my training and was now a lance corporal waiting to be posted to Hong Kong. I was down by the married quarters when SM Fletcher appeared, followed by his wife and two children. I couldn't believe my eyes: they were all desperately trying to march in unison, their arms swinging backwards and forwards ferociously. They got to the main gate when he suddenly stopped, like he'd forgotten something, turned around abruptly, and roared "About turn!" and marched them back to their house. This was a man who regularly put the brigade cats into the cells for being idle!

The best was yet to come, though. My mate Derek Smyth and I had frequently heard stories that SM Fletcher's spare bedroom was a sight to behold. "He's always looking for babysitters so he can take his missus out," said Derek. "Let's volunteer, and see whether the rumours are true."

So we did, and one night found ourselves in SM Fletcher's quarters, the children already tucked up for the night. We gave it an hour and then crept upstairs. "If they come back, just say we thought we heard a noise," I whispered. We got to the landing, pushed open the spare bedroom door and peered in. His kit was laid out immaculately on a small single bed. Next to it, on top of a bedside cabinet, were his army boots – in pristine condition inside a wooden-framed, clear glass case.

"Jesus! Look at his fuckin' parade boots," said Derek. "It's like he's displaying 'em in a fuckin' museum." Every individual eyelet sparkled like it was 24-carat gold. "He's doing it to keep the air off 'em, I bet," I whispered. "That way, they'll stay immaculate." The rumour was true. Looking back on it now, I suspect SM Fletcher knew all his "babysitters" were creeping upstairs to have a look: he'd have wanted us to know. The "boots-in-the-glass-case" legend embodied all he believed in; it enhanced his reputation.

My life during this period was so different from what it had been in the Legion. I had to go on more driving courses because I didn't have an English licence; it even took me a while to get used to the British army's way of marching. In the Legion, we marched extremely slowly, probably a legacy of manoeuvring through heavy desert sand; in Woking, we were much faster, 120 paces to the minute. In the Legion, I used to keep my palms flat to my side as I marched. In the army, fists were kept clenched. It took a lot of sessions with the peak of SM Fletcher's cap pressed firmly into my forehead, and his bellowing breath blasting directly into my face, before I got used to that.

There was only one elephant in the room, lurking big and fearful in the shadows, never going away. I was still drinking. It was only "social": we weren't under the strain of staying alive. But my pals cottoned on to my mood swings under the influence, and exploited my weakness whenever it amused them. One night we headed over to a popular pub in Aldershot, and at some point in the evening I went off to the gents. I was followed in by three civvies – complete strangers – who turned on me as soon as we walked in. One of them tried to push me back against the sinks, while another started mouthing off. It was like being on a parachute plane and seeing the green light come on: the guy holding me got elbowed straight across his nose, blood spurting out immediately; the bloke mouthing off got a heavy kick between his legs. He doubled up so much my eyes started to water, never mind his. The third – wisely – turned, and ran out before I'd even looked at him.

I lurched back into the bar, a bit dishevelled but unmarked, where my mates were pissing themselves laughing. "We knew that'd happen," said one of them. "We told those blokes you'd been slagging them off, and they should go and sort you out. We knew you'd handle them." As far as my "mates" were concerned, I was the novelty tough guy who could explode on command. I logged that, and it bothered me. But it didn't get in my way. By the time I'd completed training, I had full UK licences for any vehicle or motor cycle, and I'd risen to the rank of lance corporal. I was probably getting about £20 a week, which seemed good money at the time. Enough to support a wife and kids, because after one of my weekend trips home, Brenda had fallen pregnant again.

In January 1960, I was posted to Hong Kong. Julie and Brenda followed a few months later once married quarters had been found – just in time for my son, David, to be born in the military hospital.

I was a driver for a while, repairing and maintaining vehicles and then, later on, chaperoning commanders and officers and VIPs. I even escorted Princess Alexandra on one occasion – she was visiting a showpiece housing estate that had just been built and was all the rage. Everyone thought it'd be a blueprint for Hong Kong's overcrowded slums and apartments, although I think it's been demolished now. There was no trouble and no incidents; the locals were over-awed to see her and behaved with incredible respect and admiration as she walked past, occasionally stopping for small talk.

I couldn't hear much of what she was saying, but I was struck by how young and incredibly elegant she looked. I was about the same age as her: she was surrounded by youth and hope and vitality and privilege, whereas I'd killed and witnessed torture, brutality and depravity. Our lives could barely have been further apart. Yet here she was, dependent, for an hour or so, on me. Oh, the stories I could have told her! I wasn't begrudging her life for a second, and I truly felt privileged be in her company. She really was radiant. But she definitely looked like she belonged in Monte Carlo; not a housing estate for the masses in Hong Kong.

The military police were based in two main camps: one in Kowloon, where I was, the other on Hong Kong Island. Life was relatively peaceful: we were even given a maid to look after the house and children, allowing Brenda to become a PA with the old BOAC airline in Hong Kong. It was an excellent opportunity for her; our life was looking pretty secure.

Increasingly, I was sent out on night patrols, mainly around the teeming bars near the Whitfield barracks. My job was to round up squaddies who looked the worse for wear, ones who were maybe drifting towards trouble spots or brothels they weren't meant to be in. The absurdity of it all, of course, was that I was drinking and shagging more than they were. Nevertheless, my job was to stop the other squaddies from behaving like I was.

Everybody was dressed in civvies, but I could spot a squaddie a mile off. Our farcical conversations would usually go something like this:

"Evening sir, are you from one of Her Majesty's Forces?"

"Nah, mate. Nah, not me. I'm with the merchant navy."

"Are you absolutely sure about that?"

"Yep, certain," would be the answer, usually in a heavily slurred voice.

"So how come you've got an army ID card in your shirt pocket?" It's no exaggeration to say that would be the dead giveaway in nine out of ten cases. But I'd been in their position, I still was, and I wasn't looking to get heavy. "I'm afraid you're in an out-of-bounds area," I'd say. "But on this occasion, I'll put it down to an innocent mistake. Now get out of here."

There were exceptions, though. Sometimes, they'd be fighting drunk – beyond reasoning with – so they'd be arrested, stuck in cells, and handed back to a duty NCO the next morning at whatever regiment they'd come from. A scenario I was all too familiar with.

MARTIAL LAW

It was around this time that I experienced martial arts for the first time. I'd been working with the Ghurkha military police section in the New Territories and noticed that judo classes were being held on the ground floor of an old two-storey barn-like building close to the Chinese border. I decided to enrol.

After each session, I realised all the local Hong Kong pupils disappeared upstairs for some reason. "Where they all going?" I asked my instructor, an elderly, slightly built Chinese man. His appearance really was deceptive; he must have been well into his 70s, and his face and body seemed as frail as you might expect. But he was fighting fit all right: I'd seen him hurl the young kids in his class around like they were rag dolls.

"Don't concern with them," he replied, in faltering, imperfect English. "Nothing for you." But I was intrigued and decided to sit in a bar opposite until they re-appeared, about two hours later. To my amazement, I spotted someone I knew walking out on to the street, an Aussie called Kevin Velmar, who worked at a local bank I used. "Oi, Kev, what you doin' here, mate? Tell me, what goes on up there?"

It was a "Hung Gar" kung fu class, he explained, extremely violent and tough. "Who's your teacher?" I asked. "The same guy who takes your classes downstairs," he answered. "He's a Grand Master. He really knows his stuff."

The following week I begged my instructor to let me join in, and didn't stop nagging until he relented. "OK, OK, but you stick rules," he replied. I followed them all upstairs and walked into a large studio room, only this time there were various footprints positioned across the surface of the wooden flooring. Each combination of footprints formed a stance – each with its own distinct name, such as the horse stance, reverse stance and cat stance.

Straightaway I was instructed to bow and show respect and salutation every time I walked into the room. Then, I was positioned in the horse stance. For the next two months solid, all I was allowed to do was stand at the back, motionless, in the horse stance, and watch everyone else train. When the class ended, and the students walked past me to leave, they took it in turns to kick me – hard and unrestrained – on the back of my legs while I remained standing. The idea was to firm up my calf muscles, but they were trying to unbalance me as well. Next, they let me change to a neutral stance – for another two months – and then a forward stance, for the same period. Only after six months of this was I allowed to try some of the basic techniques and sparring I'd been watching.

About a year later, the instructor organised a competition night. One of the categories was four against one – freestyle – and they wanted me to be the one. I agreed, believing it would be non-contact. I was wrong; I naively stood in front of my four opponents and they kicked and battered and punched and elbowed me until I collapsed on the floor, my chest heaving wildly. It felt like my lungs had ruptured and would never pump oxygen again. I gasped frantically for air but there just wasn't enough. The more I gasped, the less I seemed to inhale and the more I panicked. My throat made a strange croaking sound as it pleaded for more oxygen. An ambulance was called and I remember lying in a hospital bed and lifting my head slightly to look down at the skin below my neck. It was covered in huge, violent, purple bruises. It looked like my skin would never be the colour of flesh again.

That was how my first proper introduction to the martial arts ended. The problem was, my fellow classmates had done this to me – and I suspected they'd done it on purpose, probably thinking I'd never come back. They didn't know about Grey Wolf. I lay in my bed and thought "Fuckin' bastards. They haven't seen the last of me."

Three weeks later I returned. They weren't in the least bit apologetic, but they were definitely surprised to see me. Kevin took me aside and said: "Right, now you know what the score is. They wanted to hurt you. It was deliberate. They think you're playing at being one of them. Next time they ask you to do a routine like that, kick the shit out of them. Put them down. Hurt them. Don't pull punches like you did before. Only then will they respect you.

"Oh, and just one more thing," he added. "You may notice some of the lads who trained here, some of the really good ones, aren't around any more. That's because they went to Singapore to fight in the death matches. They won't be coming back."

I carried on and reached Black Belt grade about a year later. I even won the south-east Asia championship in Hong Kong, against Chinese opponents. Not long after, the instructor organised another competition night – and once again, I was asked to be the "one" in a four on one. This time I laid three of them flat out, including two of the original opponents who'd put me in hospital. I kicked and punched without restraint, and when they went down and got back up, I waded in even harder. I got their respect that night.

I worked for an anti-vice unit for a while and a big part of our job was to tackle the alarmingly high rates of gonorrhoea among British soldiers. At one point, it was calculated that 67 per cent of the garrison had a sexually transmitted disease – over the next 10 months we brought that figure down to 20 per cent. Every time a soldier reported sick, the special treatment centre would ring anti-vice. We'd interview the soldier, find out where the girl was, and get her treated as well.

We even spread out into the brothels and bars where the girls worked, and issued them with clinic cards, so they could have regular check-ups. It was a policy that worked; the alternative would have been to try to close down the brothels – an impossibility in such a seething mass of tightly packed buildings, where there were way too many door fronts, entrances and exits to hide behind.

The more I patrolled, the more I got to know the best places to hang out myself: the bars and brothels that were well out of sight, deep in no-go districts. I'd go on benders, drinking heavily, and then end the night with one of the prostitutes or bar girls who I knew had a clean clinic card. I'd stagger back at ridiculous hours in the morning, stinking, retching, falling down – everything I would have arrested a squaddie for. I wasn't being a good husband, or a good father. I'm ashamed to say I preferred the company of alcohol to my family, and shagging prostitutes and whores whenever the urge came.

Understandably, Brenda tired of my lifestyle and behaviour, but somehow we held our relationship together for the rest of my service in Hong Kong. I worked with the Gurkha military police for a while and spent some weeks in Borneo. Their loyalty to the British army was unwavering and, if they were given a task, absolutely nothing would get in their way. Their devotion and commitment left a permanent impression on me; even now, I help raise funds and organise events for a local Gurkha welfare society in Cornwall.

I returned to the UK in 1965 and was posted to the London District Provost Company as a duty driver. Brenda and the kids went back to Birmingham to live with my parents for a while, but came back when I secured married quarters near Richmond Park.

I had some laughs during this period. For a while I was stationed at the Kensington Palace barracks, where legendary comedian Spike Milligan would frequently turn up at around two o'clock in the morning, usually announcing his arrival by swinging on the giant wrought-iron gates at the entrance and yelling out something stupid in one of his trademark "Goon Show" voices. We'd let him in and he'd sit in the guard house with the NCOs, one minute talking normally and seriously about anything and everything – and the next, diving straight into one of his comedy characters, usually the infamous Eccles, leaving us crying with laughter until sunrise. We all suspected he couldn't quite let go of his own previous army life – he'd famously served during the Second World War – and while he never failed to make us smile, his remarkable intelligence also left us in awe.

We also had a good laugh at the expense of the aristocracy – not that they knew anything about it. One of our night-time duties was to guard Lancaster House, in The Mall, where the Prime Minister frequently attended heavyweight meetings and there were regular conferences between commonwealth heads, VIPs and international dignitaries.

The centrepiece for these conferences was an enormous, highly polished table that must have been at least 30 feet long. It was some piece of furniture, with a surface as smooth and glossy as a billiard ball. Once you'd got used to all the grandeur, however, guarding somewhere like that became incredibly dull – especially at three or four o'clock in the morning. So, to relieve the boredom, we'd stick an old mat upside down on top of the table, sit on it – and then take it in turns to be propelled along the surface like a sledge. We even called it the "slalom" – the idea being to see who could reach the end of the table without swerving or falling off. I nearly always veered away to the left, but I did make it to the end once, to great cheers and laughter.

I can honestly say we never left a mark on that table, but it made us smile to think that the toffs had absolutely no idea what had been going on the night before their conferences. We even held our own mini concert shows in there, as well. The entrance to the house was a huge, wide hallway with two grand staircases that curled elegantly up either side to a balcony above. We'd take it in turns to go up there, and either sing songs or crack jokes while the rest of the unit watched from the hall down below.

Another laugh came very much at my expense. I was still chaperoning senior officers and personnel around when I fell head first into a set-up. I was instructed to take an officer to a medical centre, where he had an appointment with an extremely eccentric but high-ranking doctor. I was asked to remain in the waiting room; about 20 minutes later, the doctor marched out of his office, looked at me, and boomed: "What on earth are you doing here?" Suddenly, there was absolutely no sign of my passenger. The doctor was distinctive in a loud, exaggerated way, with sweeping silver eyebrows and immaculately groomed silver-grey hair. He exuded authority, this was his territory, and I suddenly felt like a trespasser. "I was told to wait here," I mumbled. "I'm driving the patient you've just seen."

"Well, get into my office immediately," he commanded. I walked in, not sure what on earth to expect. "Right. Roll your sleeve up." He then produced a syringe and plunged it straight into my exposed arm. "There, that's a TB jab. Nobody sits in my waiting room without getting treated," he boomed. "Now get out of here before I jab you with something else." I returned to the barracks, bemused, and told everyone what had happened. They fell about laughing. "You fuckin' idiot. It was a set-up!" They'd got me – good and proper.

Later in the year, I joined the military police mounted display team, based in Aldershot. This comprised four horses with four riders, and four motorbikes, each with a driver and pillion passenger, and we spent the following summer months going round county shows up and down the country. The horses and bikes would do high-speed crossovers in front of one another, then there would be a tent-pegging display. The horse riders would each carry lances, like cavalrymen, and have to scoop up pegs that had been left in the ground; meanwhile, the motorbike pillion passengers – I was one of them – had to lean over and grab the pegs with our hands. I ended up badly injured during a training session when the bike I was on collided with another as we tried to cross over. I was sent crashing on to my back, substantially worsening the spinal injuries I'd already suffered in Algeria. I never really recovered; I still endure terrible back pain every day.

Although Brenda and I were still together at this time, I was also surrounded by women from the Provost military police training school, and I made it my mission to hook up with one of them – a girl called Beryl. She had fair hair, long legs, and a very seductive charm. Every weekend Brenda would go back to Birmingham, so I'd bunk off with Beryl, and smirk over how devious and clever I was being.

Inevitably, however, Brenda found out – just after I'd been posted to the mounted display team. We split – I still deeply regret the way I treated her – and Beryl and I got engaged, marrying soon afterwards. Wife number two. My behaviour hadn't gone unnoticed, though, by my army bosses. They weren't impressed, and my military police career soon fell into a sharp nosedive. I was posted to Wales as a driver-cum-bodyguard, and hated the remoteness and boredom of my working life. I even ended up guarding heavy-duty tanks and military vehicles at a huge training base in Castlemartin, Pembrokeshire. This wasn't what I'd dreamt about; my contract with the army was coming to an end so, in 1967, I left – feeling hard done-by and disillusioned.

STREET OF FEAR

I was only ever frightened in Civvy Street.

In the military, I faced death, human abomination, hell – but was never frightened. No matter how relentless the training or how brutal the punishments, I rose to the job, made the right decisions, and came out – alive. It was the polar opposite in Civvy Street. No matter what I did, I blew it; no matter who I married, I screwed up.

In Civvy Street I felt alone, unprepared, untrained and ill-equipped. A man with no family. People and problems crushed me. Inside a year, I lost three jobs and two wives. In the end, Civvy Street drove me to Vietnam. That's how bad Civvy Street was.

Beryl fell pregnant almost immediately after I left the military police. We moved to Plymouth in Devon, because her family were originally from there, and bought a small house. I applied to join the local police force, but even that plan was doomed. The city police had just been merged into a new, combined Devon and Cornwall constabulary – and they couldn't guarantee me a placement in Plymouth. We didn't want to move elsewhere, having just bought a property there.

I tried working for a credit management company. I was hopeless; I was bored and disruptive, and it was no surprise when the manager gave me a week's notice. My relationship with Beryl deteriorated rapidly: to be fair, I think neither of us were really suited to each other. We argued; she was angry I hadn't clung on to the job; the more we rowed, the more I chose to hang round the local bars instead of going home. Inevitably, I met someone else – another Cornish girl, Joanne – and she became wife number three soon after. I think Beryl was simply relieved to get away from me.

Next, I landed a job driving dust carts for the local council. The money was good, but I was only a reserve driver, and I suddenly hit a stretch of three days when they didn't need me out on the roads. I was still being paid so they gave me a brush, shovel and mobile bin, and told me to clean the streets by hand instead. It wasn't what I'd signed up for. On day three, I was stood in a shop doorway sheltering from pouring rain, my bin crammed with wet leaves and rubbish, when a supervisor unexpectedly turned up. "What you standing there for, doing nothing?" he barked.

"I'm waiting for the vehicle to unload my bin so I can carry on – plus it's pissing down," I replied.

"Well, don't just stand there doing nothing, it doesn't look good."

I was wet, cold, and ready for a row. "What's the point? My bin's full, and everything inside is soaking wet in any case."

"At least it'll look like you're working," he snapped back.

"That's fuckin' stupid."

"You can't talk to me like that. When I say jump, you jump!" he replied. With that, I took the bin and unloaded its contents straight through the open window of his van. That was the end of that job.

Joanne didn't give up on me straightaway. She was working for a local company, Texas Instruments, and got me on a 12-hour shift, every night, helping manufacture integrated circuits. We were given targets, and had to complete so many circuits each shift. The supervisor was a squinty little bloke with terrible eyesight: the lenses on his heavy, black-framed glasses were so thick they made his eyeballs look three times bigger than they actually were. He always wore a white coat, like a junior doctor, which he put on when he came to work, fastening every button so it'd cover his lemon, or sometimes pale green, Bri-nylon shirt. I often wondered how long he'd have lasted in the Legion – about as long as I lasted at Texas Instruments probably.

One night he came over and barked: "You've got to up your rate of productivity!"

"Why?" I enquired.

"Because there are others doing twice as much as you." I protested that I always hit my allocated target each night. "I want you to do more than that. I'm going to be watching you every night from now on," he warned. That was it. I demanded to leave on the spot, but he refused to open the office doors until I'd completed my shift. At that point, I grabbed him round the neck and held him, wriggling like a little toad in a science class, perilously close to the grinding production machinery. "How'd you like to become a fuckin' integrated circuit?" I enquired. He screamed for a security guard, and I was eventually let out. I got home around 3am; Joanne panicked when I crept into our bedroom, thinking it was morning and she'd overslept. Then the penny dropped. "You bastard, you've fucked it up again, haven't you, Bob?"

My third job could, and should, have been my salvation. It might have even altered the entire course of my life, because I loved it so much. I was working in the great outdoors, planting and managing trees at a large reservoir way out on Dartmoor. It was wild and exposed terrain, the weather could be brutal, but somehow getting cold and soaked in those surroundings didn't bother me like it had cleaning the streets. I adored the big, wide, open outdoors, and on the rare days when the clouds vanished, and I was engulfed by Blue, well, it wasn't hard to imagine being back in Montana.

Then it all went horribly wrong, and I got trapped by union politics. I'd finished my shift at 5pm one day when a union convenor from head office came over and ordered me to attend a mandatory meeting. "Nah, thanks," I said. "I'm off home." He wasn't having it, we rowed, and he threatened to sack me. In a blind rage, I stormed off, saying: "You can stick your fuckin' union up your arse."

What hope was there for me? I was 29 years old, already on wife number three, heavily dependent on alcohol, and utterly unable to hold down a job. I couldn't take orders off little people whose only way of feeling big and empowered was to boss me around. I'd spent the most impressionable years of my life surrounded by officers and commanders who issued orders that determined who got to live – and who died. Those were the big calls. Those were men were under real pressure. Would they give a fuck about productivity targets at Texas bloody Instruments?

I'd seen the extremes. I knew what life was like on the edge; how it felt to be exhausted at the end of the day because you were simply trying to stay alive. I knew what bodies blown apart by bombs looked like; I'd lived with the screams of men and women and children being tortured or dragged from their homes. There were no little men in white coats and Bri-nylon shirts in the world I'd encountered. Their stupid ideas of punishment would be to order you to attend a union meeting, or increase your productivity. My idea of punishment was to lie for 24 hours in a grave that I'd dug with my own bare hands in blistering heat.

I'm not saying I was yearning for all that again. I just couldn't see an alternative; it was the only world I knew. The more I tried Civvy Street, the more I craved the structure and regime of military life. I think I still do. It was in my DNA before I was born, and it was expertly mined and nurtured by the Legion. I never stood a chance. I wasn't hungering to kill people, I wasn't trying to die, but if those were the prices I'd have to pay for belonging to the only club I wanted to be in, then so be it.

The problem was, I didn't have an army, or a war, to join.

Part Four

VIETNAM

The wolf can make strong emotional attachments to other individuals; it can also be one of the most vicious and bloodthirsty of all animals. When prey is vulnerable and abundant, they may surplus-kill, regardless of hunger and appetite.

THE PHOENIX PROGRAMME

I found myself a war to join in October 1967. That's when I went to Vietnam. I'd taken the train from Cornwall to London, knowing that ultimately, the journey would be leading me to Saigon. I'd no idea, though, that I would end up working on a controversial CIA-run assassination programme responsible for the deaths of almost 40,000 Viet Cong.

I'd failed abysmally to hold down jobs in Civvy Street, and I'd heard on the grapevine there was a private contract company in London recruiting mercenaries and sending them off to Saigon. I didn't know any other English soldiers who'd done the same thing and, once I was in Vietnam, I only met ones who'd attached themselves to either Australian or New Zealand units. There was no other way they could be there because – as everyone knows – the British government never officially supplied English soldiers to fight in Vietnam.

In many respects, it was like joining the Legion all over again, although this time I was signing forms in an anonymous third-floor office amongst the grand, aristocratic buildings of London's Pall Mall. "It's a 12-month contract and you'll be paid $1,800 per week," I was informed. "Plus, you can claim unlimited expenses for any equipment, clothing or personal stuff you might need out there." It was good money. "We'll also take full care of your insurance premiums. Your wife and children will be well catered for if anything goes wrong."

I remember those words "if anything goes wrong" very clearly and, as I stared out of the window and looked out towards the junction with St James's Street, gridlocked with cars, black taxis and red double-decker buses, I realised I was in a part of London that looked very familiar. The Kensington Palace barracks, where I used to be based with the British army, weren't far away at all.

Six days later, I was staring out of the window of a US government-chartered World Airways Boeing 707 that had taken off from Okinawa, in Japan, on my way to Saigon, where I was to join the South Vietnamese army as a military advisor for one of their provincial reconnaissance units (PRUs). Below me, in the darkness, lay Saigon; but the only lights I could see were the fluorescent flashes of flares and tracers exploding intermittently across the night sky. If it had been New Year, or bonfire night, it might have been beautiful; instead it was a chilling reminder of what I was flying in to.

We landed at the Tan Son Nhut air base, the outline of its main reception building barely visible in the sinister blackout. It was a spooky way to arrive into a new country. I was met by a US military advisor, who was standing at the exit clutching a lopsided piece of cardboard with my surname scrawled on it. I remember thinking how knackered he looked, like he was wishing he could jump straight on to the plane I'd just landed in. "Hi Bob, I'm Hal, pleased to meet you," he said, trying to force a smile across his weary face. We shook hands, he helped me load my bags into the back of his jeep and, as we drove to my hotel in downtown Saigon, he started to tell me about the CIA's Phoenix Programme.

The Viet Cong, he explained, had successfully infiltrated jungle villages and hamlets, removed the local elders and politicians, and installed their own civil leaders who were quietly recruiting new soldiers – or stashing arms and equipment. In response, the CIA had devised a strategy of using local sympathisers and secret police to identify the Viet Cong ringleaders, so military units could go in and "take them out". Most of the military units were from the South Vietnamese army (SVA), largely because they could speak the local language and understood the local customs better than the Americans. "It's working pretty well," he said, turning sideways to check I was listening. "With our help, the South Vietnamese PRUs are dismantling Charlie's infrastructure and the Viet Cong power base in the villages is collapsing." I didn't need him to explain what "take them out" meant. It was understood.

"We know all about your military record with the British Army and the Legion, Bob," he continued. "You're exactly the sort of person we need to advise the South Vietnamese units on the ground so when they go into the villages, they successfully neutralise the Viet Cong targets the secret police guys have identified." I didn't ask him to define "neutralise", either.

"Any questions?"

My mind was racing. It had been a long flight, I was desperate for a drink, but I understood the basic principles. "So, will I be receiving information directly from the CIA?" I asked.

"Not directly – those guys stay in the background, although they know what's going on – for sure. I've regularly seen them checking reports and talking to the South Vietnamese commanders." Then, Hal added: "The secret police hand their information into local Phoenix offices and when enough information has been gathered on a specific target, it's handed down to a PRU like the one you'll be with. You'll always be able to call in US marine back-up and resources whenever you need it though, Bob."

Hal explained I would be stationed at a South Vietnamese compound not far from the main US air base at Da Nang. "Your unit will have roughly 25 men – but, be warned, they'll be tough fuckers. Most of them will be ex-prisoners who've been allowed out so long as they fight. Take my advice, Bob: show them respect, and they'll be on your side. Treat 'em like dirt and they'll turn. I promise you, you won't have met anything like this lot before. Most of them will be South Vietnamese, or the local hill people – Christ, they're something else – then, there's the Chinese and the Chinese-Vietnamese, and the converts who've deserted the Viet Cong and switched sides. You never really know for sure whose side they're on."

Hal continued: "Oh, and one more thing. Don't forget: the South Vietnamese can't stand the Chinese-Vietnamese – even though they're both on the same side." He paused. "You getting all this, Bob?"

I was still grappling with who was who when he added: "But don't worry. You'll also have a US marine advisor working with you as well. He'll look after you, just fine."

We continued talking. I was warming to Hal, even though he was worn down by it all. He clearly knew how everything worked, and he left me under no illusion: my mission was to help my PRU kill, or capture, Viet Cong agents and leaders. There would be a command structure above me: intelligence would be funnelled into a Phoenix district office, where files would be kept on suspected Viet Cong activists. When sufficient information had been collated, their names would be handed to me. That's when I would help "neutralise the target".

There were three categories of Viet Cong, Hal explained: A, B and C. Category A were the ringleaders; B the highly positioned local politicians and leaders who turned a blind eye to Viet Cong activity in their own villages, who never warned where the booby traps were hidden; and C, the women – maybe even children – who might go shopping for unusually large quantities of food or medical supplies. They might even have stashes of gold, blue and red cloth hidden away to make Viet Cong flags, or they might have a transistor radio somewhere that only received Liberation Radio, the voice of Viet Cong propaganda.

"The secret police guys have informants working for them at all sorts of levels," he continued. "The intelligence they get is proving to be pretty fuckin' accurate."

That was the end of my pep talk. We pulled up outside my hotel. I leapt out, grabbed my bags and checked in. My head was still spinning and I headed in a daze straight for the lobby bar, where I sank my first Vietnam "33" beer. It certainly wouldn't be my last.

I got up early the next morning; I wanted to explore, and headed out into Saigon's heaving streets. The heat was overwhelming, sweaty and oppressive; the dusty roads and pavements were throbbing with Honda motor bikes and three-wheel Lambretta scooters, all weaving desperately around hordes and hordes of people and animals, all utterly oblivious to any vehicles on the road. Chickens, dogs and pigs roamed as freely across the streets as did men, women and children.

Scruffy, grey, flat-roofed buildings, largely bleak and featureless and square, rose in higgledy-piggledy piles to house a chaotic jumble of cheap shops, cafes and dark offices, all of them sweating and overheating as rickety ceiling fans creaked and groaned and struggled to breathe any fresh air into the buildings. I didn't see much that reminded me of the grandeur of Pall Mall: this was an entirely different, dishevelled world. I came to realise that downtown Saigon was a sprawling concrete jungle in a country where the jungle was everywhere.

I lost count of the hands that tugged at my jeans, the blind men and the beggars, often missing limbs, their broken bodies slumped in gutters as Saigon trampled all over them. Shoeshine boys were on every corner, and absolutely everywhere there were hustlers, offering drugs, sex, their wives, their sisters, even their mothers. Anything you could ever crave was get-able – in return for the mighty dollar. All this was overwhelming, and I stopped at a roadside café where I ordered a French coffee with sweetened condensed milk and watched the world pass by.

That's when I first really noticed the women, young and old, most dressed in regulation black leggings, or short pastel mini dresses. Some of the older ones were crouched uncomfortably on the pavements behind baskets piled high with fruit; many of the younger ones walked round in pairs, giggling and pointing, and looking so sweet and innocent. They all had black hair, which the older ones hid under oversized lampshade hats to keep the sun away. It was impossible to believe they might be the enemy.

I continued wandering around until I eventually reached the US embassy, which I wanted to see just out of curiosity. From a distance it looked like an old-fashioned department store about five storeys high, with a bold, curved frontage and distinctive yellow walls on a corner of Ham Nghi Boulevard – a surprisingly leafier and more ornate district. The surrounding buildings were grander – nearby stood the Majestic Hotel and the landmark Saigon Palace building with its domed roof. The only tell-tale embassy signs were the sentry boxes outside and small dumpy rows of concrete pillars that stopped vehicles getting too close. Two years earlier a car bomb outside had killed 23 people and injured 183, and the building had become notorious overnight – which is why I wanted to see it.

The following day I was met by a cheery South Vietnamese army officer at my hotel. He only spoke faltering English but he never stopped smiling, possibly because it compensated for his lack of vocabulary. Nevertheless, he managed to explain we'd be heading for Quang Nam province, where I would be based. "You get meet men," he said, smiling again.

What he didn't tell me was that it would also be where I'd meet my best friend for the first time.

THE MAN WHO TALKED HIMSELF TO DEATH

I never knew or understood what loss or grieving truly meant until Vietnam. I'd seen soldiers, who'd become friends, die in Algeria, and I had killed there myself, but none of those deaths meant anything to me. It was the same for a while in Vietnam – I saw soldiers from my PRU die, I watched US marines being blown apart or sliced apart by booby traps – and I certainly killed Viet Cong targets, one of them with my bare hands. Once again, none of these deaths affected me. I could always walk away and carry on. I never once considered whether their families were grieving for them somewhere. I wasn't bothered. But all that changed when I saw my best friend die. My first, my only, best friend. He still is – even though he died 49 years ago.

When my best friend died, I experienced grief for the first time and I never recovered from it. Every cell in my body wishes I could have died in his place. I should have, I deserved to; he was just a kid, 24, with so much life ahead. Me, I was 30, there was already nothing worthy or virtuous about my wretched existence, I contributed nothing to the planet other than bullets and death. It was my duty to get the kid, my best friend, through

Vietnam, and return him to his mom and dad in America. That was our unspoken pact. We would have stayed friends for ever and maybe I would have visited him over there.

I failed.

Vietnam became personal the moment I saw my best friend's slaughtered body, blown apart by a rocket-propelled grenade. His death made me flirt with savagery. I lusted for revenge; all l wanted was to kill. Or be killed. I truly didn't care who got the bullet. In fact, I prayed it would be me. I disconnected from my humanity, if it was ever there; I witnessed depravity and human carnage and I hated myself. I still do.

I've seen artist's impressions of what "hell" is meant to look like; I've seen Hollywood's interpretations of it, too. None of them ever came close to what I saw and smelt in Vietnam. In fact the smell was often the worst, and you don't get that from looking at photographs. My Vietnam stank. It stank of hideous, rancid, gut-wrenching, vomit-inducing rot. First, there was the human rot – the all-pervading smell of fear; the smell of dead bodies; the smell of shit constantly being burned in the compounds and firebases. The rot's worst odour, though, was the malodorous stench that accompanied atrocity. Each time I witnessed something that exposed how far man can sink, how cruel man is capable of being, the smell became too toxic to breathe. Inhale, and it seeped into your pores, it bedded into your soul – and it made you compliant. That's when you became immune to the smell of atrocity; that's when men would lose control and become wild, uncontrolled animals armed with grenades and M-16s and AK-47s and rocket-propelled grenades and Bouncing Betties and Claymore mines and bloody bows and arrows with poisoned tips. I inhaled when my best friend was killed. That's when I rotted.

Next, there was the jungle rot. The insufferable heat, the humidity, the monsoon mud – shitty, clinging, filthy mud that would try to suck you into the core of the earth. The ceaseless jungle, layer upon layer, endless, unconquerable; giant trees and prehistoric vegetation and, behind all that, the damp fetid smell of moss and the constant drip, drip, dripping of distant water that sounded like it was way off somewhere – but maybe was your own sanity turning to liquid.

Everything in the jungle wanted to kill you: the Viet Cong, the North Vietnamese, the snakes, the evil-eyed reptiles you thought were long extinct, the parasite tics and geckos, even the razor-sharp elephant grass waiting to cut you to shreds.

The "fuck-you" lizards.

Every night we'd lie in our bunkers and hear the "fuck-you" lizards talking. They only knew two words and they repeated them incessantly all night long until they ricocheted around what remained of your scrambled brain: "fuck you, fuck you", until miles upon miles upon miles of deranged jungle reverberated to a chorus of "fuck you".

Then there was the bamboo. I saw unsuspecting soldiers fall into booby traps and become speared on evil beds of sharpened, angled bamboo sticks. I saw the sharpened ends protrude out of gaping flesh holes. You couldn't lift the trapped bodies off so you watched blood cascade – and you listened to the terrible screams of death.

Everything that I did or witnessed in Vietnam between October 1967 and October 1968 was sick and rotten but one moment, more than any other, embodied the futility. I saw a man talk himself into dying.

He was a marine driver and our unit was tagging behind his M35 two-and-a-half-ton Reo truck, heading on a routine patrol up into the Ba Na hills that rose high above our compound near Da Nang. We were in a much-smaller jeep and I was sat in the back with three or four other PRU soldiers. Everything seemed calm and I dimly remember staring out at roller-coaster mountain peaks that jutted in and out of white, low, hanging clouds. "Christ, we must be high up here," I said to my best friend, who was sat next to me. If you climbed high enough, there were precious moments like that when it was hard to believe Vietnam was at war. When you dared to remember the human you used to be. I was allowing myself to drift into this unexpected and rare serenity when suddenly there was an almighty explosion.

The truck in front lurched heavily to its right and one of the front wheels catapulted high into the air and went hurtling down into the war somewhere far below. Our jeep screeched to a halt – sending us crashing into each other at the back – but as we untangled ourselves, I could clearly see smoke billowing out from the front of the truck. "Fuckin' land mine!" I yelled, and jumped out to see how bad the damage was. As I ran round the side of the truck, I saw a marine tumble out of his driver's door and slump on to the road, his back propped up against the side of the truck.

He was clearly dazed, but still breathing and just about conscious. In fact, I couldn't see any injuries on him at all, not even flesh wounds or signs of blood. But he definitely looked ashen – like a man in deep shock. "I'm dying," he muttered as I crouched down in front of him. "No, you're not," I replied, grabbing him by the pocket flaps on his combat US Marine shirt front. His helmet was still clinging haphazardly to his head. "You haven't been cut, you're ok, you must have hit a mine but it's not caused any serious damage. You're just in shock, that's all. Now come on, snap out of this, let's get you back down to base, marine."

The furrowed lines on his forehead suggested he was a bit older than me, maybe early 30s. I didn't know him, he wore small, thin-framed, round spectacles that had somehow stayed in place. Maybe he was single, maybe his parents were already dead, because he looked like a man who had no reason left for living; a man who'd simply had enough. He was running on empty, like he'd been waiting to die for some time and had prepared himself for this moment. He was a man who could no longer see any value in carrying on with life, if this was all life had to offer. The problem was, his body wasn't damaged enough to die. Only his mind was. I pulled and tugged on his shirt front and frantically pleaded with him to stand up. "What's your name, marine? Come on, mate, get up, there's nothing wrong with you, trust me, you're not hit."

He didn't respond. I'd never seen a soldier react like this before and I yelled at my best mate: "Get on to Da Nang and tell them to get a medic here, fuckin' quick. I don't like the look of this one, he's giving up."

I could clearly see the lights were going out in the eyes behind the glasses; his lips were slowly mouthing the same two words over and over but no sound was coming out: "I'm dying, I'm dying…" I tried to lift his folded body upright to convince him he could walk but as I started to pull him upwards I felt an almighty, slumping weight drag him back down. The silly bastard just died in my arms, there and then. He literally willed himself to die, and nothing I said could convince him not to. His body fell down and even though I knew he was dead, I yanked his silly round glasses off his face and slapped him repeatedly across his sallow cheeks, trying to shock him back to life. "You're not hurt, you fuckin' idiot, pull out of this." I was so angry with him; by the time the medic arrived he was long gone, and I'd been completely powerless to prevent it. Once his body was being driven back to Da Nang and we clambered back into our jeep, I remember saying to my mate: "You know what, I don't even want to know who the stupid fucker was. I don't want to know anything about him; I don't want to know whether he was a bloody orphan with no family, or that his beloved wife died of cancer or something. I don't want to know anything about him."

That's how angry I was. It was so stupid, so senseless, so meaningless. Yet deep down I knew it summed everything up. It should never have happened, and yet I couldn't stop it.

Just like the death of my best friend.

SEMPER FI

We had to become friends because we had to carry the weight of war, together. The shared extremes. Two people in an office may become colleagues because they have to make a difficult presentation together at a board meeting. We had to kill – or be killed.

The weight of war makes you confront extremes that simply could never exist in civilian life. Perhaps that's why I couldn't survive in Civvy Street. I needed those extremes. So did Frank. We had to set ambushes and survive ambushes; we had to cover each other in firefights, we had to "neutralise" targets. We had to bring back our men, alive. We had to check their ammunition and kit, we had to call in cover when Charlie was too close, and we had to get the coordinates right, or America's own artillery would be smashing into us. We had to pull wounded soldiers to safety so they might still get back to their girlfriends and moms and dads; we had to pump morphine into men with heads and chests and souls blown to fleshy shreds.

We had to shelter from incoming mortars and bombs together, when all that's between you and death is a flimsy canvas roof or some unconvincing sandbags. When you're hiding in a bunker and the ground is shuddering so violently you're sure it will implode at any moment and drag the pair of you into its molten core, you discover the true nature of the person lying next to you. That's when you know whether that person can be your friend. As explosions pulverise and smash and destroy all around you, when your life is so utterly in the lap of the gods because all it will take is one mortar to land exactly where you're lying and the game is up, then you see the measure of the man. How does he cope with the prospect of death? Amid the chaos, does he find the calm to issue instructions, to safeguard his unit, to make the decisions that swing between life and death? Or does he scream and cower and try to hide?

We had to confront atrocity. We had to see soldiers speared by booby traps. We had to work out whether we were savages. We had to kill with our own hands. We had to kill when we could see the faces of the soldiers we were killing, when they were so close, we could see their fear and their fanaticism. Could we be pushed too far? Would we cross the line between killing for duty – and killing for sport? What were our extremes of war?

When we weren't at war, when there were no patrols to go on or no mortars to endure, we had to find ways of living, together. So we went on rest and recuperation, together. Drinking and screwing whores and drinking again and finding ways to laugh, together. In fact, the humour was probably the bond that united us most strongly. The humour was as extreme as the war. We found humour in situations that were sick and gory and tragic. We laughed at the same things when others might be repulsed. We found humour in mutilated Viet Cong bodies. Grotesque humour in grotesque deaths.

Most of all, we took the piss out of each other. Endlessly, brutally. Frank was a ginger and he tried to grow a beard, but it just wouldn't grow. "That's cos you're still a fuckin' baby," I'd tell him. "They sent me to war and gave me a fuckin' child. No, no, they didn't – no, worse, they gave me a fuckin' puppy. You're a fuckin' puppy. Here puppy, sit puppy, there's a good puppy." And I'd ruffle his hair like a dog, and call him puppy for days on ends, and we'd laugh and find it hilarious. It was impossible for us to wound one another.

We'd even find humour when death was uncomfortably close. I'm not ashamed to say I found mortar attacks terrifying because I felt so utterly helpless and vulnerable when they came in. There might have been a distant "thump" but you never knew how close the mortars were until they were actually exploding all around. Then you'd yell "incoming mortars" and dive into bunkers and slit trenches and wait to see whether your time was up.

Mortars caused such devastation, especially the shrapnel, giant clumps of sharpened metal flying around looking to decapitate and maim. Mortar attacks were so indiscriminate: if they chose, they could land, bull's eye, right in the trench you were lying in, and that would be the end. I've seen soldiers walk away from mortar attacks without a scratch, even though the explosion may have been metres away. I've seen others torn in half by flying shrapnel far from where the mortar landed.

Lying there, helpless, in a mortar tempest felt like hell to me. In fact, I became so used to the hopelessness of it, I'd become punch-drunk. Sometimes, if I was lying in our hootch trying to get some sleep, I'd say: "Fuck it, mortar", and just turn over. What was the point of scrambling into a slit trench and praying nothing would hit? "Hard-core, hard-core, man," Frank would say, usually taking a long-drawn-out drag on the weed he liked to smoke. Maybe he was trying to use it all up quickly, so it wouldn't be wasted if a mortar landed. I'd reply: "Christ, I've just realised what the problem is. They can see your fuckin' ginger hair. It's your fuckin' fault. You're like a great, big, ginger beacon. You're a fuckin' useless ginger."

I was only six years older than him, nothing really, and yet the more we got to know each other, the more I felt like the big brother. Paternal even. We never spoke about death, we never discussed what we should do if one of us was wounded so badly he wouldn't want to live. We never discussed Blue stuff like that. It just hung in the air. An unspoken pact. We would look out for each other, that's what we'd do. Always.

In calmer moments, he'd tell me about his family: his dad ran a family accountancy firm in Middle America, he had two older sisters, and his mum had stayed at home to raise the kids. "Show us a picture of your sisters then," I'd say. "Are they as God-damned ugly as you, Jarhead? Bet they'd fancy me, though, wouldn't they, eh? Bet my accent would get them all hot? Bit of English, eh? I might come over to America after we've finished here and see what I can do for them..."

He made out to wallop me, but instead fumbled round in a tattered, brown leather wallet and dragged out a grainy black and white photo. His sisters were beautiful. Blonde and pretty, and too good for me. Suddenly I wanted to abandon the joke. Instead, I held the tiny snap in my hand and just stared at their innocence. How could they possibly understand, how could they begin to comprehend, the weight of war their kid brother was carrying?

"What you going to do when you get back home?"
I asked instead.

"The old fella wants me to pass accountancy exams and carry on the business once he's retired. I dunno. He's made good money but hell, accountancy. I mean, it's so fuckin' dull."

Frank had joined the US marines and taken to the way of life straightaway. Like me, he'd breezed through training; unlike me, he could speak fluent French, although I still remembered a few words from the Legion. "That's how come I got the short straw and ended up covering your fat arse," he explained. "They got it into their heads French might be useful round here."

Then he added: "Oi – Monsieur Bob. *Vous etes un fuckin' imbecile, n'est-ce pas?*"

Our military backgrounds provided another source of constant piss-taking and rivalry. Every morning, without fail and before he'd uttered any other words, he'd wake up and roar: "Marine Corps, *Semper Fi* – hoo-rah!" He'd say this so loudly it felt like an exclamation to every single Viet Cong soldier across Vietnam, even though it was only aimed at me – especially if I was still dozing. Then it would be an even greater source of amusement; he'd punch the air with joy if I suddenly leapt up and mistakenly squealed "incoming mortar".

I needed a response, of course, so – not to be outdone – I'd take a giant gulp of breath, push out my chest and retort: "Airborne – hoo-rah!" Like I was Sergeant Major Fletcher on the parade ground in Woking. It seemed to matter, this declaration of loyalties and convictions; it seemed more than an early-morning let's-get-on-each-other's-nerves game. It felt like we were reminding each other of what we were, what we were doing – and why we were there, together.

Out of everything we did, that little ritual is the one thing I cannot let go of, even today. It seems so stupid, really, so irrelevant and small, but every night – before I go to bed – I shout out to my two German shepherd dogs. Heather gets "Airborne – hoo-rah!", while Liken gets "*Semper Fi* – hoo-rah!" because he's a mud marine, he loves water and rolling in mud.

Semper Fi.

Always loyal.

THE HILL PEOPLE

I'd remembered Hal telling me about the Hill People when I first landed in Saigon. "Christ, they're something else," he'd said, and those words stuck in my mind for some reason. They certainly were "something else", too – primitive, hardened survivors, like the Northern Cheyenne. They lived out in the wilderness, in inhospitable places beyond the extremes and, just like the Northern Cheyenne, they were an embarrassment Vietnam wanted to forget about and ignore. They were left abandoned in the mountains, out of mind and out of sight, but suddenly expected to lay down their lives when war came. Their faces were lined and toughened, and their children looked old beyond their years. I often thought the Hill People's skin was so leathery it could be used to make suitcases that would last for ever. They were ferocious fighters and, thank God, they were on our side.

They would take us sometimes up high into the Blue, along myriad trails that were impossible to scout or fathom, until we found their villages and their families. The views up there were staggering: way below us would be a vivid green valley of paddy fields, flanked either side by giant green steps of rice paddies that were built into the foothills and rose like mighty staircases leading up to the mountains. The mountains themselves rolled on and on for miles and miles in every direction, unfolding into higher mountains, universally coated in uninterrupted swathes of dense jungle that were only broken by deep ravines and gorges, and more valleys of bamboo and elephant grass.

"Jeezus Kerr-ist, take a fuckin' look at that," I'd say to Frank, but he'd already be rolling up another joint, in a hurry to inhale the weed, the views, and the crystal-pure air in one giant gulp.

We'd sling our weapons and bags and war paraphernalia on to the roughened earth outside one of the village shacks and sprawl out like a bunch of adolescents on an adventure trek somewhere. The war wasn't there. Charlie wasn't there. And America wasn't there, either. Grey Wolf was, though, and I felt closer to the Northern Cheyenne in those moments, in those places, than at any other time in my life. We'd laugh and chat and gossip and be human all over again until the village women – dressed universally in black with brightly coloured ribbons and bandanas – would emerge with bowls of sweet rice and roast pig that had been cooked the Native American way on open fires. You could taste the smoke with every mouthful and yet that food felt like a banquet. We'd make eyes at some of the girls, and talk about fucking them because nobody spoke English, but we were guests and we were being treated like royalty and even though our daily lives trod the thin line between savagery and humanity, we remembered we could be civilised sometimes.

I adored the Hill People, I trusted them like I trusted Frank. I felt as though I belonged amongst them. They lived how I wanted to live, how I'd been taught as an eight-year-old to live. It's hard to shed what's ingrained into you when you're a child, isn't it? Their way of life was the Native American way: every day was a balance between surviving and killing for food and defying poverty and belonging to each other. They refused to be beaten, and – my God – they were profound killers. Their weapons were the weapons I first learned to kill with – bows and arrows and hunting knives and spears. The only difference was, they knew how to put poison tips on the ends. In the middle of firefights, when my twentieth-century bullets had missed their targets, I'd see dazed VC soldiers staggering around with arrows and spears sticking out of their chests and necks and arms, their horrified faces bemused by the shock of knowing they were about to die from weapons that belonged to the medieval era, killed by the audacity of the Hill People. They would let me play with their bows and arrows sometimes and just holding them up and taking aim felt more natural to me, more instinctive, than any AK-47 I'd ever clutched.

There were six or seven Hill People in my unit. As Hal had warned me, the rest really were a right mix, many of them ex-prisoners. There was South Vietnamese, Chinese, Chinese-Vietnamese, and converts who'd defected from the North – or decided they no longer wanted to fight on Charlie's side. They were the hardest to fathom, and we could never be 100-per-cent sure about their loyalties. There was always a suspicion they were keeping their options open just in case America abandoned Vietnam and they needed to be in Charlie's good books again. I remember Frank coming back from Da Nang one day, in a right old state. "We've got to be careful," he whispered. "I was talking to some of the guys over there and they said some of the converts had switched sides in the middle of a fuckin' firefight. Soon as they thought Charlie was winning, they started shooting at our guys instead."

I have to say that never happened to us. Our PRU was based at the Chi Long camp in the provincial capital of Quang Nam, Hoi An. The base was also used by the 51st ARVN regiment and was very much a satellite for the colossal marine headquarters at Da Nang, where thousands of Americans were based in a military city, about 17 miles away, accessible over the Han River by a series of road bridges. We weren't alone in our camp – other units were also based in the same compound. We'd regularly fly in and out by helicopter; from the sky, the camp looked like it had been dug out of an old quarry on the outskirts of the town. The ground was dusty, rough and rock-strewn, and metal-mesh fencing topped with coils of razor wire ran in an uninterrupted circle around the entire perimeter. An area was designated for helicopters, the ground there flattened and levelled by their constant coming and going. Sometimes I'd lower my eyelids until I could only see a blurred outline of the world. I'd look to the skies as a swarm of Hueys flew in and I'd imagine they were giant missile-carrying bees, trained by the CIA to plague Charlie. "Fuckin' hell, it's amazing what those guys in Washington can do," I'd murmur and Frank, not sure what on earth I was mumbling about, would give me a hefty kick up the arse. "You been on my weed, you sad old bastard?"

Although Chi Long was our unit's HQ, we spent most of our time on the sprawling American firebases scattered throughout Vietnam. From these, we could launch raids and ambushes on nearby targets identified by the secret police. There was never a shortage of artillery firepower on these bases; supplies – usually from Da Nang – were constantly being flown in on helicopters. There were times when it felt like a non-stop production line as the Hueys disgorged crates of weaponry and then picked up the wounded – and the body bags. Typically, vast stocks of ammunition were housed in huge storage bunkers, again smothered by sandbags, while wooden guard towers rose above triple-layered rolls of barbed wire to keep a constant eye on the perimeter and key approach points. At the heart of these firebases often stood five 105mm M101A1 artillery howitzers, each one positioned at the points of a giant star formation. Those beasts, with their giant wheels and huge main barrel angled up to the skies, would go off endlessly, either providing us with cover when we were heading into enemy stretches of jungle, or providing cover for other units as well.

Wherever we were, we usually slept in hootches, dug into the ground with a canvas roof and surrounded by a knee-high rectangle of sandbags. Nearby would be bunkers and slit trenches where we'd hurl our quaking bodies whenever the mortars started to pound. The Chi Long camp had some more solid buildings within it, like old single-storey factory units with corrugated tin roofs, and these housed offices, a medical centre, radio communications and the main canteen. I had command of the radio within our unit. Grey Wolf was my call sign and I had the authority to call in US artillery or air support whenever we needed it.

Not everyone in my unit could speak English, so Frank and I relied heavily on the senior sergeant, Cam, who was fluent. The three of us became close and we felt honoured when he introduced us to his wife and two teenage sons when they visited our compound once. Maybe all sergeants come from the same stock, whatever their nationality: unlike most South Vietnamese, he was stocky, ferocious like a bull terrier, and hard with his troops – but it was clear to see that he had their respect. If he said leap, they would, and that was good enough for me. He was with me when Frank died; I know he managed to get his family out of Vietnam when the war ended, and the last I heard they were living somewhere in America.

Whenever we could, we travelled everywhere in an old beat-up M-38 A-1 Jeep, with two human skulls perched permanently where the wing mirrors should have been. I'd picked up the Jeep from Da Nang and I'll never forget Frank's reaction when I drove up to our hootch. "Who the fuck are those two?" he said.

"I don't fuckin' know. I thought they were pals of yours," I replied. "If you don't know them, then maybe we should give them some new names. What d'ya reckon? You're always singing 'Homeward Bound' when you're stoned, so how's about Simon and Garfunkel?"

Frank wandered round the front of the Jeep and peered close up at each skull in turn. "Tell you what, I've got a much better idea. Let's call 'em Laurel and Hardy. After all, they look like a right pair of Charlies to me."

So that's what we did. Laurel and Hardy came with us everywhere, and that Jeep became a bit of a trademark within our unit. We dressed up to the image as well, because we had the authority and freedom to wear what the hell we liked. At first, we'd worn regular-issue South Vietnamese army uniform – tiger stripes and jungle boots – but within weeks it was all rotting. That was the jungle: it seeped into your clothes and into your skin until everything started to peel and fade, or blister and stink. "Why the hell are we wearing this shit?" I said to Frank one day. "Let's drive Laurel and Hardy over to the PX and get some proper gear."

The PX, or post exchange, was an Aladdin's cave really, of clothing and goodies at the US Da Nang base. I imagine it was the marines' equivalent of Walmart. It stocked everything. Our daily uniform became a cowboy mix of Levi's jeans, sweatshirts, basketball boots and bandanas – not because we were trying to be fashionable, simply because it lasted much longer than the army stuff.

It embarrasses me now, but I guess Frank and I were a bit guilty of role-playing: a couple of rootin', tootin' gunslingers from the Wild West, out to show those commie boys a thing or two. For a while it felt like a game as we drove around the bases, wearing our bandanas and T-shirts and jeans, with our AK-47s slung over our shoulders. We even stuck bandanas and sunglasses on Laurel and Hardy sometimes. "There ya go, fellas, that'll keep the sun off your pretty heads," cracked Frank, and we'd think that was pretty hilarious and scratch the tops of our heads and waddle around like the comic pair used to.

Our Jeep was armed to the hilt, too, like a mini fortress on wheels. I always carried a Browning semi-automatic shotgun everywhere, pump-action, and an AK-47, because I believed it was more reliable than the M-16s. I also had an old MAT-49 submachine gun, which I'd picked up in Da Nang and had probably been captured from Charlie. I'd used them before in the Legion, they were easy to grab and use from a vehicle because they weren't long or cumbersome. I also liked to have as much ammunition and spare magazines with me as possible, just in case we needed to go out on foot somewhere.

Then there were the knives. We were issued with American M7 bayonets, which were designed to stick on the M-16 rifles. But I much preferred knives. I still had the old Bowie knife that I'd bought in Birmingham and carried through the Legion with me, plus a survival knife which was essential for slashing through thick jungle undergrowth. Then there was an arsenal of grenades we kept in our Jeep – fragmentation grenades, smoke grenades if we needed to be seen by the Hueys, and even tear gas grenades if we needed to hurl something down tunnels. I also carried some C-4 plastic explosives – that stuff was like making bombs out of Plasticine.

That wasn't all, however. Frank liked to use an M60 machine gun and we also carried an M-79, which was like a shotgun, only it blasted out grenades. We called them "thumpers" because that was the noise they made when they were fired.

I couldn't begin to count the number of maintenance rods and steel brushes and the amount of oil we went through; I was particularly hard on any members of the unit who didn't keep their guns in pristine condition. It was something that had been embedded into me by the Legion. If I found a soldier hadn't bothered to clean his weapons – even immediately after a firefight – I'd kick the shit out of him, just like the Legion did to me. I remember once doing an unannounced spot check and finding an M-16 that hadn't been rodded, so there was still residue clogging up the main barrel. I went ballistic. "What fuckin' use are you to me?" I yelled – so loudly,

I swear they heard me over the river in Da Nang. "What if we're in a firefight and I need you to save my life but when you shoot, your rifle jams. You're not a fuckin' soldier. You might as well go fight for Charlie right now. You on his side or something?" I was so furious, I kicked him hard in the balls and he collapsed in agony on the ground, squirming and writhing as he clung on to his testicles, like he needed to know if they were still there. I didn't care how much pain he was in; that bastard could have cost me my life, never mind his own.

We also carried webbing kit to hold personal stuff and water bottles. You needed water as much as you needed bullets. Other essentials included a flak jacket, toilet paper and a medical pack, which included bandages, morphine and even aspirins. When we were out on patrol, we mainly ate C-rations: a typical 24-hour pack would have tiny tins of sausage or burgers, biscuits, coffee, chocolate and even boiled sweets. I always took curry powder with me — it just made everything taste better. We also ate lots of rice whenever we entered the villages. By comparison, the Viet Cong seemed to survive off far less. Whenever we took prisoners, we'd often find they were only carrying handfuls of rice, which they'd live off for days.

Back at base, we'd mainly eat all the American stuff that makes you fat — doughnuts, fries, steaks, hot dogs. Comfort food, I suppose, always washed down with as much alcohol as we could lay our hands on. I must have drunk gallons of 33 beer but increasingly I needed to spice it up, so I'd drop in spirits — even the local rice whiskey, "Ba Xi De". My God, that stuff was poison: it was like drinking liquid rust. I never really knew what was in it, and I didn't really care. I was already at the stage where I'd sink a couple of beers every morning for breakfast. Then, soon as I could, I'd top up with whiskey or spirits. It wasn't long before I was going through a bottle of whiskey every day. That was easy.

BODY COUNTS

It seems unbelievable now, but we were given targets. The sort you get in offices and factories – like I had at Texas Bloody Instruments – such as the amount of washing machines you must build, or clothes pegs you must sell, by the end of the week. The only difference was, our targets were body counts.

Our targets were how many Viet Cong our PRU should kill by the end of each week. The figure varied depending on what our schedule was, and it was usually unattainable. If we were planning an ambush, and maybe a couple of small-scale raids on individuals, we might realistically take 15 to 20 lives. The target would always be higher, though; I lost count of how many times it was set at 100. It was absurd. Then there were times everyone forgot about the targets because our units had taken too big a hit and nobody gave a fuck about targets any more and we all wanted the same thing in any case, to kill as many Dinks as we could.

Usually the targets were set at the beginning of each week, when I'd receive an intelligence report from the Phoenix district office. These reports would be sifted through and analysed by my bosses and then, when they had enough information on key individuals or units, they'd be handed to me. Sometimes I'd go to the office myself to pick them up, and other times an envelope would be biked over – or even arrive on a Huey with a load of supplies.

Once I'd digested the contents, it was my job to head out and "neutralise" the targets. If we brought back prisoners then fine, they'd be interrogated, but they wouldn't count towards the target figure. So nobody ever said to me: "Why didn't you bring them back alive?" Instead they'd say: "How many?" and I'd maybe reply "Four" and they'd smile and nod and make a note, and cross it off that week's productivity target.

We had to prove how many we'd killed, too, which meant bringing back evidence. Usually, that would be documents and ID we'd find on dead bodies, or it may be more personal stuff like photos or watches or wedding rings or chains. There is something cold and repulsive about frisking a dead man's body to see what he was carrying. Especially if that body is missing limbs or spilling intestines, or it's just plain mangled-up. That was a weight of war, one of the extremes.

In the end, we got immune it: sometimes I'd see soldiers cut off fingers and hands if that made it easier to grab the bracelets and rings. Sometimes the evidence would be heads or ears. That was after Frank died, when the extremes became blurred and I no longer cared.

Once I'd studied the intelligence report, I'd decide how and when to approach a mission. There were other South Vietnamese commanding officers in my unit but they would always look to me for guidance and strategy. How many men would we need? How would we get to the target area? When would we go – nearly always at night, I knew that answer already. Night time was the deadliest time for everybody in Vietnam. We might spend the daylight hours on reconnaissance patrols, or wandering into villages where we didn't really expect to find very much; but when we had a purpose, a mission to execute, we wanted the cover of darkness as much as Charlie did when he chose to attack.

Wherever possible I favoured a small group, so I'd maybe only take five or six South Vietnamese with me – plus, of course, Frank. I can't recall any missions when he wasn't by my side. Instinctively – and no doubt because we shared the same language – we plotted and planned the operation together before trying to explain it to the rest of the unit. Nearly always, Cam was with us, too – one, because we increasingly trusted him, and two, because he spoke such faultless English.

Usually, we'd be either driven in Jeeps or airlifted to somewhere close to where our target might be. More often than not, we'd be taken by Huey. I was OK with that – walking across trails and swamps was torturous, every step was an intolerable strain in case you trod on something that would explode in your face or slice you apart. Flying over the jungle was much more bearable, even if you were a target for rocket-propelled missiles and machine- gun fire. I'd take my chances in a Huey any day, and I think most soldiers were the same. Sometimes we'd run towards a chopper simply because it was there – it represented a means of instant escape, even if there was no tangible threat around. The Hueys became as much a part of the landscape as the jungle itself: every day soldiers were either clambering in or out of them, going into firefights, or leaving them behind; the wounded and the dead were being lifted in and out alongside crates packed with ammo and rations.

I would peer out of the open doors of a Huey and hope to see scorched swathes of jungle where napalm might have left its calling card. The more jungle razed by napalm, the more I smiled. I hated the jungle, it was on Charlie's side, not mine, and there was way too much of it. Sometimes vast areas stretching all the way up to the mountains would be reduced to charred, smoking stumps, and I'd chuckle and think: "Where you going to hide now, Mr Charlie?"

Frank, however, detested going anywhere by helicopter. He hated how quickly it could fly us into danger; then he hated how quickly we'd all jump out and disgorge our kit. "It's all too fuckin' quick," he insisted. "Like we're in a hurry to be abandoned in the middle of nowhere. That's when mistakes get made. That's when we give Charlie the upper hand. He can see us coming down and he knows where we must have got off. I mean, even Charlie can see a great big fuckin' Huey landing in his back garden. It's too bloody obvious." That much was true. It was always a sobering moment to be left behind, as the Huey you'd just arrived in soared rapidly back up and disappeared pretty bloody quickly over the tree tops. "There goes our lifeline. There goes our only way out. We're on our fuckin' own now, Bobby boy," Frank would say. "Let's just hope those Phoenix knobs got their coordinates right. I mean, are we even in the right place?" I'd look around at the hostile jungle surrounding us and curse that it hadn't been napalmed like the other bits I'd seen from the Huey. Nobody would see us die here, nobody would hear our screams or watch our bodies fall. Nobody would care very much. How ironic, we'd probably be the body-count targets for the Viet Cong. "Christ knows where we are," I'd say, just to make him feel worse. "Tell you what. You stick with me. That way, if Charlie fires, he'll hit you first, cos he'll see how fuckin' ugly you are. Jarhead."

Sometimes our target would be a specific individual; other times it might be an entire Viet Cong unit. In those cases, we'd lay an ambush and wait for Charlie to walk straight into our trap. Those operations were often on a much bigger scale, and I'd maybe take a unit of 20 with me.

Ambushes could go any way: success, failure, or a complete waste of time. Ambushes made you hate the jungle even more because it always wanted to ambush your ambush, like it was a gigantic booby trap waiting to screw you over. It was always there, watching and waiting and mocking. You could lay an ambush and take positions and lie waiting there for days on end with absolutely nobody turning up. Twenty of you eating and sleeping and pissing and shitting in the same place. Twenty, armed to the hilts, trying not to make a sound, trying not to emit odours that the jungle would carry on a rare breeze towards Charlie's gaping nostrils, twenty men trying not to breathe or rustle or chomp or scratch or fart. Men who smelt too clean were also a danger; maybe they'd had a shower and splashed on Old Spice before they'd been called out. Those were unnatural odours the jungle would waft towards Charlie.

Had I been there before? Sort of, when I was in the Legion waiting for six days to kill my Algerian target. That was different, though: it came with heat and discomfort, but it didn't come with the jungle. The jungle was a giant, sweating, stinking, inhaling, exhaling gland.

At some point, nearly always, the rain would come and we'd shelter feebly under our ponchos, all the while trying to keep a grip on our AK-47s and weapons, all the while watching the ground beneath us turn into mud, mud so strong it would slowly start to suck everyone into the reddened earth until our battle was with the ground, as well as the jungle, as well as Charlie. The rain would be monsoon strength, always. I'd never seen rain like it anywhere else before Vietnam; it was like being in a mortar attack, only the shrapnel was relentless spears of water – widespread, indiscriminate, deadly accurate, and impossible to repel. Even the jungle groaned under the rain, and we'd hear stuff it was impossible to believe. We'd hear giant trees groaning and twisting and turning and edging towards us; we'd hear sweating vegetation relaying messages to Charlie; we'd hear invisible creatures load AK-47s and rocket-propelled grenade launchers and hear them laughing with the rain. Then the mosquitos would show and bombard us like B-52s spewing napalm, diving suicidally straight at us, circling us, going away and coming back and trying their damnedest to fly kamikaze into mouths and ears. Those fuckers just didn't care, they were on Charlie's side, too.

Then sleep would want to have its say. Sleep would want to fuck us just like everything else. We'd arrange rotas but when your own turn for sleep came round, it was a nerve-racking battle with your own brain, one half screaming for you to shut out all the lights, the other yelling: "Stay awake, don't close your eyes, those bastards are out there, waiting for you." In the end, you thought you might be sleeping, but really you were just listening and waiting.

The jungle always had you by the balls; all you could do was lie there and wait, just in case Charlie wandered into your trap. Usually, an ambush would be set along a length of trail. At the entrance, I'd have placed a light machine gun, usually an M60, with another covering the exit. Then we'd lay the Claymore mines and Frank and I would always have a laugh about them because the outside casing carried the words: "Front Towards Enemy".

"Which dozy fucker came up with that?" I'd say. "That one of yours, Frankie? 'Front Towards Enemy' – is that to help the dozy marines? Very good. But why didn't you put 'Place right way round or you'll blow your own arse up'? That would have been clearer, surely? What d'ya say, Frankie boy?"

"Fuck you, Meathead," would be his sharp reply.

The Claymores were nasty buggers, though. They were attached by wire to a clacker, which you held in your hand. When Charlie was near enough, you pressed the clacker – click, click, boom – and the Claymore would explode and spew out a sweeping arc of steel balls that could devastate flesh and bones. I saw Claymores reduce entire swathes of jungle to clumps of stubble.

Another nasty little surprise was the Bouncing Betty, which we also used for ambushes. Step on one of those and you'd hear a tell-tale click – just enough time to realise your head was about to be blown off – before it shot up from the ground and exploded in mid-air, right in front of you.

Charlie used them a lot. In fact, my first experience of them was while I was on a routine day patrol and my unit was walking in single file along a trail. Suddenly I heard the click from somewhere up front, and then the explosion. Next thing I knew, we were all ducking as a human arm hurtled back along the trail over our crouching bodies. "Medic!" I screamed. "Medic to the front, man down!"

Within seconds a voice from the front shouted back: "That *was* the fuckin' medic. He's gone."

Once an ambush had been set, the unit would then dig in along one side of the trail, ready to open fire if the targets showed up. If they did, they'd instinctively run towards the end of the trail where the M60 was waiting to cut them off. One thing was for sure, they'd never surrender and if ever we were going to hit the body-count target, it would be then. Usually, however, nobody showed up, and we were left sinking deeper and deeper into the mud, soaked to the skin, heavily bombarded by the Charlie mosquitos, the Charlie bugs and the Charlie leeches. Then there were the snakes, especially the venomous green pit vipers, with their evil over-sized eyes. They were only a foot long but they were killers, too.

If we weren't setting an ambush, or targeting an individual suspect, we'd go out on patrol, looking for any sign of Viet Cong activity or presence in the villages. That's when your mind became acutely aware of booby traps. Charlie just loved sharpened bamboo. I was on one patrol when there was a tell-tale snap, the ground caved in and a soldier fell on to a bed of acutely-sharpened sticks, angled upright just like the howitzers at our base. I can still see his impaled body, threshing and bleeding wildly, with five or six sticks protruding out through his chest, neck, groin and legs. At first he screamed, then his mouth seemed to freeze so it looked as though it was permanently screaming and yet no sound was coming out. Mercifully, he died relatively quickly – but I know others weren't so lucky. Once they were impaled there was no way of getting them off and their death could be slow and torturous.

We did the same, though. We learned off Charlie. We'd even piss and shit on the ends of the sharpened sticks, so if – by some miracle – a victim survived, his wounds would inevitably turn septic. That was common – primitive but effective, and absolutely no way to die. Every footstep could be lethal. The jungle scrambled your senses to the point where seeing, hearing, smelling, tasting and touching were no longer enough. There was too much for just those five defence mechanisms to handle. How does a man stay alert for the minutest twitch, the tiniest unnatural sound, when all around there's a ceaseless cacophony of noise from the jungle? How does a man hear the clicks and clacks of buried mines before they've actually activated? How does he spot leaves and branches on the ground that have fallen irregularly because they are covering booby traps? How does he contend with the heat, the rain, the snakes, the leeches, the disease, the rot – and then contend with Charlie himself? Where the hell was he? What if Charlie just suddenly appeared, what if the elephant grass just parted like the fuckin' Red Sea and thousands upon thousands of deranged Viet Cong poured out, hurling grenades and firing AK-47s straight at you? "Fuckin' hell, Frank, why can't we just napalm the entire fuckin' country?"

That's what the jungle did to you.

KILLING BY HAND

When you kill a man with your bare hands there is an adrenalin rush. The rush of putting your own life on the line, of not knowing for certain whether you are stronger, faster or wiser than your opponent. Every single sense and instinct in your own body is alive, and tuned in like never before. All the switches you carry are on. I was never more aware of my own life, my own humanity – physical and mental – than when I was trying to kill someone with my bare hands. Then, as you feel your opponent's body weaken and his life ebb away, there is the strangest, most addictive sensation. You become acutely aware of your own life surging on and, like a drunkard who thinks he can do absolutely anything, you begin to feel immortal.

For a few magical moments, your surroundings become bright and vivid and servile. You are the master of a techno-coloured world; everything is eternally beautiful, a beauty you desperately want to grab and hold and preserve for ever. You become intensely conscious of your own breathing and suddenly you can feel the air in your lungs, clean and invigorating and life-affirming. You want to touch that air somehow, it's the purest, cleanest oxygen ever, and you inhale it greedily because it reminds you that you're alive. It's as though your entire body is a battery, and you've sucked the current out of your opponent and used it to recharge your own sapping supplies, depleted from the exertion of conquering and surviving.

I experienced all of this when I killed with my bare hands. I felt the adrenalin, I felt myself gambling with my own life – him or me, no weapons, man against man to the death. Then I felt the surge, the transferring of his current into mine, then the beautiful relief and ecstasy of winning. I was never more alive.

I've no idea how many people I killed in Vietnam. When I ordered in an air strike, or artillery fire, and the bombs and rockets that rained down ripped people apart, did it mean I'd killed them because I sent over the co-ordinates? Is their blood on my hands? There is a sense of detachment when you kill people you never see face to face. You never hear their pleas or their pain or their panic, you don't experience the discomfort of seeing them die. You might think "poor sods" when you see a B-52 spewing out the firepower from hell but, even then, it's only because you're thanking God you're not on the receiving end.

Up close is different. When you kill someone you can see, there's an aftermath. It may simply be the memory, the eternal knowing that you killed someone whose face you saw. The face makes it personal. The face has a habit of leaving an imprint in your brain that won't go away. When you close your eyes at night and pray, sleep erases everything, the face comes back to life, and you remember the detail of what you did. If you're lucky, you're not haunted by it – other than it won't go away. That's how I used to be. I killed without flinching and, even if I saw the face, I didn't think it bothered me. It just embedded. Things changed, though. I suffered the delayed reaction, and now I'm haunted by the face of every person I ever saw killed, including the ones who died alongside me, or followed me into firefights. They give me night terrors.

I remember the first time I killed with my bare hands. I'd taken a small unit to the huge Los Banos firebase, a heavily guarded US compound built on a prominent, dusty, rock-strewn hill overlooking Lang Co Bay, off Highway One. Like all the military bases, it constantly reeked of burning human shit. Every day the latrine oil drums would be doused in petrol and set alight. If ever a smell summed up the Vietnam war, that was it.

The firebase's elevated position meant you could see for miles in all directions and a network of Claymore mines, booby traps and roll upon roll of razor wire made it feel hostile and impregnable, although – God knows – Charlie tried his damnedest to breach the defences.

We operated from there many times. A railway line ran along the base of the hill and sometimes you'd hear an old steam train wheezing its way between the impoverished farms and paddy fields below. "Talk about two bloody worlds," Frank said. "Here's us with all our hi-tech weapons that cost millions of dollars, and there's the fuckin' enemy with their steam trains and water buffalo."

The latest Phoenix report had identified a Viet Cong leader who was living on the edge of a nearby hamlet, just on the inner fringes of a vast stretch of jungle to the west of the highway. I'd found a decent drop zone where I could take four or five men in a pair of jeeps. "From there, we can literally crawl through the jungle until we reach the hamlet," I explained to Frank. "We go tomorrow night."

Everything went to plan and we could clearly see the target's house as we edged our way through the undergrowth. He must have been high up in the community – his home stood alone in a clearing, it had recognisable walls, and even a colonnaded veranda that supported a sturdy bamboo roof. I was beginning to think it was all a bit too easy. Through the surrounding network of drooping branches and elephant grass I could clearly see lights were on in the house – and the back door was wide open. I glanced towards Frank, who was about three metres away to my left, and saw him frantically pointing to something to my right. An armed guard, his back towards me, the unmistakable outline of an AK-47 slung casually over his left shoulder, was standing close by. I'd been so busy trying to peer through the open back door, I'd completely missed him. "Shit!"

I took a couple of deep breaths and realised the advantage was still with me. The guard had clearly not heard a sound. I couldn't shoot him, though. That would immediately alert anyone in the house, and I'd no idea if there was anyone inside with the target.

I turned to Frank and held up my hands. He understood. I slowly removed my AK-47 from around my shoulder and inched into a position where I was near enough to make a sudden lurch towards the guard before he'd realise what was happening. Just like I'd done in Montana, I gradually stood up until I reached a point of no return. Without any hesitancy, I stepped forward, my feet momentarily crunching the fallen bracken on the ground, and swiftly wrapped my right arm around his neck. I could feel his Adam's apple squashing under the pressure. He gasped, a choking, throaty rasp; the catastrophic pressure was cutting dead his air supply, and I could hear a lame gurgling somewhere deep within his throat.

At the same time, my open-palmed left hand went flat against the back of his head, ramming it forward heavily. I then pushed all my weight into his back and kicked out my own legs backwards and upwards so I'd lift up and then fall forwards – forcing him to crash face-first to the ground under my weight. On the way down, I heard the back of his neck snap; I even thought I could feel the bones and sinew crumbling and yielding and breaking.

As we both dropped down hard, I suddenly felt a shower of blood splattering against my eyes, face and down the front of my shirt. We thumped on to the ground, my head cushioned into the back of his shoulder blades. I scrambled back up, away from his limp body, and looked – disbelievingly – at his neck. It had completely ripped open along the back, like a piece of torn cloth; his head had flopped forward and was barely connected any more to the rest of his body. I'd never seen anything like it – in fact I thought it was impossible to tear a man's head off – but I just about had.

For once, even the fucking jungle fell eerily quiet, as if I'd stunned it into silence. It was like the jungle was taking a breather of its own, checking it was all right, before saying: "Jesus, has that really happened? Have you torn his fuckin' head off?" I looked down, my heart pounding, my senses blazing as a torrent of adrenalin surged through me with monsoon force, and I saw the guard's face for the first time. It was young and innocent and fresh and weak. His eyes were still open, just like all the others.

He was just a kid – maybe 18 or 19 – short and slightly built. My weight alone would have crushed him. I knelt down and looked at the split across his neck and, as I did so, Frank passed by. Like me, he wanted a second look and, as he crouched, I could see the faintest sign of a smirk spreading across his face. Grotesque humour in grotesque moments. I'd put my life on the line. I had no way of knowing how the guard would react under attack, whether he knew how to wriggle free and overpower me. Kill or be killed. In the immediate aftermath, I felt the familiar rush of knowing I was still alive, I was the one left breathing.

But the tension stays acute in those moments and humour – or alcohol – is the only refuge left. It's neither arrogance nor strength. It's simply a nervous reaction, a way of dealing with the act of killing. Dark humour is an antidote to the shock and the stress and the rush. It's what you do at the extremes.

Frank's smirk broke my tension, my adrenalin levels subsided, and I felt my mouth start to crease and submit slowly to laughter. Before we knew it, we were both sat there, cross-legged and giggling, like a pair of schoolkids. It was only when Cam walked past with the rest of the unit that we regained some composure. "I didn't think that was fuckin' possible," said Frank as we stood up. Then, looking at my face and shirt still splattered in blood, he added: "Try to be a little less messy next time. Really, we can't take you anywhere these days."

It turned out he was the only guard on duty that night, although we didn't know that until Frank and I crept in through the back door, while the rest of the unit kept guard. The target was fast asleep on a makeshift bed in the main room; once we realised there was nobody else around we kicked him awake, stuck an AK-47 in his chest, and persuaded him to get up without a struggle. The panic and terror on his face convinced us he was a local politician of some sort, not a trained soldier. He was shaking with fear, and made no attempt to struggle. I called in a couple of my unit and they ransacked the rooms, finding documents and propaganda leaflets stuffed in cupboards, drawers and bits of pottery. "Tut, tut – you been helping the Bad Man. You in bad shit now," said Frank, dragging the target out. Once he was in the Jeep, we stuck a sack over his head and drove him back to the firebase where he was handed over for interrogation. "You gotta hand it to those Phoenix guys," said Frank. "We always find something, don't we?"

Another killing that turned personal came when Frank and I joined up with another PRU. They were going out on an ambush and I volunteered to give them some radio support. Naturally, Frank insisted on coming along, too. About 30 of us were helicoptered in to a stretch of jungle that had already been razed months earlier by an artillery bombardment. It felt like landing on a great big open wound, everywhere torn and bruised and gaping. We were still working on laying an ambush when, to our surprise, Charlie turned up earlier than we'd expected. A dishevelled, spontaneous firefight broke out – soldiers firing wildly at each other with little cover or protection – but they were a small unit and wilted quickly. Some fled for whatever cover they could find among the sparse trees and undergrowth that hadn't been napalmed, but a group of three were determined to fight to the bitter end. I was kneeling alongside two of the PRU soldiers – one of them had an M-16, I had my favourite AK-47, and between us we swiftly took out two of the group as they charged towards us. But the third kept on charging, even though he'd clearly lost his gun and could only manically wave a knife at us. At that point, the second soldier I was with – a guy I knew called Gerry – stood up and said: "This little Dink's all mine."

Gerry was a Filipino – short and skinny but extremely fit and agile. If anyone looked like a killer it was Gerry: his face was almost skeletal, the skin stretched tightly over his jaw bones. Everything about him was hard and chiselled and impenetrable. His eyes were never soft at the best of times, nothing in them ever showed a capacity for mercy or compassion. Now, those eyes were blazing. They were the eyes of a wild animal, zoned in on its prey; nothing else could exist in the world again until that prey was ripped apart. I'd seen that look in men before. Crazed, obsessed: it was a look that went way beyond the extremes into a place where there were absolutely no rules, no reason, no restraint. No humanity existed in that place. Gerry had smelt the blood and was intoxicated.

Gerry was also extremely talented at martial arts – which is how I'd got to know him – and an unbelievable knife fighter. Most people armed with a knife just stab or plunge or lunge with it. Not Gerry. A knife for Gerry was simply an extension of his arms. Combined with the lightning-fast martial arts movements he knew, Gerry was quite simply lethal.

The pair started to circle each other and Gerry immediately used his phenomenal Hung Ga speed and movement to start slicing his prey. Silver flashes of steel exploded like tracers in front of them. I'd seen Gerry use a knife before; he had incredible hand speed and could make the knife disappear into a blur so you never knew for sure where it was at any moment. The Viet Cong soldier was simply bedazzled by the swirling and ferocity of Gerry's arm movements. Within the blink of an eye, he'd flashed his knife down and cut his opponent's knife clean out of his hand.

Gerry was simply winding up: this was only the start.

He then started working his way up his opponent's right arm with swirling, deadly curves and arcs that were impossible to follow, each flash leaving behind another slice on his opponent's skin. Next, he whipped his hand round the back of his opponent's right leg, cutting it expertly – almost delicately – until the soldier was hamstrung and collapsed onto his right knee.

It was like watching a deathly dance – there was artistry and balance and even beauty in Gerry's movements. He carried on with a symphony of swirls until his knife reached his opponent's shoulder – and then he paused. Briefly. Like an artistic pause. Just enough time to let his opponent maybe think it was all over. It wasn't, though, for next came the crescendo: Gerry flicked his knife straight across the soldier's throat, so its surface layer sliced open, leaving behind a perfect, symmetrical line of blood. Still not finished, Gerry then worked his way back down his opponent's other arm, all the while his knife a flashing flurry of swift criss-crossing flicks and turns, until he reached round again and hamstrung the left leg. The soldier was left bleeding heavily, kneeling with both knees on the ground.

I looked at Gerry's face and instinctively knew what was about to happen. He could smell death and he wanted it badly – only death in itself wouldn't be enough. He wanted death to hurt. He wanted it to be cruel and vicious and drawn-out so it became torture as well. He wanted his opponent to die in a way that everyone in Vietnam feared. Agonisingly and slowly, maybe with little drops of mercy thrown in so his opponent might dare believe, might even pray, that he'd be spared, before another vicious slice removed any lingering hopes.

Gerry's eyes were choked with undiluted hatred and bloodlust; his opponent had no resistance left, his body was immobile, his face contorted, his voice wanting to scream but his honour – or maybe it was his surrender to certain death – muting any sound that might have bellowed from his voice. A smirk started to spread across Gerry's face; this was sport, and he was enjoying the annihilation. He was looking at his opponent like a butcher might look at a cow, like he was in an abattoir sizing up the best cuts.

I felt my right hand grasp my Colt 45. Now I was in a similar place to Gerry. I was submerged in the moment, shorn of reason – angry, wild and impulsive. I stood up, and walked towards the kneeling soldier. Gerry saw nothing, he couldn't have, he was too consumed by death and hatred. At that moment, the fucking president could have walked in and Gerry wouldn't have noticed.

I carried on walking until I stood directly behind Gerry's kneeling target. I remember looking at the back of the target's head, and seeing a dark shimmer of black stubble that ran down to his neck. Maybe he'd had long hair once. His head looked a bit like the place we were in. Maybe his head had been napalmed like the fucking jungle. I raised my gun and at the very moment he would have felt a cold circle of steel pressing into his skin, I pulled the trigger. The back of the soldier's head burst open in a shower of blood and flesh and his body slumped forward, on to his kneeling legs.

Instantly, a wild, piercing, anguished scream rose up from the clearing and echoed round every charred and blackened tree and root and wretched living or dying creature left in that bombed-out crater. "Noooooooooooooooooh. Fuckin' nooooooh. You Charlie-fuckin'-loving bastard; you fuckin' commie traitor. He was fuckin' mine!" He yelled the word "mine" so loudly it felt like a shiver across Vietnam.

Next thing I knew, Gerry was charging towards me, his knife angled and poised and ready to kill. I lifted my gun again and aimed it straight at his face. "Don't fuckin' do it, mate. One more step and you'll be on the floor with the fuckin' Dink." I was willing to shoot all right, because I knew he was willing to slice me to death. I held the gun right at him and he stopped, looking hard into my eyes to see if I was for real. He could see the same madness in my eyes that I could see in his. He backed off.

Gerry calmed down straightaway, like it had all simply been a light on/light off moment. That's what made him a natural killer, I suppose. Like me, he didn't do recrimination or remorse or self-doubt or analysing. But he was still determined to have the last word. "Don't think I'll ever forget this, Bobby boy!" he spat out, venomously. "Just one fuckin' word of advice. Never – ever – turn your back if I'm around. You got that? You got that, you commie-lovin' bastard!"

BAD KARMA

The more patrols I went on, and the more villages I went to, the more I noticed the terror in the faces of the locals. This alarmed me at first – our PRU had not been involved in any atrocities up to this point, although we were aware that sick stuff had happened. In my mind, we were trying to protect the villagers from Viet Cong infiltrators.

One evening I asked Cam about this and he told me about an American patrol he'd once tagged along with before I'd arrived. His story made a lasting impression on me, mainly because he started it nervously, clearly worried I might think he was being treacherous or anti-American. I knew he wasn't, he was simply telling me what he'd seen with his own eyes. The more I saw and learned about Vietnam for myself, the more I believed Cam's story. I could see for myself the locals were frightened; Cam simply explained why they were so afraid. His story also underlined just how much the Americans failed to understand local customs and traditions and language – with the catastrophic result that they often made enemies out of the very people they were meant to be protecting.

This is what he told me:

The Americans headed into a village and everything seemed fine. The local kids – they were all bare-chested and skinny – ran down the trail towards us hollering "My, My" (Americans, Americans) and waving their hands high in the air. The Americans were fully armed with rifles and grenades and knives and ammunition, but they tried to look calm and friendly and even smiled – a bit awkwardly though, like they weren't really sure.

They patted the kids on their heads and handed out sweeties until they got into the middle of the village where mums and old men started to appear from their huts and shelters. It was a desperately poor place – most of the huts looked like they'd been pushed and pulled together straight out of the jungle.

I must admit, Bob, I did occasionally spot a dark glance between maybe a young woman and an old man, but it'd only last a second and, in any case, everyone was putting on a big show of being happy to see the marines – so maybe I was wrong. I don't think I was, though.

Then one of the Americans asked: "Who's in charge here?" and, eventually, the village leader appeared, smiling and friendly-like. He was old – maybe 70.

"Is the Bad Man here?" the Americans asked.

"No, definitely not, no Bad Man here. I give my word." That's exactly what he said, and everybody around him smiled and nodded.

Cam stopped his story at this point and, as an aside, explained: "It's very important you understand this, Bob. It is the Vietnamese way to never give bad news first – or even at all. Vietnamese people like to say what they think people want to hear. It's much better to say everything is OK and perfect because, if you don't, it's bad karma and not polite."

He paused, then continued. "Please, please remember that, because it doesn't mean they're deliberately lying. It's simply the way they are. Do you understand?"

I nodded and let him continue.

The Americans peered into a few of the huts, still clutching their M-16s but still smiling. They couldn't see anything wrong – and neither could I, except for the glances. I definitely noticed there were no young men around, though – just young mums, gripping babies across their chests, and old men, who looked bemused by everything. The Americans started to head out but, just as we were leaving the edge of the village, rifle fire suddenly burst out from the jungle and one of the marines was hit. We all dived for cover and eventually got the sniper. There was nobody else.

The Americans were furious, though, and stormed straight back into the village, looking very, very angry. The village leader was hauled back in front of them. "Why didn't you tell us about the Bad Man?" they yelled. "Why did you hide Charlie from us? This very bad, now we must make village safe."

I thought they were going to tear the place apart but instead they radioed base and an hour or so later, Hueys started to arrive packed with supplies and provisions. It was incredible, the kids were running around screaming and laughing again, and the grunts were hauling boxes and bags of food and stuff into the middle of the village. I couldn't make sense of it.

Once everything was unloaded and the Hueys had gone, the Americans gave the village a final search. I swear, Bob, if there were boxes of AK-47s and ammunition anywhere, they were well and truly hidden. There was no trace or sign of anything, no bunkers, no underground tunnels, nothing. The Americans gave the village leader another lecture before leaving: "You're settled now, we go, you carry on but we will come back to check everything stays ok. You must tell us if Bad Man comes back." That sort of stuff. It was very tense, Bob.

We went back two or three times over the next week or so but stopped after that. Then, maybe a month later, we returned – the same unit, with me tagging along. And exactly the same thing happened all over again. Just as we were leaving, one of the marines stepped on a booby trap and fell onto bamboo spears that went straight through his body. He had no chance and all hell broke out.

The Yanks charged back into the village and this time tore it apart, storming into huts, kicking stuff around, smashing bits of furniture and chairs to bits, tipping boxes upside down and hurling contents and clothing all over the place. They even smashed up the pots and jars filled with the rice and food they'd supplied just four weeks earlier. "Why didn't you tell us about the fuckin' booby trap? Why didn't you tell us Bad Man had returned?" they yelled. They were so angry, so deranged.

I watched them chuck grenades down wells in case Charlie was down there; they even killed chickens and pigs and cows like they were suspects as well, like they knew something they weren't telling. It was insane. Then one of the Americans roared: "How come there's so much fuckin' food in this place. You been hiding it for Charlie? Why you got so much fuckin' stuff?"

The old leader was desperately trying to calm the Americans down and kept protesting his innocence. "We didn't know! Bad Man not tell!" he kept screaming. It was too late, though – the Americans weren't listening to him any more. Everyone was screaming and begging and pleading and the women were running around trying to hold on to their babies or grab their kids. It was mayhem. Then someone got hold of a flamethrower and started burning the huts. I could see him smirking like a crazed teenage kid playing with a new toy, the flames spewing out everywhere. The Yanks wanted Charlie to see the smoke rising above the trees. Pretty soon the whole place was just a pile of ashes and blackened, smouldering branches.

Soon after, the Hueys returned to pick us up, and I saw the Americans scattering calling cards for Charlie to find. On the card was a drawing of a dagger plunged into a stomach. I remember looking down as we took off and I could hear the weeping and wailing of the women and children drifting up with the smoke. Inside my helicopter, the Americans were busy adjusting their ammunition belts and grenades, like it gave them comfort somehow.

That was the end of Cam's story, but once he'd finished, he added: "What do you make of all that then, Bob? Nobody was killed, or raped or attacked, but then they were just a bunch of old men and mums and kids – people we're meant to be protecting. They had next to nothing in the first place, but even the bits and pieces they did have were burnt to the ground.

"I'm telling you, that's why Charlie keeps getting the upper hand. He'll have gone back to that village afterwards and said: 'Just look what the Americans have done for you'. And they'll listen.

"Who are the bad guys, Bob? The Americans talk to the villagers with contempt, I hear them taking the piss – 'Dink this, Dink that' – like they're just deformed little people. I can see the mockery in their eyes; I can see them letching at the village women and laughing at their poverty. They only have sarcasm, they grin and make dumb faces. They think nobody notices. Is it any wonder the villagers listen to the Viet Cong?"

He took a deep breath. "And in any case, where the fuck is Charlie? I never saw him. He's there, and he's not there. Just like those kids. Do you think Charlie is the fuckin' kids, Bob?"

It was quite a story, but it wasn't until I started going into the villages myself, and saw the terror in the eyes of the locals, that I realised how true it was.

BONFIRE NIGHT

A lot of our work involved random patrols and recon missions, much of it mundane. That's when we might wander into villages, and I'd see the terror Cam had told me about. But every day wasn't a battle or a firefight or an ambush – another reason why giving us body-count targets was so ludicrous. Often, infantry patrols spotted unexpected trails or tracks but didn't have the time to check them out. So, we'd go along and follow up, just to see if they led to Charlie. If they did, we might deal with the problem ourselves. Alternatively, we might send over coordinates so our big artillery guns could hurl over mortar and shells, or we'd call in an air bombardment and afterwards we'd go in to sweep up the pieces. That's when we'd be confronted with the gruesome realities of the Vietnam War. That's when we'd find limbs hanging from branches, the blackened remains of children and women who'd run out of places to hide when the bombs showered down. Sometimes I'd see soldiers vomiting because the devastation was too gruesome, especially if it had involved napalm.

The more villages we came across, the more we began to understand how persuasive Charlie could be. Installing their own people in key civic roles and positions was a clever way of spreading the Viet Cong message and controlling local resources. The villagers both trusted and understood what their leaders were saying, whereas the Americans simply came across as arrogant imperialist invaders, most likely to piss off as soon as it suited them. Even when we did find a leader who was working for Charlie, or a village that was providing shelter, it was impossible to know whether they'd been terrorised into doing so, or whether they'd simply been put in an impossible position of taking sides in a war they didn't want.

It wasn't our job to worry about such matters, but sometimes I sensed the Vietnamese soldiers in our unit struggled to maintain their morale and belief that America would stick around. "I've got to give these guys something to smile about," I said to Frank one day. "Find me a stretch of jungle that's nearby, one we know for sure is uninhabited, and let's have a laugh."

Frank grabbed a map and stretched it out on a table inside our hootch. "There," he said, tapping his fingers up and down on a spot not too far from our base. "How's that? Trees and shit everywhere, but not a village to be seen. Now, what you planning?"

"I want to give everyone a surprise. Let's get some crates of 33 sorted, stick 'em in the jeeps and head out over here tomorrow night," I said, pinpointing a hill on the map that was directly opposite the stretch of jungle Frank had found. "I'm not telling you what the hell I'm up to, you'll just have to trust me. Tell the men we're heading out on a job at 11pm tomorrow and everyone has to meet up by the jeeps. Top fuckin' secret. Got it, Frankie boy?"

"Yes sir, Mr President," and he clicked his heels to attention and saluted.

So we all met up at 11pm the following night and headed off along a narrow mountain road until we reached a high enough spot, about 45 minutes from our base, where there was a wide enough ledge for us to park the jeeps and sit, waiting, in the pitch darkness. Cam – who was in on my secret – leapt out of his jeep and started handing out the beers amid great surprise and enthusiasm. Frank still hadn't a clue what was going on. "Oi, Meathead, you finally gone loopy or what? What the fuck you up to?"

I'll never forget Frank's face five minutes later when the sky suddenly erupted into a blaze of flares and tracers and the purpley-orange glow of napalm, like a great big firework display. "Happy fuckin' bonfire night!" I yelled, and within seconds everyone was hollering and whooping as America inadvertently staged a spectacular pyrotechnic show – just for us. I'd called in the heavy stuff to bombard the jungle Frank had found on the map. "You'll be in deep shit for this," said Frank, his jaw practically collapsing on to the floor, but I was too busy laughing and whooping with everyone else to care. Suddenly, the unmistakeable roar of a mighty AC-130 gunship filled the skies and the hulking black outline of the monstrous Lockheed slowly obliterated the horizon, spraying thousands of rounds of tracered ammo into the innocent jungle below. "This, my friend, is the most expensive morale-booster ever staged," I said, winking at Frank. "You could have got Elvis Presley over here every day for an entire year for less dollars than this. And d'ya know what? Nobody will ever know they're hurling all those bullets and shit at a pile of fuckin' trees. Just to give us a laugh! Here's to fuckin' Vietnam," and we clashed our 33s together and laughed with everyone else and marvelled how colourful our weapons of destruction could be.

Even my morale was lifted by the absurdity: the cost, the irresponsibility, the risk, the impudence, the fuck-you-all of it all. Frank rolled up a joint, lay back on the front seat of our jeep and said: "You know what, this is mellow. Good job, Meathead." He was right. It was mellow. The flares and tracers were painting random, luminous patterns across the black sky, like someone was playing with a gigantic Vietnamese Etch-a-Sketch. For a few moments it was possible to believe we were watching something artistic and beautiful. I knew I'd get away with it: as far as America was concerned, it was a genuine H and I mission – harassment and interdiction to blow up one of Charlie's hiding places. Only thing was, we knew Charlie wasn't there and so we pissed ourselves laughing.

MORTAR TERROR

Mortar attacks still terrorise me today. Every night I collapse out of bed – usually around 3am – and hit the ground, just like I did in Vietnam, my arms and hands clutching the top of my head, my body shaking violently as my bedroom floor is being blown to pieces. In Vietnam, it was the not knowing that was the worst. Not knowing if you were going to die. Not knowing if you'd be left blinded, or without any arms or legs. You never saw a mortar attack coming at you, you couldn't defend yourself against it, there was no shooting back. Just an eerie, soft sound – poompf – somewhere away in the distance. Poompf. What an inadequate, comical-looking word, a word that doesn't begin to hint at the death and destruction it preludes, because after the "poompf" came the explosions and the carnage.

I dreaded the nights in Vietnam. I dreaded the moon. The moon was a huge spotlight, switched on by Charlie so he could introduce the main, terrifying act. We might feel invincible during the days, pouring in and out of Hueys, adjusting and parading our weaponry, but Charlie came out at night – and he used the moon to illuminate us and then he used his mortars to blow us apart.

"Incoming, incoming!" we'd all universally scream, and

everyone would instinctively hit the ground, hit the trenches, hit the earth as mortar shells rained down like deadly, flaming meteorites plunging straight out of the clouds.

Only hitting the earth wasn't enough. You wanted to be much deeper than that. You wanted to be inside the earth, so you'd dig at it violently with your outstretched fingers, and stretch full-length along its crumbling surface, trying to be a part of it and not just on top of it, where death was sweeping violently across its outer layer. If the earth got into your mouth and you tasted it and even swallowed it then that didn't matter because maybe that meant you were really deep inside it.

Then came the aftershocks. The earth would boil and shudder and implode and explode as the mortars slammed into its defenceless crust, spraying sludge and slop and slime everywhere. The shells would be so heavy the ground would sway with each strike. The earth would start cracking and yielding and suddenly it was no fucking good any more, no shelter at all, and you might end up buried alive if you stayed inside it. So you'd get up, in a sort of deformed stooping-crouching position, like the fucking Hunchback of Notre Dame, and look around for somewhere better to hide. That's when you'd see the bodies and the limbs of the soldiers who were whole and alive just seconds earlier. That's when you'd hear the screams of the ones who'd already been maimed and ripped apart but not entirely killed. That's when your training and your ability to be a soldier in the most horrific molten extremes kicked in.

"Frank, three o'clock to you, man down," and I'd see him running along in that demented, crouching stoop, clutching a medical kit, hoping to save a life. I'd head for Cam and between us we'd try to work out where the mortars were coming from so I could hit the radio and send over coordinates. "Grey Wolf to Da

Nang. Heavy incoming, coordinates 6712 – request immediate overhead artillery. Men down, need urgent medevac back-up." I made that call so many times.

The pounding carried on as you waited and prayed that the coordinates were correct and the big guns in Da Nang could end the onslaught quickly. Still crouching, still incapable of completely letting go of the earth, still thinking you might need to get back into it somehow, you'd watch hideous distortions of steel and shrapnel zipping through the air hoping to maim and kill. The fear and the tension would be so acute your sight would somehow stretch to points beyond its usual lines of vision. You'd see behind you; you'd see into blind spots along your sides – you'd become aware of angles you never knew existed. All from a crouching position as you kept close to the earth.

And still the pound, pound, pounding, continued. In fact, it never ended. It'll still be there tonight.

Another piercing scream would rise above the explosions, someone else would be hit, so I'd scramble off in my crouching run, one hand desperately trying to clutch the helmet on my head, the other gripping a medical kit.

Even though I was never physically hit, mortar attacks always left me scarred. My body would be shattered by the noise and the screams and the terror and the shudderings and the scurrying around trying to help the wounded or issuing fire control orders or making radio calls. At some point I might notice Frank, crouching like me. He'd maybe grabbed some binoculars and he'd be trying to see if the bombs from Da Nang had landed yet and I'd pray he'd yell out: "It's over, Charlie's hit. Charlie's fuckin' hit." Sometimes he did, sometimes he didn't. It was a wonder any of us survived mortar bombardments.

Firefights were different but they also give me night terrors now, just like the mortars. I have a recurring dream and it always ends the same way. A firefight breaks out, it's an ambush and my unit's caught by surprise. I look around and suddenly I am the only person left, everyone is dead except me and I'm enclosed by a perfect circle of Viet Cong soldiers, all staring directly at me and screaming insanely. They're heavily armed yet none of them are firing. Instead, they move slowly towards me and, as they approach, the circle gets smaller and tighter around me. I dive to the ground and fire manically in great sweeping, circular movements and I see some of them fall but then watch in horror as they stagger back up, laughing and pointing at me and there's not even any blood on their black fatigues. I throw grenades and their bodies fly high into the air but land straight back to where they were standing, unscathed, and then they carry on moving towards me. Now they're really close, I can see their teeth and their eyes and smell their breath and their circle has closed in on me completely, shutting out light and air, night and day, like a noose drawing tightly around my neck. They don't shoot me because I'm choking and suffocating without them having to lift a finger, until – right at the very end – I say one last, dying word. It's always the same word. It's always: "Frank".

When a firefight begins, especially if it's an ambush, the first split seconds are the moments that determine your fate. The decisions you make then are the difference between life and death.

My first instinct was always the same. Sheer fuckin' terror. Then an automatic lunge towards anything that might provide cover. If we were in a clearing, or on a trail, we'd dive into whatever undergrowth the jungle offered, men diving in any direction into swampy water, mud, elephant grass, anything. My second instinct was to shout for Frank, to establish where he was and what –

between us – we could do to organise the unit. When you can feel bullets caressing your temple, when you start to feel the ground violently shattering as grenades tear it apart, when you see men crouched down vomiting because they can't deal with the sudden shock and then you see other men slumped, dazed, against a mangled reptilian tree root and you can tell just by the smiles on their faces they've been hit – badly – but they're smiling because they want to believe they'll be ok, when you see all that, then hearing a voice you trust, who will die himself if it means getting you out of this hole, well, it's the greatest adrenalin rush of them all.

That was why Frank and I were inseparable. He was the only one I trusted completely in a situation like that. He had my back and he knew I had his. That's why we immediately looked for each other when a firefight broke out because between us, we knew, we could keep ourselves – and the unit – alive. I've never trusted anyone like that since. Every day I placed my life in Frank's hands and he did the same with me. *Semper Fi.*

"M60 cover, six o'clock!" I'd roar and suddenly the unmistakeable, rapid, blast of ammo ripping into a mound of bushes where I'd seen a shadow of movement, no more, would tear through the air as Frank unleashed its full destructive power. That salvo would buy us time; now we could establish who was where and who was in trouble.

Each time there was a firefight, it felt like we had licence to do whatever it took to survive and win. If that meant going beyond the extremes, if that meant going crazy, then nobody gave a fuck because survival was all that mattered. I never thought about the morality of it. I simply wanted to kill instead of being killed myself.

In one firefight, I dived alongside a member of our unit and screamed "Cover me!" I'm certain he nodded but as I scrambled up, there was no machine-gun fire coming from behind. I looked round and there was a hole, plumb in the centre of his throat. Everyone in Vietnam dreaded being hit in the throat. I never sensed the bullet pass me, I never heard it land, I never heard him die and yet I was right next to him as he was killed. Death is like that in a firefight: it comes and it goes – just like that. You don't freeze, or think, or debate it. I didn't try to wake him up, or say a prayer, or re-arrange his body into some sort of dignified position. I just shouted at someone else to cover me, we were in a fuckin' ambush, and I needed to kill Charlie before he killed us.

I'd see soldiers fall, I'd see them being killed or maimed and my first, immediate reaction was always the same: Thank God that wasn't me. Then I'd carry on trying to live. The enemy was there, it was trying to kill us all and in that moment, we would do whatever it took to prevail.

Generally – and with the notable exception of the Tet Offensive, when Charlie nearly wiped us out – firefights fizzled out once we'd established good cover and our M60s had dealt with the main source of attack. Charlie would simply slip back into the jungle as quickly as he'd arrived. Then came the sweeping up; the picking up of dead bodies, the picking up of anything with a heartbeat – even if it was torn apart. That's when you'd see men with legs sticking out at insane scarecrow angles and you'd go over and try to convince them everything would be OK and they'd be "on their way out of here any moment now". I'd radio in medevac support and, to be fair, that usually arrived pretty bloody quickly. Whoever was flying those Hueys was some kind of genius because I'd see them land on patches of land where I'd struggle to park a jeep.

Mopping up was often the worse; in the heat of battle there isn't time to count the bodies, you're too busy fighting back, trying to organise the unit, trying to fire in a coordinated way. In a firefight you hear the sounds of bullets and grenades and rifles and they usually drown the sounds of dying men. That comes in the aftermath. That shatters the silence when the artillery has stopped. I would say 99 per cent of wounded men screamed for their mothers as they fought to stay alive. Sometimes those men won that fight, too: I've seen soldiers with horrendous wounds – limbs blown off, chests split open, disfiguring head injuries – and they somehow survived.

Frank and I would rush over and slap morphine into them, and then wait for the medics to take over. I was clearing up a site once when I had to load a badly wounded lieutenant into a helicopter. I didn't know him; his chest was torn apart and, as we lifted him, a waiting medic tried to hook him to a drip. "Here, quick, climb up, I need your help," he said urgently, looking at me. I jumped in, the medic grabbed my hand and immediately placed it inside the lieutenant's chest – under his rib cage – and made me grab a soft, squashy ball inside. "Feel that," he said. "That's his heart. Now keep pumping it – in and out, that's it – and don't stop pumping it until we land."

I did as I was told, keeping my eyes firmly fixed on the lieutenant's face the entire time. I didn't want to see what I was doing. The Huey took about 15 minutes to land and that's a long time to look at a face when you're trying to keep the rest of its body alive. He was young, whoever he was, yet – like everyone who was young in Vietnam – all the youth had been sucked out of him. What should have been fresh, virgin skin was now a ploughed field of creases and lines and where there should have been colour there was simply ashen grey. I must have seen hundreds of faces like that.

It wasn't until we touched down, though, that I fully realised what I was doing. My hand had been covered in shit and mud and the slime of battle, yet now it was inside a man's ripped body, pumping his heart, trying to keep him alive. If I'd thought about it while we were in mid-air, I'd have probably thrown up. The adrenalin keeps you in the moment, though. You only become sick and squeamish when the adrenalin disappears. That's when I needed alcohol.

I never found out the lieutenant's name but I bumped into the medic about two days later. "Could you tell me what happened to that guy in the medevac? You know, you grabbed my hand, stuck it inside his chest and made me pump his heart while we were flying back to base," I said.

The medic scratched his head and thought for a while, clearly trying to picture who I was talking about. The youth had been sucked out of his face, too; he must have seen so many bodies; he must have been weary like all of us. "Oh, the young lieutenant," he suddenly responded, like a light switch had just flicked on in his memory bank.

"Him. Yes, yes, I remember now. Did you know him? Sorry, I can't remember his name. Was he your friend? I'm afraid he never made it. We lost him shortly after we landed."

That's combat. That's why I never questioned the morality or worried about the extremes in the heat of combat.

PLAYTIME

One night, Frank and I got wasted and I told him all about Bob
Rose, the Northern Cheyenne, the French Foreign Legion, Gian
Falconie, and the murder I never committed. He thought the
murder bit was hilarious. "So, you ran away from home because
you thought you'd killed someone and then nearly got blown up
yourself in Algeria? Then it turns out you never killed anyone, so
you'd joined the Legion for no reason at all? Fuckin' classic!"

There were moments when the two of us tried to escape the war,
when we'd head for Saigon or Bangkok for rest and recuperation.
We fought side by side and we played side by side. Wherever we
went, it was always the same ritual: Frank would get stoned and
I'd get pissed and we'd both end up screwing whores, sometimes
the same ones on the same bed in some dingy room above a seedy
neon-flashing bar. I still had a full head of black hair, and was
pretty lean and fit, so pulling girls wasn't too difficult. Frank,
however, was less successful. "You're too fuckin' ugly," I tried to
explain. "In fact, you're the God-damned ugliest marine here. It's
not your fault. Try to watch how I do it."

He got his own back one night, though. We were in Bangkok and
I slept with a stunning whore – her straight, jet-black hair was

so glossy it even lit up the dingy room we were in – but I was too drunk to fumble about with a condom. Instead, I used the sleeve of my shirt, trusting that would give me enough protection. Frank and I headed back to our grubby hotel later that night and I gave him an uncensored account of my conquest: "So I just used my shirt sleeve," I explained, and we fell about laughing. When I woke in the morning, however, I felt a terrible itching in my groin. I looked down anxiously and the entire area was covered in a vast, hideous rash, like I'd been rolling around in nettles all night. "Jesus, shit, I've got the clap!" I screamed, jumping out of bed, panic-stricken. Frank roared with laughter as I hopped around, looking mortified. "That's not the clap, you clown. That's an allergic reaction. Look, pops, it's time you faced it – you're allergic to women, and you're allergic to shirt sleeves."

Although we could temporarily escape the war, there were constant reminders of it all around us – even on R and R. We'd bump into other marines, and end up playing the sort of bar games that were as sick as the war itself. Freckles was one. A group of us would sit round a table, pissed or stoned – or maybe both – and someone would defecate on a beer mat and then thump the top of the table hard to see where the shit splattered. Another favourite was pissing into drinks and then passing them around to see who gagged first. We'd be in the company of men you wouldn't want your parents to meet. Men who, like Frank and I, had seen the extremes, and in many cases gone beyond them. We'd all inhabited a world of death and limitless horror and pain; maybe our games needed to be just as vile as well.

Frank and I got ourselves tattoos in Saigon – but even they were sinister reminders of the world we were inhabiting. On my right arm I have the words "Provisional Reconnaissance Unit Quang Nam". Then I have "Doh Hoh Chi Minh" – which means Fuck Hoh

Chi Minh. I also added the words "Sat Cong" – Kill Communists – accompanied by a dagger and skull. Those tattoos are still on me today.

None of us had a better world to go back to. Random terrorist bombs exploded regularly in Saigon, maybe planted by the shoeshine boys, or the girls smiling in the laundry shop, or the scruffy-yet-smiling young kids running up and down the streets with paper kites flying behind them in the hot-air breeze, or even the elderly. The old were forever staring at you, in a silently tolerant way, only there was distress in their faces too, and you suspected they were really saying: "We're going to get you for this, you motherfuckers."

It wasn't my idea of rest and recuperation. There was simply no oasis or completely safe haven anywhere, so I tagged along with everyone else and got blasted like everyone else and, like everyone else, hoped for the best. I kept in touch with my parents, I wrote home but never wrote anything meaningful, and sometimes I'd get a letter back. I saw soldiers who kept letters in their chest pockets, holding them there as if they were security blankets, close to their hearts and their childhoods, and maybe believing they'd deflect a bullet one day. I saw others who never even opened their letters because they couldn't deal with the reminders of what life used to be. Frank was a bit like that. I watched him one day sitting on the side of his bed, holding an envelope in his hands and staring at the handwriting on the front. "It's from Mum, it's her writing," he mumbled, struggling to contain the tears welling in his eyes. I couldn't take the piss, not then. He looked at me and I smiled weakly, then he put the letter down on the bed cover, unopened. I've no idea if he ever read it.

I had my own fledgling family back in England: wife one and wife two and my kids. I'm ashamed to say I shut them out completely. It was far easier to play freckles and get pissed than it was to spend time thinking about them.

R and R was simply something you did to make out you were having a good time. Mainly, you were too exhausted. I was talking to someone at a bar one night, he was stood right in front of me and words were coming from his mouth but all of them were incoherent, gibberish, like he was stuck in a dream and the words he was saying were from his dream and not from the conversation I thought he was having with me. Everybody craved sleep but nobody could find it. It was impossible to sleep on patrols; it was impossible to sleep on R and R, mainly because you were always on guard, always agitated. In any case, what was the point of being on R and R if you spent it sleeping? Yet sleep was all you really wanted.

BOMB US ALL

I was gambling with the lives of soldiers who depended on me. I looked at their faces as they prepared for death and I saw their eyes begging me to save them. I'd be gambling with my own life, too – and Frank's. I know now, with absolute certainty, I would never have taken the gamble if he hadn't given me the strength and courage to do so. I couldn't have done it alone.

Our unit was being annihilated; Charlie had launched the Tet Offensive and pounced, unexpectedly, pushing me into a new extreme. I called in fire on the exact spot where my own men, exhausted, battered and almost beaten, were fighting for their lives.

It was early morning on New Year's Eve, 1968, and we simply didn't see it coming. I was in a deep alcohol-fuelled sleep when the first mortars rained down but there was an intensity to the bombardment this time that went way beyond what I'd experienced before. It's amazing how the fear of death can sober you up. The Viet Cong were hurling everything at us – rocket-propelled grenades, mortars, B40 rockets – and then the cry rang out that we all dreaded: "Charlie's in the fuckin' wire!"

My first instinct was to look for Frank; we flung ourselves into the nearest trench and then tried to work out what was happening and why it felt different this time. "Let's get over to comms," he yelled. "Let's find Cam and see what he knows. This feels bad."

We stooped down and ran like fury, feeling the ground around us being pulverised as we dashed through the mayhem. The concussion from each explosion shook my face so ferociously it felt like my eyeballs wanted to pop out of their sockets. Smoke and fire and dirt made the air so dense I could barely see where I was treading, barely see clumps of shrapnel spinning and flying and hurtling through the fog, looking for victims.

I scrambled into comms, where Frank and Cam were already trying to make sense of it all. "Charlie's getting through," said Cam. "They've got boards down and they're crawling over the wire. It feels like hundreds of them this time, it's far heavier. There's too many – we're being overrun." As so often happened, Frank and I instantly thought the same thing. "We need to pull out," he said. "Let's push back into the main town. At least the streets and buildings there will give us some cover. We'll get blown to fuck staying here."

I agreed. Cam spread the word while Frank and I grabbed everything we could: ammo, grenades, M60s, AK-47s, knives – as much as we could carry and hurl into jeeps – and we fell back into the heart of the town, not just us but other units as well, still trying to work out how the hell this had happened. I radioed Da Nang, told them what we were doing, and learned Charlie was springing surprise attacks across Vietnam, including Saigon. The news made me shiver. "Fuckin' hell – it's kicking off everywhere," I said to Frank.

Charlie kept on charging. He wanted our blood and he was happy to slug it out in a street fight. We took cover behind abandoned cars; we clustered in groups around opposite shop corners, so Charlie might walk into a double-barrelled blast of ammo from each side as he came towards us. Still he kept on coming and he was getting too close: increasingly, we could see Viet Cong faces. If they got any closer, we'd be locked in hand-to-hand combat and there were way too many of them to win that. All the while, we were being pressed back towards the Thu Bon river, where we eventually bunkered down, waiting for the final showdown.

"We're getting overrun, we're fucked here!" I yelled at Frank. "We need something drastic, there's nothing left to lose. I'll have to call in cover – what other option is there?" I scrambled for the radio, held it in my hands – and then paused. It was the nuclear option. I'd be calling in America's artillery on top of our own heads, praying they'd hit Charlie and somehow work out how to avoid us. I needed to know if it was the right call to make.

I looked at Frank; he knew why. "Just fuckin' do it, Meathead, and stop having a fuckin' debate." So that's what I did. I radioed Da Nang, gave our coordinates and then waited for the marines to unleash hell from the air – right over our own heads. It would be a lottery – the ground would be destroyed and either Charlie, us – or both – would evaporate in the fires. Instead of watching it from the comfort of a hilltop and swigging some more 33s, we'd be underneath it, praying, waiting to see who would burn first. I knew what I was doing, I was calm and ready to die. So was Frank.

As we waited, we carried on firing, throwing everything we had left at Charlie. As one wave of bodies were mown down another would appear, charging relentlessly and, to be fair, fearlessly. I remember fixing my sights on one soldier who just kept on running and for a split second I was back in Algiers, waiting to assassinate my target. Just like then, I could see – fleetingly – into the man I was about to kill. His eyes were demonic, possessed. I'd seen the thousand-yard stare on many soldiers before but that kind of stare was vacant, life had deserted the body, there was nobody at home any more. This was similar, but the polar opposite at the same time. There would be no reasoning with this man racing towards me; he had locked out the world and had one all-consuming purpose: kill. I took him out, then the next one and then the next and then the one after that. They all had the same stare.

Then came the explosions; then came the shells and the rockets and the bombs, as I'd directed. The overhead bombardment caught Charlie by surprise; he hadn't called it in; he was still marauding through open streets while we crawled deep into the sludgy earth by the river bank, grateful for the chance to sink into its slime and softness, covering our hands and faces and skin into its black core. Some men praying, some thinking of home, some waiting to die.

The tactic worked. Charlie was suddenly trapped on a violent demolition site: ground and buildings imploded and exploded and shrapnel big enough to fell entire units hurled at wild angles across the streets. About 50 of us managed to scramble over to the other side of the river as the deluge from Da Nang crashed down. By the time we'd crossed over, the South Vietnamese 51st Regiment and the 1st Marine Division were ready to push back what remained of the Viet Cong invasion. It had taken a full day to survive and it was the closest I'd ever come to death in Vietnam.

There was worse to come.

DEAR JARHEAD

There was no sense of foreboding, no inner voice whispering "Don't go." Grey Wolf didn't ominously appear and stop me in my tracks and make me think something might be wrong. In any case it never worked like that. Events just unfolded, like they always do, and we went along with them because that's what you did.

It was at least five weeks after Tet but tensions were still high. None of us were sleeping, none of us wanted to be caught out like that again. We were on maximum alert, Charlie could return, and that fear alone left us in a twenty-four-hour paralysis. I'd close my eyes at night, hoping alcohol would numb my senses, but even that didn't work. I was awake to the slightest inconsistency, waiting for a scent or a sound that didn't feel right. Days and nights became a ceaseless ordeal.

We tried to continue as before, acting on Phoenix intelligence reports, raiding villages where the Tet Offensive may have been hatched, looking for clues, leftovers, anything dropped as the Viet Cong were driven back. It was hard to trust or believe anyone and yet sometimes I'd look round and stare at the locals and realise their lives weren't so dissimilar to my old life on the reservation. They lived amid astonishing beauty and yet existed amid ugliness and despairing poverty. Worse, they had war and Charlie and, just like the Northern Cheyenne, America on their doorsteps.

We'd come back from one reconnaissance patrol particularly weary and frustrated. Yet again, we were staying on one of the giant US firebases and we'd gone out on foot to check an area to see whether it had been used to launch mortar attacks. Patrols like that were often incredibly tense and therefore tiring. You had no real idea if Charlie was watching, whether he was waiting behind the undergrowth somewhere, so your senses were constantly on high alert for the slightest sound, or rustle, or trace of something on the ground. Everyone was terrified of stepping on to a booby trap; everyone was edgy and nervous – straining and listening and silently praying everything would turn out OK.

In this instance, everything was OK. We couldn't see or find anything – not even the tell-tale sign of where the base plate of a mortar might have left an indent on the ground. So we returned, frustrated, tired, yet glad to have survived.

I turned to Frank and said: "I'll get the guns sorted," and then hurled my kit over to him. "Take that back to the hootch will you, mate." Unloading and cleaning weapons was standard operational procedure immediately after any mission, so I headed off with some of the unit to a sandpit area where the guns could be stripped, cleaned and made safe. After a while, I wandered over to the communications tent, just to see if anything was coming in over the radio. I still had my AK-47 with me as I walked in.

Cam was already there. An emergency call had just landed from a US reconnaissance unit who were being overrun and needed urgent back-up. "Sounds like they're getting shot up real bad. We've got two choppers ready to go," he said. "You coming?" It wasn't a question I needed to debate: I raced over to the hootch immediately, telling Frank: "We've got a patrol stuck on a hot

DZ, they need help real bad." He was lying down on his bed but without any prompting leapt straight up and the pair of us grabbed ammo and kit before racing off to the Hueys, their rotary blades already fired up, their doors flung wide open, their landing feet – like great big snow skis – bobbing up and down on the ground, desperate to get up in the air. Frank and I clambered on board; Cam was already inside, along with two air gunners covering each side of the chopper, a crew chief, plus the pilot and co-pilot.

We didn't talk. Instead, we triple-checked our guns and fiddled with ammo, cramming as much as we could into shoulder belts and webbing. I looked out of the doors, hoping to see more napalmed jungle, and mumbled "Shit" when I couldn't see any. Frank looked over to me as I cursed and I recall thinking: "I bet you're hating this." He hated arriving anywhere on a Huey, not least a firefight. I thought it – but I never said it.

The other chopper was slightly ahead of us and, as it started to descend, it came under heavy fire. "Fuck, it's hairy down there," said one of the gunners, releasing a torrential blast of covering fire. Our pilot could see a clear landing spot but just as we were about to hit the ground, there was an almighty explosion and the first helicopter erupted into an engorged ball of flames, its aftershocks rocking us violently from side to side, its heat so ferocious we all cowered back from the doors. "Fuckin' hell, it's gone. It's disintegrated. Get out, everyone out – now – and let's get some covering fire down!" I yelled. I didn't know it then, but everyone in that Huey died.

We all jumped out of the Huey's left-hand-side doors and I instinctively ran to the rear, where I could see three US marines in the distance struggling to make their way along a trail that disappeared off into the jungle behind them. Frank and Cam took position in front of the Huey's doors, so they could give me covering fire as I headed towards the marines.

The jungle felt like it was erupting as I raced down the trail; grenades and AK-47s and M60s were exploding relentlessly and a thick, dense smell of burning petrol – probably from the blown-up helicopter – made the air feel combustible, like it would ignite at any moment. I was half-running, half-crouching and could clearly see one of the marines was badly hit; he was lurching forward in spurts, then stopping as his knees buckled, falling, then picking himself up and moving on again in another short burst. Even from a distance I could see him desperately struggling for breath, his chest heaving up and down, his mouth wide open like it was struggling to digest the petrol-poisoned oxygen.

As they got nearer, there was a sudden and violent burst of machine-gun fire. His two colleagues were mown down instantly, their bodies folding and then crashing face-first into the muddied slime underfoot. I didn't even need to check, I knew they were gone. But the injured one was still lurching forward and getting near enough for me to see his rank. "Captain, Captain!" I yelled, and his face tilted up towards my crouching body on the edge of the trail. I saw a glimmer of hope in his eyes and I pumped my AK-47 into the mangled undergrowth, praying it would give him enough cover until he reached me.

He was desperately close and he continued running and stumbling and leaning his body towards me. He was practically an arm's length away when his legs buckled and he fell flat out into the trail's slime, his face submerged into the shit, his mouth desperately trying to spit out the mud and slime he'd ingested as he collapsed. I carried on firing ferociously and leant over to feel for a pulse. I could now clearly see he'd been shot in the side of the head; the bullet had left a bloodied crater above his left ear where you could see the edges of his brain exposed. But he was still conscious, still alive, and trying to talk to me through the mud and shit in his mouth.

I dragged him full length over to the side of the trail then hoisted him up so he was leaning into me, face to face. He wasn't tall – maybe five feet nine inches – and although he was pencil-thin, he felt deceptively heavy. I hadn't anticipated that and I tore away his ammo and kit feverishly in a desperate bid to lighten the load. For a few fleeting moments I looked into his face. He was older than me – perhaps 35 – and his bony features simply exaggerated the lines and crevices across his forehead. I suspected he was fanatical; the sort of officer who believed passionately in the cause, who used his seniority to inspire and rouse his unit so they'd become ferocious committed believers in the great war for freedom. He just looked that type, even under the dripping layers of mud and sweat and blood that were submerging him now. Through those invaders, I could see the fear of death and the desperation of wanting to live all rolled into one.

I wanted to show him some dignity, to respect his rank, but suddenly all that stuff seemed utterly trivial and stupid. He was a human being clinging to life and clinging to me. In years to come we might meet each other one day. I might nip across the Pond and he'd salute me and introduce me to his family and make them honour the heroic Brit who saved his life. In this moment, though, he was no different from any other panic-stricken, wounded soldier I'd seen teetering between life and death. He didn't want to let go, he wanted to survive, but deep down he suspected he was screwed. I was his only hope.

"Captain, I'm going to hoist you on to my back, so just dangle your arms either side of my neck and hang on for fuck's sake. I'll get you out of here." I'd no idea if he was taking my words in, but

I turned my body round so he was facing my back and he half fell, half lurched on top of me, his arms flopping down either side of my chest as I'd instructed.

I then staggered back on to the trail, and – stooping for cover and stooping under his weight – half ran, half crawled towards the helicopter, which I could see not far off. "Just hang on captain, hang on in there, I can see our Huey, we can do this."

I thought we had as well, although I could see the chopper was under heavy fire; prolonged blasts of ammo were spewing out from the left- and right-hand open doors and I thought I could see smoke spiralling out from under the rotary blades. I could hear the captain groan with every step I took, I could feel his body trembling from shock and injury, I could sense his breathing getting more and more agitated. "Almost there!" I yelled, as much to me as to him, and then – suddenly – I felt a sharp, intense thud in the small of my back and I fell flat, my face and mouth plunging into the grotesque squelch, my body flattened by the captain's weight.

I instantly knew I'd been hit, I'd felt the thud, although I never heard it. You never do, I suppose. There's too much gunfire and mayhem going on to actually separate one bullet, one grenade, from the other. In fact, for a split second, there was no sound at all and for that split second I was sure I was dead. I think I mouthed to myself "I'm fucked." I looked for Grey Wolf, expecting to see his face, only this time the blurred outlines of the jungle's tentacles began to sharpen into focus. I tried connecting with my body and felt both astonished and elated when I realised my brain was functioning – I knew where I was and what had just happened. I couldn't be dead and I wanted to scream for joy when I moved my toes and fingers without pain. "Fuck, I'm ok." Then the survival instinct kicked in like an enormous avalanche tearing through me.

I wanted to live and I wanted to get out – quick. Every breath felt like another second of life and, as pure adrenalin coursed through my veins, I levered myself back up, pushing all my weight – and the captain's – on to my elbows. His arms were still dangling either side of my chest and I grabbed his hands, squeezing them so he'd know we were OK. Only there was no response and, as I rose, I couldn't feel the same weight pressing down on me.

I turned, and froze in horror as I looked down on the quagmire ground. There, mangled up in the slime and the filth, was the lower half of his body, his blood and his entrails congealing into a muddied mash of flesh and dirt. I shuddered and wanted to vomit, but then an awful truth dawned on me: I was still holding on to his arms. The thought made me retch, I let go instantly and felt the top half of his body slide down the back of my legs.

He'd been torn apart. It was horrific and gory and repulsive and no way for anyone to die. It was also war's reality. Right bang there on the extremes. Another dead body, already a statistic, already a visit for an immaculately dressed officer back home who'd get to inform the next of kin.

All that mattered in that grotesque moment was that I was still alive – partly because the captain's body had taken the hit and cushioned the bullets so they'd lost some of their ferocity by the time they hit the back of my flak jacket. That was the other reason I was still alive: the flak jacket. There were two types – one was short, standard army issue, with a collar that largely protected the back of the neck. The other was marine corps and more like a medieval brigandine: much longer, a chunky, big jacket packed with metal plates in the lining. That's what I'd been wearing. The army one would have been too short to save me.

I turned towards the Huey; it was my job now to look away, to shrug everything off and move on. I'd done it to the Viet Cong, after all; I'd killed them without stopping to think, without worrying about their families or who'd get to inform their next of kin. Now the tables were turned and I could deal with it. That's what the military had empowered me to do. To move on and go get pissed afterwards. I thought no more of him, like I thought no more about the ones I killed. The only difference was this guy, this captain I'd wanted to respect, had inadvertently helped save my life. I had extra reason to feel something, to connect with my humanity, to say a prayer or feel something religious. Maybe even mouth "Thank you" or "Sorry" over his mangled body. I didn't. My survival instinct was too powerful for that. I could still save myself, so I carried on, half crouching, half running towards the Huey.

I didn't think it could get much worse after that – but it did. The chopper was under a barrage of fire and I had to run, shelter, run, shelter in rapid bursts until I could jump back in through the left-hand-side doors. I never once took my eyes off the Huey; it was like looking through a rifle viewfinder again – all that existed in the world was me and that helicopter. Cam had spotted me approaching and reached out a hand to pull me on board, but inside was already carnage. Smoke was pouring into the main cabin area; the co-pilot was sat slumped dead in his seat, a huge slice of his neck missing, and the pilot was groaning deeply as he desperately tried to wrap a makeshift bandage round a wound that was spurting blood like a geyser from the top of his arm. The crew chief was lying flat-out immediately behind the pilots' seats, trying to give covering fire but obviously badly injured himself, while one of the gunners was firing ferociously from the left-hand doors I'd just hauled myself in through.

It was only then that I spotted the body of the other gunner, lying horizontally across the opening of the right-hand doors.

Cam was using what remained of it like a sandbag, leaning his machine gun across the gunner's torso. Smoke kept pouring in and something made me look up: wedged into the motor below the rotary blades was an unexploded rocket-propelled grenade. Pinned underneath it was the decapitated head of the gunner whose body was now providing cover for Cam. Either the RPG was a dud, or the head was the only thing stopping the grenade detonating against the motor and blowing us all apart.

"Get the fuck out of here!" I yelled, leaping over to join Cam and firing as frenziedly as I could through the open doors. Somehow the pilot, who was severely injured – way more than any of us knew – managed to get the Huey up. That's when I realised Frank was missing. At the very moment we felt the exhilaration of rising, I screamed: "Stop, stop, where the fuck's Frank?" Cam must have been waiting for my question. Without saying a word he jabbed his finger downwards over and over and, as the Huey carried on rising, I looked out and saw Frank, flat out on the ground below. Then I saw Cam mouth: "He's gone."

His body lies motionless. I am looking down and see his back is punctured by a huge, gaping hole that has ripped through layers of clothing and penetrated flesh. His legs are bent at the knees, like they might be in a sprint only there is no movement. Perhaps he's running? Perhaps I'm at the wrong angle because I am looking down and everything is crazy, inverted, and he is actually standing but I am seeing the world all wrong. Is that possible? I know I can see blood. The blood has formed a giant circle around the hole in his back. I cannot see his face and in more desperation I think: Maybe it's not him. How can I be sure? His face is buried flat into the elephant grass. If it is him, maybe he's trying to disappear into the earth, like he's taking cover.

The helicopter is lifting now, and some of the grass that was flattened by its weight is starting to spring back, providing a layer of camouflage over his still body. That's it. He's taking cover. Fuckin' brilliant. "Frank, get up, get up," I roar, but there's no reply, no movement, no sound, and I start to panic because the helicopter is getting too high and I can't reach him. "Drop down, I'll jump!" I scream and I make to climb out of the Huey's open doors but then hands start holding me back and I wrestle as the hands try to keep me in. Still the helicopter is lifting and still I can see the blood. I will him to move, I beg the Great Spirit to give him the power – Grey Wolf, I need you – give me a sign, a flicker, anything, because if you do I'll leap out right now, and I won't care how high up we are. I'll break my legs, my neck, my spine – it doesn't matter. I want to bring him back. I have to. It's our pact.

His body gets smaller as we climb and now the rage kicks in. I grab an M60 and pump round after round after round into the compliant trees and undergrowth. They saw it all, the bastards. They were part of the ambush. I keep firing, wildly, aimlessly and each pump of ammo, each vicious release, feels like an exclamation of my rage. "You bastards will pay for this!" I scream, and I see the jungle sway, but it's not in fear. The jungle isn't trembling. No, it's laughing at me. It's fuckin' laughing at me. It has won. It has taken the only thing that mattered.

I do the only thing left to me. I step beyond the extremes towards savagery.

I never saw Frank's body when they brought it back. I didn't want to know if it had been hacked and mutilated. I wanted to believe it was still whole. I wanted to believe it still wasn't him. I knew that wouldn't be the case. Cam later told me he'd been hit by a rocket- propelled grenade. "He died instantly," he told me.

I never wrote to his parents, either, although I imagined their distress many times. I imagined the knock on the door of a neat little colonial-style house in mid-America, the solemn face on the veranda – the officer in immaculate, starched uniform with shining brass buttons, respectfully holding his peaked cap under his armpit – the low, muttering voice, the stunned silence and then the sobbing. I imagined a mother's scream and her daughters' tears as they all held each other, not ever letting go of one another ever again. Then I imagined a father's loss and the abandonment of everything he'd dreamt about. A father who simply prayed his son would one day take over the poxy family accountancy business and enjoy a safe, decent life, maybe with kids of his own.

They didn't know me and what could I possibly tell them about their boy, anyway? That he was a good bloke, no – much more than that – that he was my best friend, that they should be proud, that I trusted him with my life, that I called him Jarhead, that we had each other's backs only I didn't quite have his back enough because he died and it's my fault he's dead. I can't send them a letter like that.

Sometimes I think about writing to Frank himself; sometimes I grab a piece of paper and write "Dear Jarhead". Then I get stuck because the name alone makes me see his motionless, blooded body again and I feel my hand instinctively reaching out, wanting to lift him away from death and pull him into the helicopter, the one that lifted me to safety. When I see all that – and I see it constantly – I know I'll never write to him because I can't find words that are big enough, that carry sufficient weight, to erase that memory and, in any case, I don't want to erase it. I want to feel the pain of his death every day of my life until it's my turn to die. I want his death to hurt me eternally.

If I could write to him, though, I'd want to tell him how gut-wrenchingly sorry I am and how I wish I was dead and not him – and that's the truth. I really do. I want to swap places with him right now. Every day I try to work out ways I could have stopped him dying. I always come to the same conclusion: I should have stopped him coming with me on that mission in the first place. He never needed to be there. If I ever wrote to his parents, I'd be sure to tell them that. "I should have insisted he stayed behind," I could write, and in my heart I'd believe that to be true. "He would have listened to me."

I'd like Frank to know his death made me think about death, properly, for the first time. One person died that day who saved my life and yet I still looked away. I was still a cold killer. The other person was Frank, and I've never looked away since. His death changed everything. I'd like him to know that when I mourn for him I am mourning for my own death, too, because I must have been dead to kill like I did, to see so much death and not be crippled by it. I'm also mourning now for all the other deaths I am responsible for. When I killed targets, I never saw human beings. I do now, and that's because of Frank. His death brought life to a sliver of humanity deep within me, one I didn't think I had, although it took a long time for it to emerge. He'd piss himself laughing at the irony of that but it feels important, all the same.

I'll never write to Frank. It would be inadequate and useless and weak because it wouldn't alter anything. It would just be my self-indulgence, my guilt. In any case, he'd only tell me to stop whimpering. "Jesus, Meathead, grow a pair, will you." Everybody I've spoken to – family, friends, shrinks – assure me his death was never my fault, and maybe they're right. It's just I'll always blame myself until the day I die, and that's the way it is.

SUICIDAL

Hate. Every particle, every atom, every tiny blood cell consumed with hate. Hate coursing through me: I want to hurl myself out of the helicopter like a human bomb and, as my body hits those bastard jungle trees, detonate the entire jungle and scream "Fuck you!" Instead, I sob violently and scream hysterically and fire wildly out of the Huey's open doors as it limps back to base. Then I make a vow.

I will kill myself. I have no interest in life. I want death. I do not want to carry on, knowing how worthless and empty my existence is. I hate myself; I detest the aberration I have become. How did I sink this low? Was I ever human? What vile, dark space is sufficiently grotesque for me to crawl into?

I am to blame for his death. I am certain of that. The perfect killing machine I became has paid the ultimate penalty for all the death and destruction and misery it triggered. I could have been killed or mutilated in action and some perverse voice within me would have said: "Well, that's what you signed up to, Bobby. Kill or be killed."

This is far worse. This cripples; this suffocates. This is the worst retribution I could ever be handed. I have to spend the rest of my life certain that I am to blame, and I cannot face that. This is the ultimate weight of war.

Only five of us had survived – me, Cam, a gunner, the crew chief and the pilot – and God only knows how he hung on in there. He was as much shot to pieces as the smoking, wheezing, bullet-strewn, invalided hulk he was somehow flying. Why didn't the grenade pegging the other gunner's head to the motor detonate and blow us all to smithereens? I wish it had.

We landed; I grabbed as many bottles as I could and headed for the hootch where I drank, violently. In the end, when I'd run out of beer and spirits, I mixed meths with red wine. I even added antifreeze. Nobody came near me and, on the seventh day, I grabbed my Browning semi-automatic shotgun and stuck its black, shortened single barrel into my mouth until it pressed, hard, against the palate – blocking my air passage and making me gag.

Cold steel inside my mouth: I was close now. I clamped my teeth tightly around its harsh metallic circumference, wanting to preserve this new possibility, this new gateway to death. I sat there, in an alcohol-fuelled daze, and looked down the length of the rifle to my hands, one clawed over the surface so my thumb could push down on the trigger, the other holding the butt end. How funny. I'd never seen a rifle from this angle before, not even goofing around. I'd never registered its sleek, streamlined beauty; I'd never been this intimate. Now I could see and feel the ingenuity.

I closed my eyes and imagined I was back in the Huey, looking down at his body. Only everything was wrong: now it was mutilated and butchered. The parts that had given him life, identity, the parts that made him strong and whole, had been dissected and removed. The jungle, too, was different: it had been plunged into an eerie, unnatural blackness, with a sinister hint of shapes and movement somewhere deep within. The evil moon was there, rejoicing in the fact that its only role in this macabre vision was to illuminate the torn remnants of his body. Demonic creatures drifted in and out of its spotlight: I saw hideous cross-breeds of alligators and snakes, and huge distortions of wild beasts, their mouths gorging on flesh.

I pressed my teeth ferociously against the steel barrel of the Browning and, mercifully, the hellish image vanished. All that remained was a body, motionless, flickering in and out of sight under flailing elephant grass, and a helicopter, belching smoke, rising − slowly − until it disappeared into The Blue.

My thumb started to tease the trigger; I started to apply gentle degrees of increasing pressure, toying with my own life. All I needed was to press firmly − as I'd done countless times before. But I couldn't. Why couldn't I take my own life just like I'd taken the life of everyone else and then walked away? Maybe that was it: I couldn't kill myself because I always needed to be able to walk away, unaffected. That's what had made me the perfect killing machine, after all. But if that was the case, how come I couldn't walk away from Frank's death? Why was I permanently looking at it, refusing to move on?

I let go of the trigger and pulled the Browning out of my mouth. I looked at my watch and realised the gun had been there for twenty minutes. Perhaps Grey Wolf had been with me. Or maybe it was Frank, and for the first time I allowed the faintest shimmer of a smile to invade my face. If Frank had seen me with a gun in my mouth, he'd have said: "Take that fuckin' thing out or I'll shoot you myself."

I carried on drinking. The blackness hadn't gone. Over the next couple of days I held the gun to my mouth twice more, each time playing with the trigger, each time pushing it to the point of no return, each time backing down. Was it a game? Was I trying to show the world how hurt I was? "Look at me, I'm grieving so badly I want to commit suicide." Was it a cry for attention? Only nobody was looking and nobody really cared. I was told – when I eventually crawled out of the hootch – that nobody dared approach me. One military policeman had apparently debated whether to shoot me himself. "You were dangerous. Wild, like an animal. We were getting scared," I was told.

After ten days, when I physically had nothing else to drink, I abandoned the idea of committing suicide. Instead, I decided to go down fighting. I'd let Charlie kill me. I still hungered for revenge. If I killed without restraint, if I went way past the extremes and embraced savagery, then I'd not only take more life and get payback for Frank's death, I'd increase the chances of getting myself killed, too. That's what I decided to do.

DEATH WISH

I descended towards savagery. I didn't care if I died and I didn't care who I took with me. I just wanted payback. I hated so much. I hated myself even more. I craved brutal, ugly revenge and I craved my own death in equal measure. Sometimes I would look into the eyes of the Viet Cong and see they actually *wanted* to die in the great struggle against America. I was like that. I wanted to die as much as they did. Maybe more.

I went on patrols with a new attitude. There were no second chances for anyone. I was much more like Gerry. Shooting someone in the back of the head wasn't an act of mercy like before. It was a swift and effective means to an end. I'd go looking for trouble. I hadn't got a buddy any more so I craved firefights. I craved putting my life on the line. I only had two or three months left until the end of the tour, so what the hell.

I took suicidal risks. I'd walk into firefights with no thought of cover and I'd shoot manically, ammo blazing. I was willing Charlie's bullet to find me. Come on, you bastards. But it never did, and word got round that I was charmed.

"Follow the *Dai Uy* (captain), he never gets hit," I'd hear my PRU soldiers say to one another. So that's what they did. All the frightened soldiers, all the ones who shouldn't have been there, who were way too sensitive for war and actually thought if they kept their heads down they might just be OK, they all started following me. The trouble was, it never worked like that. War was never fair. They were the ones who died, their virgin bodies crumpled and shattered on the ground while I carried on blasting away. I regret their deaths so much now. I'd turned a blind eye, I'd forgotten my responsibilities – I wasn't just leading myself into danger, I was leading them into it as well.

I was a living a charmed life. No matter what I did, what crazed risks I took, I never got hit. Grenades, bombs, mortars, land mines, they'd all erupt near me, around me, beside me, but they just plain didn't get me. In the end, word got round about that, too. There was something spooky, not right, about the *Dai Uy*. I sensed the soldiers were getting nervous around me; I sensed they were whispering behind my back, and not in a good way like before. I sensed they feared where I was leading them to.

I carried on drinking ferociously: it helped maintain my anger levels and it replaced the adrenalin when the adrenalin subsided. It blurred my conscience, too – if I had one – so I wouldn't dwell too long on what I was doing. My drinking wasn't social, like a-few-beers-with-the-lads stuff. It was full-on brutal and aggressive. I even started pouring Brasso into my 33s. I spoke to nobody and I befriended nobody. Nobody was going to get anywhere near Bob Rose ever again.

I even brought a head back from one patrol. One of the PRU soldiers had hacked it off to prove we'd taken out a Viet Cong suspect. "Here, *Dai Uy*, grab this," and he handed it to me like it was a football. I didn't flinch. I held it by the hair – black and lank – and dangled it by my side as we all climbed into a Huey. Then I placed it on one of the side seats and stuffed a cigarette in its mouth. Three of us and a Viet Cong head in a Huey, just chilling, and we giggled like schoolkids and asked if it was enjoying the ride and whether it was having a good war so far.

When we got to camp, I headed for the MP office to file my report, still dangling the head from its hair as I walked along. The guy at the desk was stood smoking a cigarette and studying some paperwork at the same time; he didn't even look up. I started my report in the usual way – "We engaged a VC unit at such-and-such a place..." – and I gave him the location and all that sort of stuff. Then, just to make sure he was listening, I lifted up the head – bits of sinew and flesh covered in dried blood still dangling from its torn neck – and plonked it straight over his paperwork. "Don't suppose you could spare a light for my mate here? He's been dying for a smoke," I grinned. The guy made to vomit, turned deadly white, and then reeled backwards before fainting on the floor. That really made me smile. That was a bit of grotesque humour.

I'd started to make my own lead slugs, which were bigger and therefore more lethal than the standard issue ones. I even opened up the cartridge of my Browning so it could accommodate my larger bullets, but I never expected what happened on one ambush. A Viet Cong unit walked straight into it but one of their soldiers broke clear of our cut-off point and was heading straight towards me. He was getting too close so, just as he drew level with a tree, I unloaded my Browning, pumping my new lead slugs straight into him. I got him, he was definitely dead, but I couldn't understand why he still appeared to be standing – and, more bizarrely, holding his AK-47 at the same time.

"Heh, come have a look at this, everyone!" I shouted. "How the fuck's he hanging on like that?" A small group of us gathered round, like a group of student doctors pondering a patient, and eventually worked out that the slug from my rifle had gone through his spine and pinned him upright against the tree. When we pulled him away, his body completely folded like it could be packed into a suitcase. We weren't in the least bit interested in who he was, we didn't stare at his face and ponder the meaning of life, loss, war, mortality. We didn't give a fuck about him or his family. No, we were way more fascinated by the physics and science of how his body had reacted to my larger bullet.

The more I lost control of my unit – or rather the more I turned a blind eye – the more our weekly body count shot up. I started to notice some soldiers had what looked like strange beads dangling round their necks. It was only when I got closer that I realised they were human ears they'd hacked off Viet Cong bodies and strung together to make macabre necklaces. They even gave me one to wear. Until then, Frank and I had directed our PRU in a professional, military manner, engaging the enemy when necessary, or when thoroughly planned. In the process, we'd both come to like the men – more than we probably realised at the time. We never had a moment's problem with them, nobody ever turned against us. They respected us and we respected them. Yes, many were hardened prisoners; that was their deal for getting out. We never judged them on their previous lives, though, only on what we saw and how they behaved with us. We treated them the same as everyone else and we gave them respect.

Now, their discipline was disintegrating and it was hardly surprising. It must have been a nightmare for them to see me losing control. I was no longer the leader they needed. I was no longer their protector. All I wanted was to die – and they could see that. I wasn't giving them direction; I was putting them in situations that were too close to the extremes. They had little option but to fight ferociously if they wanted to survive. They were suddenly being confronted with dangers Frank and I had always tried to navigate round or avoid. I was leading them into combat situations that invited death and, because they were still loyal soldiers, they kept on following me – even if it meant being dragged towards savagery.

Were we war criminals? What's war crime? When soldiers lose discipline and kill indiscriminately? That's easy to say round a bloody coffee table but when you see soldiers getting speared on sharpened bamboo sticks, when you're watching limbs and arms and chests and heads being blown apart, when your best pal is slaughtered and the captain you are trying to piggyback to safety is being mown in half, do you really think there's time to find the relevant sub-clause on how best to react in the bloody Rules of Engagement book?

Are we expected to proffer a hand of friendship towards the enemy? Isn't that the stuff politicians and religious nuts must sort out before they send us all to bloody war in the first place? Who is the enemy – us, them, Lyndon Johnson, Ho Chi Minh?

I had no time for such debate in any case. I was too busy preparing for death. I felt a strong need to reconnect with my Northern Cheyenne spiritual beliefs and everything I'd learnt from Great-gran and the elders on the reservation. I believed – and still do – in the Great Spirit as the Heavenly Father, a God as such, but not like the church's version. I thought about the Great Spirit a lot and about my next life in the spirit world. Going there didn't frighten me, in fact I was preparing myself for that journey. The only thing that truly worried me was not reaching it in one piece. That was the same fear my dad had. The fear of being decapitated, or mutilated, or speared on a booby trap, worried me immensely – simply because it meant I wouldn't be whole in the next world.

My reality check only came when I started to notice that the glances were intensifying among my unit. My soldiers were increasingly falling quiet whenever I walked by, conversations were suddenly stopping if I entered a room, smiles were suddenly being replaced by looks of dread. At first I thought it was my paranoia. Perhaps they'd been spooked by some frenzied Viet Cong soldier who they feared was wild and out of control in the jungle, some beast who would kill them in vicious, brutal ways.

The whisperings and the glances wouldn't go away, though, so one night I wandered over to Cam and said: "Is there something wrong with the men? They always seem to get uneasy when I'm near. Are they spooked about someone? Have you got any idea?"

I liked Cam. His men were still loyal to him and he spoke openly and honestly. I'd never forgotten Frank and I meeting his family, and I knew he was proud to introduce us to them. But now he looked like he was struggling to find the right words. Maybe he was stuck for a translation, although I knew his English was excellent. "Come on, you can tell me, just be honest. What's up with everyone? Why do they look so nervous? Who are they worried about?"

His reply probably saved my life. It stopped me in my tracks, and began a healing process that, even now, isn't complete. "My friend," he said gently, compassionately. I looked into his eyes and saw only humanity. "My friend, it is you they are worried about."

He coughed nervously. "The men... the men believe you want to die – and that you will take them with you."

I AM NOT
AN ANIMAL

I held a gun to my mouth for a fourth and final time the following night, having spent the entire day drinking wildly. Cam's words drilled into me and ricocheted around my skull until they were all I could hear. *"The men believe you want to die and that you will take them with you."* It felt like my epitaph.

This time I loaded my Colt 45 and held it under my chin, pressing it upwards into my jaw, so it jammed against the bone and rammed my rows of teeth hard against each other. This time I needed to *feel* how worthless my life had become and how much I deserved to die; I pressed deep into my skin until it felt like the entire structure of my face was being pushed to breaking point and would shatter and crumble at any moment. I wasn't seeking sympathy – there was nobody there – and I wasn't wallowing in self-pity. I was wallowing in self-hatred.

Tears started to fill my eyes. The physical pain pressing against my skull, and the demons trying to press me towards suicide, meshed together in a watery blur. I wept freely and, in my mind, I started to see an eight-year-old boy. He'd shot a deer with a bow and arrow, the animal was prostrate on the ground but not yet dead. The boy held a knife in his hand and stood over the creature as it twitched and strained to hang on to life. The boy knew what was required; before cutting the deer open, he solemnly blessed the creature and thanked it for surrendering its life so that he – the boy and his family – could eat and exist.

I desperately wanted to talk to that boy. He had courage, he'd made the bow and arrow with his own hands, he'd channelled his young, undeveloped mind and skills into killing to survive and he'd accomplished it – yet remembered what he'd killed for. He'd even remembered to kill with honour, to respect his target but not let that respect cloud the primal need to survive. I felt I knew this boy. I had his values once.

"I'm not an animal," I murmured. "I'm not an animal," and I kept repeating those four words over and over as I continued pressing my chin into the Colt 45. I needed to cling on to something. I needed to find proof that the words "I'm not an animal" were accurate. So I clung on to the certain knowledge that I'd never found pleasure in killing; it had always left me feeling cold.

I'd never killed for sport or for fun. The killing I sank into was always based around military requirement or expectation. That's what I'd been programmed for. I'm not saying "I was just doing what I was told". I'm simply stating the reality of what my role was – and what I was being paid for. I was given information by Phoenix, I was told who or where Charlie was, and I "neutralised" as required. In the end, as I sought to single-handedly avenge Frank's death, my PRU's body counts rose dramatically. But nobody castigated me. Nobody said: "What d'ya shoot him for? Bring 'em back alive next time, will you."

I may have reduced the distinction, the line, between following orders and killing for sport to a sliver, but that sliver was everything. I needed to cling on to that sliver. It defined me. That sliver was my extreme and I never crossed it, of that I am certain. I pushed it to its limit when Frank died but my own men woke me up to the danger: I was way too close to the place where Gerry had been. My one-man crusade hadn't worked. Killing – and trying to get killed – wasn't bringing Frank back, wasn't winning the war, wasn't solving the whole fucked-up mess. I certainly wasn't getting any closure or pleasure from it.

Even when I behaved more like Gerry than Bob Rose, there was still a distance between us. He had crossed the line, he could kill and even thrill to the act of killing and then feel vindicated once his target had been slaughtered. That wasn't me. So I clung to that thought as I sandwiched the Colt 45's ivory grip between my hands – and I've clung to it ever since. I never turned into Gerry. There was never a smile on my face.

I'm not saying the coldness is acceptable, either. As I get older and think longer and harder about my life, I realise the coldness bothers me a lot. A voice deep inside keeps asking "Why didn't you feel pity or remorse or sadness?" I don't think I'll ever be able to answer that, mainly because it strikes to the core of what made me a soldier. If I'd developed a conscience, could I have carried on being a soldier? Would I have even survived? Developing a conscience would mean I'd have to question the definition, the role, the DNA of what I understood a good soldier to be; I'd have to question my training and what I believed the military required from me. Then I'd have to question whether we'd all be better off without soldiers altogether. I'm not ready for those sort of questions. That's Blue stuff.

Realising I'd never turned into Gerry, and believing that was important and meant something, was enough as I sat holding the Colt 45. It might not be enough now, but it was enough in that moment. Suddenly, I let go of the gun – once and for all – because I knew I'd unravelled something true about myself.

In fact, I never used a gun again. The end of my tour was only a couple of months away and I was even due two weeks R and R before leaving. I'd got to know a couple of marines in Da Nang who were both Native American and we'd spoken a few times about our backgrounds and beliefs. I told them all about my childhood and Grey Wolf, they listened intently and I could tell they understood. They nodded and agreed when I told them about the Great Spirit, they told me similar stories of their own childhoods. One of them was Southern Cheyenne – Charlie "Chuck" Walkswell. I could see it in his face: his eyebrows ran in an almost horizontal line, framing his eyes so they appeared bold and strong. His face and jaw were chiselled and firm – youthful, but not childish. The other was Sioux and similar in so many ways, except for a heavy dark shadow that made it look like he was permanently wearing a black eye mask. I can no longer remember his name, just that swarthy shadow.

We were getting pissed one night in the PX when they both told me they wanted to do a sun dance. "We need someone to help us, though. Will you do it?" I agreed; I had nobody else to spend R and R with and the thought of doing my own spirit quest appealed. We headed for a stretch of jungle outside Saigon that was considered safe and camped for a couple of nights.

It was exactly like I'd seen as a child. I cut incisions in their chests with my knife, which I'd sterilised first over a fire. Then I lifted the skin up, and slid bamboo skewers through. Both of them were already in a trance-like state, their minds submerged solely in the spirituality and seriousness of the ritual. Once I'd pushed the skewers through, I ran parachute cord round the ends and hung the rest of the cord over a tree branch until they were leaning back, their feet still on the ground, their bodies suspended.

They were controlled and composed throughout. Their faces winced in pain but they remained silent, neither speaking nor screaming. They simply switched off and stayed like that for the remainder of the day and through the following night. I sat quietly with them, relying on the fact that we had no food – just water – and, by the afternoon of the second day, I too was slowly slipping towards stupor. I remember listening intently to the sounds of the jungle until it felt like an entire orchestra of creatures were inside my head and I could pick out individual sounds with incredible clarity. I'm certain I could distinguish between each of the species – I could tell if the tiniest ant was crawling painstakingly through the undergrowth or a snake was wrapping itself quietly around an overhead branch. I was tuned in to all of it.

Just when this clarity was at its most acute, when I felt connected to every living thing in the jungle, Charlie Walkswell let out an anguished cry – the flesh on his chest had torn open and jolted him out of his stupor. About an hour or so later, the same thing happened to his pal and their sun dance came to an end. I helped cleanse their wounds, which would leave scars they'd both be proud of for life. They each offered their torn flesh as sacrifice to the Great Spirit and we all departed in silence. They never told me what they'd experienced and I knew it wasn't my place to ask.

I AM BOB ROSE AND
I AM AN ALCOHOLIC

I came back from Vietnam an alcoholic – and extremely violent. I was suffering severe post-traumatic stress disorder, but nobody told me that. I didn't even know such a condition existed and I certainly didn't know how to get it treated.

If there had been another war to join, I would have joined it straightaway. I knew no other way. I was a soldier who could take life and then carry on as normal, like it was just a regular day job. To stop the doubts, to make sure I didn't question my morality, my life, my values, I drank. I suspected something within me was disturbed and agitated, and alcohol was a way of drowning such negativity. I didn't want to ask myself questions that required anguished soul-searching – for one thing, I had nobody to tell me it might be a good idea and, secondly, why would I wish to undermine everything that had made me a ruthless yet reliable soldier? The military had trained and honed me and given me the structure, discipline and framework to do my job exactly as they dictated, legally. I was content with that so long as I didn't expose myself to remorse and guilt.

However, what the military didn't teach me was how to survive once all the weapons and bombs had been packed away and the fighting had come to an end. Without the military's framework I was lost, and drinking was the only solution I knew. Without the army, I was simply an alcoholic killer, set loose on Civvy Street. I look back on those dark days now and shudder. I was more of an animal on Civvy Street than I ever was in Vietnam.

The night terrors started immediately. Grotesque visions would haunt me: I'd come under mortar attack, more violent and deadly than anything I'd experienced before. These images were so vivid, so sharply defined, that I'd not only see them, I would hear them as well – the screams, the pleas, the dying. I was so terrified of going to bed, I'd drink even more in the hope it would keep me awake longer, or knock me out for good. It never did, and the nightmares always found a way of breaching my defences.

In Algeria and Vietnam I'd relied on alcohol to fill the gaps in between firefights and bombardments. Drinking had restored my adrenalin levels then – so I did the same when I came home. I used alcohol to get me through the days and nights. I'd either end up dead through alcoholic poisoning, or end up in prison for killing someone I mistakenly thought was the enemy.

Incredibly, three unforeseen and unconnected events steered me away from destruction. First of all, I attended an Alcoholics Anonymous meeting; secondly, I discovered the martial art American Kenpo; and, finally, I met Sheila.

I know with absolute certainty that American Kenpo, and the woman who became my fourth wife, saved my life – and continue to do so every day.

I returned to Birmingham immediately after Vietnam, and tried to pick up again on my faltering marriage to Beryl, even though there had been precious little contact between us while I'd been away. I worked for a short while with the Austin motor company – on security – but Beryl and I eventually moved to Plymouth because that was where her mother lived. However, there was another drama to contend with before we moved, this time involving my own mum. We'd gone off for the afternoon somewhere and decided to stop for fish and chips on the way home. "I'll go and get them, you stay here in the car," Mum said as I drove up.

I watched her walk in and noticed a gang of 17- and 18-year-old lads pushing and shoving and generally larking around inside the chip shop. I immediately sensed trouble and sure enough, saw my mum get knocked to the ground. The red mist descended: I charged in and floored the lad responsible straight away. Next, I heard a bottle smash against a wall; he was clambering back up, this time clutching a shattered bottle in his right hand, its jagged glass edge pointing directly at me. I reacted instinctively; my right foot kicked him so hard between the legs it lifted his entire body and sent him hurtling back into the shop's plate-glass window. Even now, I'd do the same thing all over again. Nobody got to mess with my mum.

The police came and were largely sympathetic – they recognised the lads and most of them already had criminal records. The court was slightly less understanding and believed the defence's claim that the lad was still kneeling when I launched him into the window, and therefore I was guilty of GBH. "You lost control," the defence said. "No, I didn't," I replied. "If I'd lost control, he'd be dead now. I knew exactly what I was doing." Ultimately, it was my word against theirs; the judge gave me a five-year suspended prison sentence.

Beryl and I moved to the Southwest soon after, but our relationship really was doomed. I was sinking more and more into depression and alcohol, which I was stashing around the house. We agreed to separate and I carried on drinking until, completely out of the blue, I received a letter from an old army pal who was running a soup kitchen in London. "Why don't you come over one weekend and see what we do," he wrote. I was unemployed at the time, it seemed like a good idea, so off I went, arranging to stay in Aldershot where I still knew a few ex-military drinking buddies.

We met up on a Saturday night near Charing Cross station, where he worked. We reminisced for a while, then headed off in his car with giant stainless-steel containers of soup perched on the back seat and boxes and bags crammed with bread rolls and cheap plastic cups in the boot. He eventually stopped under the arches of a railway bridge, where large groups of men – predominantly – were either huddling around braziers or simply lying flat-out on sheets of cardboard, their heads and bodies barely visible underneath layers of old rags and clothes held together by scraps of string.

I helped him unload the car and then watched as a queue slowly formed and he started ladling the soup into cups and handing them over with pieces of bread. It was a sad and sorry sight, a picture of humanity at rock bottom, men wearing rags, men who stank of firebase latrines, men who had no dignity or pride or reason left in their lives. After a while their faces blurred into one another until they all looked the same: filthy, unshaven, desperate, starved. It was their eyes that told the real story, however. It was when I looked into their eyes that I saw the most horrific truth of all. When I looked into their eyes I saw myself. Alcoholics.

I think my pal saw me shiver. "What do you think of this lot, then?" he asked.

"They're scumbags," I replied, trying to hang on to my own dignity, trying to separate myself from them.

He laughed. "No, they're not," he replied. "There's all levels of society down here – men who used to have decent jobs; men who are ex-military, just like us, only they held ranks higher than you or I ever reached. There's aristocracy here, as well. And do you know what every single one of them has in common?"

"No, what?" I replied, already anticipating and dreading his answer. "Drink. Each and every one of them has been destroyed by drink. They've all lost their discipline, their self-pride, their self-worth, and it's the drink that's done it to them. And do you know what, Bob? You're heading in exactly the same direction. You're just like them."

"Don't be ridiculous, there's no way I'm as bad as this lot," I tried to argue.

"Yes, you are. I see it in your eyes. The army life held you together, but now it's gone you're falling apart and drink is making it worse. I know how much you drank in the army, but the discipline of fighting and serving was enough to get you through the days. I can tell you're still hitting the bottle just as much now – maybe even harder. I've seen too many people, down-and-outs, with the same deadness in their eyes."

He was right, of course. I went back to Aldershot and spent most of the following day thinking about what I'd seen and what my pal had said. I even went off to the pub in the evening, intending to have just one drink, but something stopped me walking through the door and I turned away instead. The next morning I discovered there was an Alcoholics Anonymous meeting being held in a local church hall and I decided to go along. I sat at the back and watched a group of people, maybe fifteen, sat in a circle, just talking. I couldn't tell what they were saying, although at one point someone stood up and I could make out the words: "I am an alcoholic".

I left before the meeting ended and went back to the pub the same evening, determined to prove I was above all that sort of nonsense. But once again something stopped me at the door and I turned round, knowing I would have to go back to that church hall and sit within the group myself.

So that's what I did. For an hour and a half I simply sat there, listening – first to the organiser, who was saying stuff that resonated and made sense, and then to individuals within the circle. Many openly wept as they talked, some broke down, incapable of completing their stories. One, I remember, was a girl who looked way too young to carry so much sadness. She was paper-thin, unnaturally so; alcohol had drained her face of colour or softness and she looked gaunt and haunted. Her parents had abandoned her when she was born and she'd spent her entire life in care homes, unable to find any meaningful, lasting relationships. "I started drinking when I was ten," she said, and I felt a sudden acidic rush of bile flood into the pit of my stomach. "A year later, I was nicking stuff from shops and by the time I was fifteen I was mixing spirits – anything – into beer. I'm homeless now and you're the only people I talk to." She later admitted she was seventeen and a half.

Silence descended over the group as she finished her story and sat down. For seconds that felt like hours, nobody spoke – and that's when I made my move, that's when, for the first time in my life, I did something courageous. Shuffling my chair backwards I stood up; everyone turned their heads towards me, including the girl who had just spoken. I inhaled heavily and heard myself say: "My name is Bob Rose and I am an alcoholic. I need help."

Help is what I got, too, but it could only be temporary. I stayed on in Aldershot for a couple more weeks and attended more meetings. I talked, they listened; someone else talked, and I listened. There was nothing judgemental. Nobody got angry when I told them what had driven me to drink and, in any case, I never gave them the full, gory details. I wasn't ready for that. They had their own reasons for being there, I had mine, and that was all we needed to connect with each other. I really threw myself into those two weeks – including going into a self-enforced detox. That was truly horrendous: I was still sleeping at a mate's house and, thankfully, he kept an eye on me and kept me stocked with water, which was just about all I could stomach.

Detox put me through excruciating mental and physical agony. First came the cramps: at times it felt like my body was tearing itself apart. I'd thrash around on my bed trying desperately to push blood back into paralysed limbs. Then came the vivid hallucinations, just like the ones when I was in the Legion penal camp. I saw myself being eaten alive by gigantic alligators again, their repulsive eyes mocking me as I watched my legs disappear into their engorged mouths; I felt zombie-type strangers stabbing me in the face and throat; I'd wake up screaming in the middle of the night, convinced snakes had wrapped themselves around me and were squeezing me into a slow, torturous death. This horror lasted at least four days; I could never put myself through it again. All my deepest, wildest, most deranged fears confronted me.

I returned to Plymouth desperately needing more help. Talking to an AA group had been an incredible first step, a turning point even, and I'd survived detox without going back to the bottle. I was resolute and determined but I knew I hadn't begun to confront what was really building up inside: the regret and the remorse.

I couldn't get Frank's death out of my mind. I still can't.

Everyone simply expected me to slip back into civilian life seamlessly. Vietnam wasn't a war the British had fought in, so there was little understanding or sympathy or appetite for what I'd been through. It was down to me to shrug it off somehow, but the AA meetings had convinced me I needed help. I needed someone to listen to me; then, I needed that person to cure me. To let me get everything off my chest, then tell me it would all be OK. Someone who could help me walk away from the memories, just like I'd always been able to walk away from the killing. Now I was returning to the people I had seen killed, trying to undo it all, trying to connect with revulsion and remorse.

I saw two shrinks in Plymouth – one was a psychiatric doctor, the other a nurse – and they both made the same mistake. They both said exactly the same thing. They sat there, listening to me talk all about it, looking concerned and professional, and then they said: "We know how you feel."

That was it. "Fuck off. You can't possible know how I feel. What have you done, what have you experienced that comes remotely close to my life? Where did you serve? Who did you kill? Have you suffered endless mortar attacks? What horrors keep you awake at night?"

I carried on. "Have you ever pumped a man's heart with your bare hands through his open chest, torn apart by a grenade that's ripped him to pieces? Or flown in a helicopter that's got someone's head stuck in the motor? When did you last look at the slaughtered body of your best friend and blame yourself for his death, every single day? Do you ever see the face of a man you shot in the brain and heart after you'd watched him through a viewfinder for six solid days until you knew so much about the fucker you felt like he was bloody family?"

Pause for reply. "'No', did you say? Then don't try and tell me you know how I feel."

Part Five

AMERICAN KENPO

The wolf is a guide who can help you discover when you are being misguided. If a wolf appears to you at a time of doubt, it is to reassure you that the path you're about to take is the right one.

DANCE OF DEATH

It was impossible for me to settle into a "normal" life. I didn't belong in Civvy Street. Civvies didn't see the world like I did, their relationships were completely different, they hadn't got the same values, outlook, humour. They hadn't experienced the extremes.

The extremes made everything else seem so trivial and irrelevant. The military had left me scarred and damaged – but I can't deny it had also exposed me to a bond of camaraderie that could never exist on Civvy Street. When you're fighting for your lives together, when you need each other to survive, you develop bonds that are real and deep and immensely powerful. Like the bond Frank and I shared. That bond still survives, even in death. Military bonds are the ultimate test of loyalty and brotherhood. Nothing else even comes close: you trust each other with your lives. You are brothers. *We gallant few, we band of brothers.* I believe in that. I really do. Frank was the brother I never had.

I couldn't stand the petty disciplines on Civvy Street, the little people with their little rules and regulations, the clocking in and clocking out, the office politics, the jumped-up little squirts who thought they could mimic sergeant majors because they had a sliver of authority in their trivial little factories or offices. I hated these people. They had none of the qualities of real leaders of men.

I tried working for a credit management company in Cornwall, processing bad debts. Next, I gave being a milkman a go and, finally, I sold gas fires for the gas board in Plymouth. In fact, that's how I met my third wife, Joan: I sold her a gas fire and delivered it to her home. Joan was blonde, chatty with strong opinions, and we clicked straight away. Given my job at the time, I suppose you could say she was my favourite flame.

I still needed some sort of structure, though, so I joined the Royal Marine Reserve, based in Plymouth's Stonehouse barracks. We used to train one night a week. Phase one was a doddle for me, learning about the marines, basic soldiering and weapon-handling. Phase two, though, was an intensive two-week course at the Royal Marines commando training centre at Lympstone. I was determined to pass the commando course, which involved a tough time trial round the Dewerstone Rock – where I'd laid my dad's ashes. I got through all the runs, the climbs, the jumps, the speed marches and the agility tests, and made the rank of corporal. After that, I stayed with the reserves for eight years, becoming an instructor myself and pushing lads over the same Dewerstone course. I even wore full uniform when Joan and I got married.

I managed to stay off the bottle throughout, but I badly needed something to replace the alcohol. Violence was an obvious substitute. I'd already experienced Hung Ga kung fu in Hong Kong, so I decided to join some traditional-style karate classes in Plymouth's Mayfair Centre. It was a way of keeping fit – and topping up my aggression.

It was 1974 by now and there'd been an explosion of interest in the martial arts thanks to Hollywood stars Bruce Lee and Chuck Norris. Elvis Presley was already heavily involved with American Kenpo and, guided by its legendary founder – Senior Grand Master Ed Parker – he reached honorary eighth degree black belt in the same year.

I was discussing this one night with a black belt at the Mayfair centre, Tony Burrows, when he casually said: "There's a bloke near here who teaches that American Kenpo stuff. You should go see him – he's called Phil Hegarty."

The following Sunday I headed for the Memorial Hall in Landrake, Cornwall, proudly wearing my black belt. It was like every village hall, with a highly-polished tongue-and-groove pine floor and a small stage at the end for amateur dramatics. As soon as I walked in, I noticed all the students had white belts, with small yellow tips on the ends. That meant they were beginners. I introduced myself to Phil and asked whether I could join in his class. "I do Hung Ga," I told him, trying to sound experienced and slightly superior. He was unexceptional at first glance: shorter than me, stockier, maybe in his 40s, with short black hair. His dark, piercing eyes were comfortably the most powerful characteristic about him: they held their stare and drilled right into you. It was a stare that said: "Don't underestimate me, sucker, or I might have to put you in your place."

"No problem, you're very welcome to work out with us," he replied, finally taking his eyes away from me to look at his other students. I joined in and enjoyed the session – the techniques were similar to stuff I'd done before, so I found it relatively easy.

"We'll do some freestyle sparring now," Phil announced as the session ended. I'd noticed he was a first-degree brown belt – a level below mine. I knew he'd clocked the black belt round my waist but he still turned and said: "Who would you like to spar with, Bob?"

Even I thought it would be unfair to pick out one of the white-belt beginners, so I replied: "Can I spar with you?" He smiled, nodded and we stood, facing each other. In the blink of an eye, I was crunched up in agony on the floor; he'd kicked me where it hurts the most. "Christ, watch your control!" I squealed.

"That was controlled," he replied, and from that point on I was like a statue, utterly frozen by the speed and dexterity of his hands and feet. Everything he did was lightning fast; I couldn't fathom or see his movements. His hands, arms, feet became an indistinguishable blur as he whizzed and whirled around me, landing blow after blow with ease. The only thing I clocked throughout was the smirk on his face. He made me look an idiot: I was repeatedly picking myself up off the floor because he knocked me down so many times. I physically couldn't see where on earth his blows were coming from.

I felt an inch tall, humiliated, and went home to think about what had happened. I didn't stop thinking about it for the rest of the week. "That bastard has got something special to do that to me," I said to Joan, as she tried forlornly to nurse my bruised ego. In Hong Kong, I'd won the south east Asia championship against Chinese opponents – which wasn't easy – and yet he'd made me look like a novice. It was the speed of his hands; I'd never seen anything that fast before.

I couldn't let it go. I knew he had a small electronics shop in Saltash so I went over a few days later for a man-to-man chat. "Will you teach me how to do what you did?" I asked.

"Yeah, sure, but I'll tell you what. You'll have to ditch that bloody status-symbol belt of yours before you come back to any more of my classes. If you want to join us, then you'll have to put on a white belt like everyone else and start from scratch as a beginner. That's the only way I'll teach you."

I listened and begrudgingly replied: "I'll think about it." My pride was getting in the way and I didn't like the idea of giving up what I'd attained in Hong Kong. So I went home and thought about it for another week. "He wants me to start from the beginning all over again," I said to Joan, hoping she'd tell me to pack it in. But she didn't, and a little voice in my brain kept saying: "That guy's got something.

He tore you apart. Don't you want to understand how he did it? Don't you want to learn his skills?"

Two weeks later I walked back into the studio. He took one look at me, smirked, and said in front of the entire class: "Good to see you back – but you'll never last. You ain't hard enough." He knew nothing about my army life. There again, I knew nothing about him. I soon discovered he'd been studying Kenpo for at least ten years, even though he'd never taken a black belt test. I also discovered he was an illusionist and escapologist, and belonged to the Magic Circle. Add those skills, those feints of hand, with the speed and art of Kenpo, and I began to realise why he'd floored me so quickly. He may have been short but he had this uncanny ability to make himself look far taller, and therefore more menacing, than he really was. I've no doubt that was due to his skills as an illusionist. To my surprise, I also discovered he only had one lung – the other had been horrifically scorched when a fire-eating act went terribly wrong. He could only sustain fighting for a few minutes before his breathing became a problem. That explained why he was so fast and furious – he needed a quick knockout.

For the next three years, Phil spent the rest of his teaching life trying to either kick Kenpo into me – or kick me so hard, I'd give it up. He beat me over and over, he hurt me bad and even put me in hospital. That was the way he taught, he was hard and he had little, if any, control during sessions. When he kicked or punched, his blows landed; there was no pulling away. He was teaching a self-defence mechanism, pure and simple. He wasn't interested in it being competitive, like a sport. He wasn't there for fun.

Sometimes he'd practise a technique on me, smash a blow into me – then stand back with an expression that said: "I know that one hurt." He hit me once with a single knuckle blow on my nose that pushed it right over to my right eye. One of the female students took me into the changing rooms; I looked in the mirror, the nose was still quite numb, so I grabbed hold of it and dragged it back to roughly where it used to be. The girl fainted on the spot and my nose never returned to its proper position.

I was pissed off with Phil but I refused to be beaten, so I kept going back for more. "Fuck him," I'd think to myself. "He's not going to beat me, and I don't care how long it takes." He'd hurt me, but the truth was I'd enjoyed it. I needed to feel that pain, just like I'd needed to connect with it when I was fighting for my life in an Algerian hospital.

Very quickly, Kenpo dominated my world: the constant practise and the constant pain. I wouldn't settle for just one class a week, either. I'd turn up at his shop and carry on training there in a back room. Maybe I was winning him over – soon after, he started to teach me some advanced-level breathing techniques which helped me master the techniques, the stances, the hand speed and the basic principles he'd been using to make a fool of me.

Inevitably, especially with Phil as my tutor, I was becoming more and more violent. I was mastering techniques that have truly evocative names – such as Dance of Death, Mace of Aggression and Sword of Destruction – all for so-called good reason. Kenpo is a violent art and its techniques can kill. They involve lightning kicks and blows to the head and such knowledge, in the wrong hands, can be devastating. The names alone appealed to me enormously, they fired my imagination. I was captivated, and it more than compensated for the lack of alcohol in my life. My adrenalin levels were soaring again and, slowly but surely, I reached Phil's level.

One day the class had a night off and we all went out together clubbing. Inevitably a fight broke out; we were no part of it, but Phil got clobbered by two big bouncers in the melee and was carted out with a black eye. The next evening he was back taking a class when a couple of policemen turned up and, in front of us all, accused Phil of using his karate techniques in the club. "No, I didn't," he protested. "But the bouncers thought I was one of the troublemakers and they laid into me as I was trying to get out."

Then, to prove what sort of damage he could have caused, he turned to us and said: "Right, you lot, attack me in any way you want. All of you, there's no rules and nothing's off-limits." He wiped us all out within seconds; every one of us was on the floor, groaning and nursing bruises. He then turned to the police and said: "If I'd been using Kenpo in that club, you'd be here now to arrest me for murder."

Phil and I became extremely close, even though he'd been a brutal teacher. I also began to realise that he, too, had an alcohol problem that was taking him over. It takes a drinker to know a drinker and I recognised all the tell-tale signs – the glazed faraway look in his eyes, the unhealthy skin, the scent of alcohol on his breath, the excessive sweating. His boozing was spiralling and he'd repeatedly fail to show up for classes. Sometimes he'd even turn up pissed; he really wasn't a nice guy to know in those sessions. It got so bad, I started to take classes in his absence – which I enjoyed – until he actually handed the club over to me completely. I eventually closed the studio in Landrake and moved it to Crown Hill in Plymouth.

Deep down, though, I knew Phil's knowledge was far superior to the grade he'd actually reached. I began to realise there was a deeper level within him, something that had more meaning than just the wham, bam attack mechanisms he kept flinging out. I really suspected he understood levels that he'd never talked about. Then, on one of the increasingly few days he turned up, he suddenly looked at me and said: "I can't teach you any more. If you want to really advance, you'll have to go to the States."

ELVIS PRESLEY AND GRAND MASTER ROSE

In the year 2000, I became the only man in the whole of Europe and the UK to reach the highest-attainable level in American Kenpo – 10th degree Grand Master. To this day, my seniority is unrivalled and I still have students wanting to ask me questions, or teach them, from all corners of the globe. Believe me, the teaching bit isn't so easy when you hit 80, but I still manage to answer the questions.

I'd decided to take Phil's advice. I was gripped by Kenpo: it was changing me, reviving me, and – increasingly – it was making me challenge my own personal values and disciplines. Physically, I was an extremely dangerous person – but something was keeping me in check. The more violent I became, the less I wanted to use that violence. I didn't understand then why that was – but I wanted to find out. I wanted to learn more – physically and spiritually.

So that's what I did. I got in touch with the sport's world governing body – the International Kenpo Karate Association – and eventually spoke to their European director, Rainer Schulte. He came over to Plymouth, started training me, and then invited me over to the headquarters in Santa Monica, where American Kenpo's revered founder and leader, Senior Grand

Master Ed Parker, had two studios – one of them used by movie legend Bruce Lee. Mr Parker's reputation was global; he personally taught Elvis Presley and a string of A-list celebrities.

The club paid for the trip, I took a small group of students with me, and we met the main instructor there, Larry Tatum. Danny Inosanto, who worked with Bruce Lee and appeared in some of his films, was training there at the same time.

The Long Beach international karate championships, where all the big tournament fighters compete, were being staged at the same time and we were privileged to attend a demonstration by Mr Parker himself. It was a colossal event: there were 32 separate fighting areas in the main auditorium. We joined in training sessions – free of charge – and even stayed with our hosts throughout the two-week trip. All we had to pay were air fares. It was an unbelievable experience, and I felt especially privileged when I was invited to meet Mr Parker in his own home.

I'd read up on him and knew he had modernised and redefined karate. Before, it was extremely traditional and very much controlled by the Japanese, who would only let the outside world have access to basic knowledge and understanding. Mr Parker made it accessible to everybody. He wrote everything down for the first time in the Western world, explaining how the principles worked. Then he gave the techniques and movements their exciting, memorable names – like Dance of Death – so they'd be easier to remember and understand. He didn't hide or omit anything. The fact that American Kenpo is still going strong today is entirely down to him.

I felt nervous meeting him for the first time and as we walked towards his front door I remember Rainer Schulte saying to me: "This guy's a genius. You won't meet anyone like him again. This is a big honour, Bob." I treated him with enormous respect – never calling him Ed, always "Mr Parker". He was in his mid-40s; it was a period when men wore their hair long and Mr Parker certainly had a full, distinctive head of greying hair, deeply parted from left to right, hung low over his forehead, completely covering his ears and tumbling below his collar at the back. He was powerfully built and although his face was boyish, his eyes were steely and determined. They drilled deep into you, like they'd found a way of looking into your soul. We got chatting – he was easy to talk to, with a faint Hawaiian drawl – and I remember asking: "When we're learning new techniques, should we always stick rigidly to the instructions and guidelines?"

His answer made a lasting impression on me and is one I still repeat over and over to new students. "First, you must understand the basic principles and retain that information," he said. "But always adapt it to your own individual style and circumstances. No two American Kenpo fighters should be identical. American Kenpo is about individuality. It is about adapting techniques to suit your own style – that's what matters the most."

It was the nervy beginning of a lasting relationship that had its ups and downs, especially when internal politics got in the way – don't they always – but, in the end, he remained my idol. Mr Parker was not only Elvis's trainer and personal bodyguard, he also taught Kenpo to The King's personal security officers. I got to know them all over the ensuing years at various competitions. Although Mr Parker never became my own personal trainer – Grand Master Larry Tatum guided me instead – he'd sometimes watch me in the studio on the many occasions I returned to America, and pick me up on various techniques.

By the end of the two weeks, it was accepted for the first time that I'd reached black belt level, which was an enormous honour, and I returned from the US brimming with ideas and enthusiasm. My number one priority was to make Kenpo my living by opening up a network of clubs across the UK.

350 WAYS TO KILL

Make no mistake, American Kenpo is extremely violent and dangerous. I know 350 ways to kill with my bare hands. They're not really "ways", they're "techniques". Some of these techniques can kill with a single blow or touch. Many work because of the chain reaction they trigger. For example, I could punch you on your nose, and you might feel a slight discomfort; I could punch you harder, and I'd probably break your cartilage, there'd be blood and you'd need hospital attention. Or, I could punch you on the nose so powerfully, the impact would force the bone back into the brain and you'd be dead. One punch, that's all it needs. That is one of the simplest ways to kill someone.

I have come to understand how the body works and that knowledge has given me the potential to be even more lethal. I know the points an acupuncturist uses; I know where the twelve major meridians are – the energy flows that connect and balance all our major organs. Unlike an acupuncturist, who will stick needles in one part of the body to trigger soothing reactions in an entirely different place, I can use that knowledge to kill. The central line of the body is the most important – that's where the killer spots are. Press one of those and the domino effects are deadly.

I am not confessing to this because it makes me feel good. I'm not trying to intimidate. I just need to underline the potential power of Kenpo to cause devastation. Given that I could kill without remorse in the army, given that I'd consumed vast quantities and cocktails of alcohol, given that I despised Civvy Street, given that I was mentally and physically wrecked – incapable of sleep, tormented by night terrors, constantly tired and irritable – given all that, should I really have become even more violent?

What on earth could possibly stop me from creating more mayhem? Army discipline had kept me in check but now that it had gone, how could I learn new ways to kill, yet stay in control? Could I be trusted to roam the streets safely? Or was I simply a ticking time bomb waiting for the right moment and circumstances to explode – waiting for someone to press the right buttons and unleash the havoc?

Kenpo was re-arming me – but not like the army did it. Kenpo was giving me the knowledge to be violent and, in the same breath, teaching me how not to be. Teaching me the alternatives. I teach those alternatives today. When you understand what you can do, the power and the devastation you can trigger, you need control – and that's what Kenpo provides. Kenpo techniques are hard, fast and furious, and the timing requires immense discipline. If you don't have control and the self-discipline to listen, learn and practise, you're doomed.

I used to look for a fight, I actively wanted it. I could walk through hell, come out the other side, and leave a trail of death and destruction in my wake. Kenpo made me think for the first time, made me question whether violence and mayhem were the only solutions. Kenpo made me start to grow up.

Yes, Kenpo is about combat and fighting and defending yourself but the more you learn, the less chance you have of ever using that violence. At my studio in Cornwall, I teach students the following:

"I come to you with empty hands. I have no weapons but should I be forced to defend myself, my principles or my honour, should it be a matter of life or death, of right or wrong, then here are my weapons: my empty hands."

I believe in that, it defines what Kenpo means to me. That wasn't something the Legion ever preached. The military gave me guns and grenades and then desensitised me to emotion and loss. Kenpo armed me in a different way. Physically, it made me even more dangerous, more capable of killing with my bare hands than I'd ever been before. Unlike the army, however, it changed my own personality in a way that I'd never been willing to consider, or even think possible.

Instead of seeing people as targets, I saw them as human beings.

Learning Kenpo is like learning a musical instrument: you have to practise until everything becomes automatic and instinctive. There are three key stages: primitive, mechanical and spontaneous. You start at primitive because, in the beginning, you don't know how to stand, how to move, what to do. The more you are shown and the more you practise, the more mechanical it becomes. Eventually, you learn techniques so well you can apply them to situations without even thinking – and that's when Kenpo becomes automatic, the mantra of your life. When it becomes spontaneous like that, you're ready to progress to the higher skills and grades.

Everything emanates from the circle of parallel lines at the centre of a Kenpo studio floor. The lines represent angles of attack and defence. There might be 25 people queuing up to attack you but physically there are only eight angles they can approach from. The lines show you those angles; Kenpo's stances are therefore based around that framework.

Within this structure you will learn different stances, blocks, strikes, punches, kicks and foot manoeuvres, all based around the principle of the Circle and the Line. For example, when an opponent attacks, your feet should move along a circular path, your arms synchronising along similar arcs to deflect blows. Before you meet aggression with aggression, however, you are taught the following: "Avoid, rather than block; block rather than strike; strike rather than hurt; hurt rather than maim; maim rather than kill – for all life is precious."

I'm always aware of the eight angles I need to defend, and what my attack positions must be. I instinctively know my distances and widths, heights and depths – and, through that knowledge, I can contain and overwhelm an opponent. For every defence there is an offence. It's about balance, circular motion, distances, awareness of the eight angles, what you must protect, and knowing how to expose areas on your attacker. I always imagine I'm being attacked by the perfect opponent: in my case, I imagine I'm being attacked by myself.

If attack is the only option, then strike first – in rapid succession – to stun, distract and slow down your opponent. Go for the "soft" targets, such as the groin, throat, temple, testicles and stomach. The first technique you use should be enough – hit the correct nerve point and your attacker's arm will go dead. I don't need much after that: a lightning-fast hand-sword straight to the throat will put my opponent off.

The principles of yin and yang run through Kenpo: when an opponent attacks hard, counterattack soft. For example, you might parry your attacker's leg to the side so he's off- balance – then counterattack hard. This might include an elbow strike into his jaw and a hammer fist to the groin, followed by a right heel hook, foot stomp or rear kick. Or maybe you'll use your own individuality and launch into an elbow strike, perhaps followed by a right bare knuckle to the right side of your opponent's head and chop to the left side of his neck. This is the language of Kenpo.

Everybody starts as a white belt and is seen to progress by the colour of the tips on their belt, starting with yellow. Beyond that are the black belt grades; once you reach fourth degree black belt it's all about how much time you put in. After fourth, it's usually three to four years in between each of the remaining grade levels up to 10th. Each time you progress to the next level, you have to go right back to square one so you can discover stuff you missed first time round. If I have a pupil aiming to become a black belt, I will say: "You can go by the syllabus, sure, but I want to see how you've interpreted it to suit your own individuality and style." Just like Mr Parker once told me.

There are eight Forms within Kenpo, each one containing a sequence of techniques – the lightning-fast manoeuvres that empower you to block and overwhelm an attacker. Each technique merges seamlessly into another and all are given numbers and names as you progress. There are 154 different techniques in total; as I've already mentioned, all were given deliberately evocative names by Senior Grand Master Parker, such as Deflecting Hammer, Captured Twigs, Delayed Sword or Crashing Wings. Just so you'll remember them more easily.

Short Form 1, for example, teaches how to step away from an attacker and gain distance and time by using four basic blocks (inwards, outwards, upwards and downwards). Long Form 1 then teaches how to build on that defence by adding a counterpunch with the rear hand (reverse punch).

Kenpo also contains 17 Sets. These are training programmes to help practise the individual moves and skills, such as punches, strikes, blocks, kicks, breathing and stance. If a new pupil comes to me, I immediately start with these basics – how to stand, how to move, how to breathe, how to recognise the parts of your body that can become weapons – like the palms and sides of your hands, your elbows, the heels of your feet. I will get you to practise punches, blocks, hand strikes, movements, then kicks, and various fitness exercises that help your body cope with it all.

Next, I will introduce you to the techniques and I will make you practise them – without an opponent – until I'm happy they've become second-nature. In some respects, it's a bit like learning a new dance routine. You just have to imagine having a partner.

Five Swords is a classic example of a technique: if your opponent steps in with a right hook, you step inside the punch, blocking it with your right hand, which – in one rapid, uninterrupted movement – you then use to chop into the right side of your attacker's neck. Next, you pivot into a forward stance and thrust a hand sword (heel of your palm) into his face. This will set up an upper cut to the stomach with the right-hand fist. Next, with your left foot stepping outwards, you smash another hand sword to the left side of his neck, hook the back of his head and pull it down, so your right hand can pivot into a right-hand sword – and smash, this time, into the back of his neck.

The whole key to Kenpo is setting up the next move. I often compare it to playing snooker: a player isn't just sinking a red, he's working out five or six more pots – maybe more – beyond that.

After a pupil has mastered around 40 techniques, he or she can start to practise the Forms – the quick-fire combinations of techniques – again, without an opponent. This can be a ferociously-intense experience that plunges you into enormously deep levels of concentration. I have even reached a point where my body and mind are so perfectly intertwined in a whirlwind of movement that there seems to be nothing else in the world at that moment. I've then experienced a sensation of stepping outside my own body and looking back at myself completely absorbed in the Form.

When I think a student is fully prepared, he or she can start to work with a partner. First, though, it is critical to learn how to pull punches and how to evaluate distance. If you want to hit an attacker and take them out then, mentally, you must learn to punch *through* the target. In karate, for example, if you are trying to smash through wooden boards then, in your mind, you must imagine not just hitting the surface of the wood, but actually continuing on all the way. The target goes beyond the surface of what you are hitting – that is what we call "full contact".

When you are practising with an opponent, however, you have to learn the opposite of this – touch contact – so you are not continuing with the punch or kick, you are simply stopping on impact.

Eventually, my students are allowed to freestyle spar with another person, trying to hit and punch as though it is real full-on combat. However, they must still use touch control, although I have to admit, this form of fighting can get hairy the higher you progress through the grades. The serious black belt students get used to hitting – and getting hit.

I have taken students all the way up to ninth grade black belt, including my wife, Sheila. To pass each level, you must spar with six opponents for three minutes each – and they will push you to the limit. First degree black belts spar with higher grades and they will go in hard and heavy – all six of them pushing you to an exhausting finale. Usually, the last two are very high senior levels, and they will be the most demanding. In theory, they shouldn't get hurt but – in my experience – they often do because all you have left is the pure will to survive. That's my kind of Kenpo, that's when your own individuality is on the line. That's the way I was taught and that's the way I like to teach.

SHEILA

I became the UK's first professional American Kenpo instructor when I opened my first club in an old community hall in Radnor Place, Plymouth. In the beginning, Joan helped with all the admin but she wasn't as devoted, or as obsessed, with Kenpo as I was. She was helping to support me, bless her, but she didn't share my passion. She didn't need it like I did. Then, in 1977, a girl came along to one of our club sessions. She had long, blonde hair, her eyes were ablaze, but there was something about them that troubled me. There was anger and fury in those eyes, rather than fun or youthful passion for life. She'd come with a pal, but as she stood apprehensively alongside the other students, I noticed her stance: her body language looked broken. I was intrigued; I wanted to know why. We had a heavy workout and although I never spoke directly to her that night, I was always aware of her presence in the room. When I eventually locked up to leave, I noticed she was still sitting with her pal on the stairs outside that ran down to the pavement. I smiled as I passed them: she looked pale and drawn and I remember thinking to myself: "She won't be back."

To my surprise, she was; and she kept on coming back, week after week, training long and hard. Her name was Sheila and I could see she was driven. There was an intensity and passion about her training that made her stand out. Then, one night, I was about to leave when I found her sitting alone in the changing rooms. "What on earth are you still doing here?" I asked. "Shouldn't you be heading home – where do you live, can I give you a lift?"

Naturally, we got chatting in the car. Still her eyes blazed, and yet still her body language told me something was wrong. Slowly, she started to tell me about her life – she was married with two kids – and then we got to the bottom line. She'd taken up Kenpo because her husband was beating her up back home. We pulled over into a side road and sat talking for hours, telling each other bits about our lives that we'd found impossible to share with anyone else. We clicked, it was as simple as that, maybe because we were both victims, the pair of us hoping and trusting Kenpo would maybe provide the antidote to our pain.

It sounds corny now, but it seemed like the most natural move of all to put my arm round her. We cuddled and held each other, and in that moment I knew I was holding on to a soul-mate. I drove her back to her house and before she got out of the car, we kissed for the first time.

I was still with Joan, I knew it was wrong, but Sheila and I connected because we had so much more in common. Above all else, Sheila needed Kenpo in the same way I did. She was an outstanding student, too; she really embraced the Kenpo techniques and movement and philosophy. She was no pushover, either. In fact, she was comfortably the most aggressive female student I'd ever seen or taught. She embodied all the opposing forces within Kenpo, the yin and yang, the softness and the brutality. We started seeing each other regularly after training and when we both went on a weekend training course to Bristol, we knew what would happen.

Even though she was getting stronger, the abuse she suffered back home was still continuing. One night her husband came back late, drunk, and attacked her violently with a broom as she lay in bed. In fact, he struck her so hard, she suffered a fractured sternum and had to call the police.

A few nights later, the phone rang at home and I answered. It was Sheila and her breathing was agitated, her voice distraught like she might be crying. "I can't take it any more, Bob," she said. "I'm leaving him; I'm taking the boys and I'm walking out."

"Where the hell are you going to go?" I replied.

"I don't know yet. Mum's, maybe."

"Where are you now?"

"Outside my house with the kids and some suitcases."

I immediately drove round and brought them all back to our house. Joan was unbelievable in the circumstances; she had already sensed Sheila and I were close – she'd seen us together at Kenpo – but to her eternal credit, she was still willing to help a woman who was being battered by her husband and desperately needed shelter. I don't think I could have shown the same compassion had the tables been turned. Sheila put her kids to bed and the three of us stayed up all night talking, until Joan finally said: "OK, you can stay here for a while."

Sheila stayed with us until her divorce was finalised and then she got a new house. I'd spend alternate weekends between her and Joan; even Christmas with one, then New Year with the other. It was unusual to say the least, and it couldn't last. Sheila and I were totally in tune with one another, we were happy for Kenpo to dominate our lives, and she rapidly became more and more involved in running the club with me.

It was clear we needed to live together and, again to her eternal credit, Joan agreed to an amicable divorce. Sheila was the missing piece in my life. I'd found Kenpo, but Sheila helped me make sense of it all. She'd be woken by my screams of terror – shattering her own sleep – and yet she was never judgemental or accusatory.

Instead, she listened patiently and attentively whenever I wanted to talk about the horror of my life. She never pushed or interrogated. She only spoke when she knew I was ready. Yes, we were lovers and yes, we eventually became husband and wife. But our relationship transcended all that; we connected spiritually, we completed each other. I have no doubt Grey Wolf led me to Sheila because only Grey Wolf could have found and united two such kindred spirits.

Thankfully, Joan and I parted as friends, and that's how we've remained ever since. I look back on this episode now and can only marvel at her kindness and strength. Her humanity.

In the meantime, Sheila's martial arts career took off. She even went into full contact karate for a while – kickboxing – because she was so aggressive. The Legion had once seen the aggression within me and moulded me into a soldier; I did likewise with Sheila. She had eight fights and won them all by knockout. But Kenpo was where she truly excelled and she eventually became the highest-ranked female in the UK and Europe, reaching the ninth grade.

We were both determined to make a living out of Kenpo, so we set about opening a network of clubs across the UK. We used community centres and village halls; one night 200 people turned up in Exeter, such was the explosion of interest – largely thanks to the Bruce Lee films and Elvis. I was a tough taskmaster, though. I remember opening a club in a Methodist Church hall in Torquay and 60 locals enrolled. I started with a warm-up session that I'd picked up from my army days, one that soldiers were used to. For the locals, it must have felt like full-on circuit training. I thought it was terrific, but by the end I had people either doubled up and crawling around on their knees – or worse, throwing up in the streets outside. The next lesson was two days later, on a Thursday, and five people turned up.

I remember turning to Sheila and hearing her mumble: "I think you're doing something wrong."

It didn't make me any softer, though. We became a bit of a Kenpo roadshow, particularly across the Southwest, and people kept on turning up as we moved from town to town. I wasn't going to give them a censored version of Kenpo: sometimes the weather outside would be deplorable but I'd still take them into freezing snow and hail and rain and make them train.

Fortunately, Sheila's two boys were mad keen on karate as well and some nights we'd drive around the country and sleep together in our old Vauxhall estate. Pretty soon we were running clubs in Plymouth, Taunton, Exeter, Honiton, Torquay, Paignton, Birmingham, Oxford, Shaftesbury – and two in London, employing local instructors we got to know and trust.

Usually, there would be around 40 students in each class; it really had become our full-time occupation. I still desperately wanted to advance through the Kenpo grades myself, though, so I'd leave Sheila to run the clubs while I flew back to America for more tuition with Larry Tatum. My reputation began to grow as I rose through the levels. Word got round that I was some kind of expert and people started to seek me out to ask for guidance. It makes me smile, it's ridiculous really, but I was even dubbed "The Father of American Kenpo in the UK".

BREAKAWAY

Sheila and I had slowly built a network of clubs with hundreds, maybe thousands of students. In 1981, Mr Parker and his wife came over to give us an official stamp of approval.

It was a huge honour and, when Mr and Mrs Parker arrived in Plymouth, I drove them to the Holiday Inn and got them settled into their room. As I was leaving, though, Mr Parker suddenly said "Bob, I have something for you" and handed me a piece of carefully folded A4 writing paper.

"On this paper is the secret of American Kenpo, which I am now passing on to you," he said, extremely seriously. "But, whatever you do, make sure you don't read it until you get home." With that, he gave me one of his withering stares and added: "If you read it before then, I will know. Do you understand?"

"Yes, Mr Parker."

I left their room, got into a lift and strolled back to my car which was parked at the front of the hotel. The temptation was irresistible – as soon as I sat in the driver's seat, I unfolded the piece of paper. Across the top was written: "Secrets of American Kenpo karate – Ed Parker, 1981." Underneath that, in huge capital letters, was the word "PRACTICE" and then, below that, was the same word repeated over and over – all the way down to the bottom of the page – in much smaller, lower-case handwriting. I smiled and thought: "OK, thanks Mr Parker, I get the message."

I returned the next day. Mrs Parker opened their bedroom door and straightaway I feared the worst. She seemed subdued and, behind her, I could clearly see Mr Parker angrily hurling stuff into a bag he'd opened on their bed. My first instinct was that they'd had a row. I walked in, nervously, and he immediately bellowed: "I'm very annoyed. Really annoyed. You looked, didn't you? Don't bother trying to deny it, either. I know you looked because I have psychic powers. I can read your mind, Bob."

I gulped. All I could think was "Christ, I'm dead, this is the end of Bob Rose. I'll never get beyond first degree black belt now, it's all over." There was no point lying, he clearly knew, so I mumbled: "Yes, Mr Parker, I'm sorry, sir."

"So you should be!" he snapped instantly. "Don't ever disobey me again, and don't ever forget – I know these things."

We all fell silent. Mr Parker picked up his bag and we went off into the lift. He stood behind me and I was certain I could feel his eyes boring into me. About halfway down, his hand suddenly came over my right shoulder, and his head peered round from the side. "By the way, Bob. I'm not really psychic. I watched you through the hotel window as you got into your car. You just couldn't wait, could you?", and a giant smirk spread across his face.

"No, Mr Parker, I couldn't," I replied, and he roared with laughter. Many years later I met Mrs Parker at a convention and we had a good laugh together as we recalled that incident.

Mr Parker threw himself wholeheartedly into the rest of the visit, taking a training session on the Saturday and on the Sunday visiting a local Mormon church where he spoke to the congregation while European director Rainer Schulte conducted a local grading. On the

Monday, my most senior student, Gary Ellis, was presented with his first-degree black belt in the presence of Mr Parker, Schulte, leading instructor Roy Macdonald and, of course, me. It couldn't have gone any better, it was beyond our wildest dreams; it felt like we'd officially arrived and were now an integral part of the Kenpo empire.

Then it all started to unravel, and greed and politics and mistrust and betrayal soured everything. We were suddenly asked to find funds to cover the cost of the trip. We had no problems paying for air fare and accommodation – but we were also informed we had to pay for the time Mr Parker had spent with us – including his visit to the church. I phoned Schulte to query this and he replied: "He could have gone to a different church somewhere else if he'd wanted. In fact, he could have stayed in Los Angeles: he didn't need to come to England at all."

I got everyone together, explained the situation and said that we hadn't got the money. There seemed to be only one clear solution – to form our own, British, Kenpo association. So that's what we did, and the British Kenpo Karate Union was born in the hope that it could be affiliated to the IKKA.

I wrote to Mr Parker explaining what I was doing. Almost immediately, Schulte contacted our star pupil, Gary Ellis, and persuaded him to break ranks. Instead of joining us, Ellis stayed with the IKKA and convinced the Plymouth and Torquay clubs to do the same. World Kenpo was split. I was pissed off but carried on, putting all my other clubs and students under the umbrella of the BKKU. Ironically, I continued travelling to America where Larry Tatum was still willing to teach me – even though I was technically banned by the IKKA.

It was such a stupid situation, with no winners. In the end, Schulte and I patched up our differences and the BKKU became officially recognised by the international body. I later discovered that Mr Parker had never demanded to be paid for the time he'd spent with us, just his expenses. The more I continued to travel to America, the more I got to know his family, becoming increasingly friendly with his son, Ed Parker Junior.

My progression through the Kenpo system almost came to a shuddering halt in 1993, when I suffered a heart attack – and needed an emergency life-saving operation shortly afterwards. I'd taken a seminar in Exeter but had felt uncomfortable throughout the final Sunday, as though I had chronic indigestion. I remember one pupil saying to me: "Are you OK, you look really white." Sheila and I got back home late but I woke around 3am, barely able to breathe, with terrible pains across my chest. Sheila said my face had gone grey and my lips were blue; she called for an ambulance straightaway. All I remember of the journey was seeing traffic lights and passing the George Hotel, which was a mile and a half from the hospital. Somewhere in between I had a cardiac arrest; I vaguely recall a paramedic with jump leads in his hands and a distant voice, maybe his, saying: "You'll be all right, mate." In hospital, I was given a clot-busting drug to help clear the cholesterol in my arteries.

I was eventually discharged with angina, ordered to improve my diet, and told to lay off the Kenpo for "some time". A few weeks later I went to a London chest clinic to have stents put into one of my blocked arteries. Although I was sedated, I remained conscious during the operation and was dimly aware that the surgeons suddenly stopped; my artery had been accidently punctured. Somebody said: "We're going to halt now, give you another injection and let you relax for a while."

That was all I remember; the next I knew, I woke up with tubes splaying out of me in all directions, and my chest stitched up down the middle. It looked like I'd given birth to an alien. Apparently, the surgeons had taken an artery from the whole length of my inner leg and used it to replace the one that had been punctured. Without their quick thinking, I am told, my heart would have stopped. It seemed that, yet again, I'd miraculously escaped death – first in Algiers, then in the ambulance, and finally in hospital. I'm certain Grey Wolf was with me each time.

Five days later I was back on the train to Plymouth; not long after that I was back in a Kenpo studio, grading students.

I reached ninth grade myself just before the new millennium, although the founder of the Irish Kenpo Karate Union, Ambrose Maloney, helped steer me through grades six and seven. I'd never set myself the target of reaching 10th degree and when Larry Tatum called to say he was coming over in 2000 for a training weekend and seminar, I didn't attach any greater importance to his visit than normal. Everything proceeded as usual and on the final day I gathered all the students and clubs together to mark the end of the gathering.

I was just about to wind everything up when Larry, a celebrity and movie star in his own right, stepped forward and asked me to adopt the Horse Stance and place my hands behind my back. I sensed a smirk on his face and thought some of my students were sniggering as well. Suddenly, Larry's wife Jill – herself a seventh dan – appeared, carrying a black belt, and I immediately twigged what was going on. I knelt ceremoniously as the belt was presented to me and tied it proudly round my tunic. Larry then asked me to return to the Horse Stance and, as is traditional, aimed a gentle kick at me – a signal for everyone else to join in and follow suit.

I'd never expected it, and the significance of it didn't sink in at first. I was now officially the only 10th Degree Grand Master in the UK and Europe – in fact there were only about 10 of us in the world, mainly in America. To this day, I remain the most senior Grand Master in the UK and Europe.

Looking back, of course I'm immensely proud to have reached that level. I turned to Kenpo, initially, to be more violent. I suppose I'd already taken the positive step of giving up booze and that was probably way more significant than I realised at the time. But I never turned to Kenpo expecting to become a different and better human being. I did it because Phil Hegarty gave me a right old beating and I wanted to learn how to be as brutal as him. I accepted his challenge and I kept on accepting the physical and mental challenges that Kenpo itself threw back at me. I bought into it and, in so doing, allowed my soul and character and values to change dramatically.

Yes, reaching the highest possible level was an achievement, and yes, it signified how much I'd changed. The Bob Rose who returned from Vietnam would never have become a 10th Degree Grand Master. It needed something extraordinary and special to make that happen and I was lucky that the combination of Kenpo, and Sheila, came to me just when I was staring into the abyss. I was probably more proud, though, of the moment I managed to help Phil attain his first-degree black belt. He was exceptional within the Kenpo system and he never attained the level that his deep knowledge and understanding truly warranted. Instead, he wrote it all down in a personal diary; sadly, when he tragically died, his work was thrown away.

THE WALL

I kneel and hold out my right hand, pressing my palm against the smooth, highly polished gabbro stone wall in front of me. Inscribed into its surface are the names of all the soldiers who never came back from Vietnam. Frank is one of them, and for the first time since that horrific day, I am close to something that represents him, that honours him – that makes him feel real again.

I push one of my fingers into the shallow groove of the inscription, and run it slowly along the twists and turns of each individual letter. As I do so, I notice my reflection staring back at me from the wall's smooth, black, shiny surface. I take a look into my mirrored image and see Frank's name reflecting back, seemingly across my chest; I know it's an illusion and yet it feels like the reflection is uniting us once again.

All sorts of images flash before me, surreal mixes of the good and the bad. I see us laughing and clowning; I hear us trying to drown each other with banter. Then I hear the explosions and the mayhem of firefights and I see him running to help wounded soldiers or yelling instructions as men freeze and panic in the turmoil of bombardment. Finally, I see the one abiding memory I want to erase: his body, lifeless, beaten, torn and shattered.

I realise I am trembling; no, I realise I'm sobbing. Tears are falling down my cheeks, the emotion is too overwhelming. I want to be here, I want to be this close again, I want to relive the times that made us connect, that forged a bond so strong not even death could get in the way. Far more, I want a chance to be wrong: I want to turn and see it's all been a terrible mistake and he is standing behind me and we both survived together and went on to remain friends for ever, visiting each other across the Great Pond, sharing memories, laughing – honouring everyone who never came home and rejoicing in the fact that we did. Is that so bizarre? After all, I never saw his body when they brought it back. So maybe the name I'm looking at isn't his at all. Just as I'm losing myself in the possibility that he's actually still here, I feel a hand gently touching my shoulder. I freeze; the hand is small, its weight barely noticeable, and it is tapping up and down slowly. Trying, maybe, to get my attention; trying, maybe, to offer condolence.

I turn, praying to see Frank, but instead a child is standing before me, a boy – maybe nine or ten years old. He's wearing a black T-shirt and shorts and I blink a few times as the sun seems to shimmer around the outer edges of his body. I see his innocence immediately; I see his health and vitality and hope. I see that the world is waiting for him to be brilliant and – momentarily – I close my eyes and pray that his life is never destroyed by the horror that separated Frank and me. He breaks the silence between us. "Don't cry," he says, gently. "My grandad is on this wall as well and my daddy says they were all brave men and they gave their lives for us and their spirits will always be here."

I look round to see if I can see his father, wanting to thank him because his son has helped find the words I most needed to hear just then. But there's no-one around and, in any case, the boy isn't finished yet. "Wait a minute," he says, then turns and dashes off somewhere. Moments later he's back, clutching a little piece of greaseproof-style paper. "Rub your friend's name on to this," he says, smiling. "I took a rubbing of my grandad's name so I'll always be able to keep it in my room. You do the same." Then, before I'd even found time to wipe away my tears, he thrust a black-lead pencil into my hand.

It was entirely down to Kenpo that I had the opportunity in 2006 to visit The Wall – America's memorial to their Vietnam dead, in Washington DC. My 60th birthday was on the horizon and, unbeknown to me, my Kenpo students had clubbed together and bought me tickets to fly out so I could see it for the first time myself. When I returned, they presented me with an album full of photographs of my visit, even adding little messages they'd each written to me. I still have that album and cherish it enormously.

I didn't know how I was going to react when the day came to actually see The Wall and I remember stopping off for a coffee first. Half of me wanted to leave. I didn't want to see proof that Frank was dead and I didn't want to let in the memories. Seeing The Wall would only underline what I didn't want to accept. The other half of me knew I owed it to my Kenpo students – and possibly to myself, too – and, thankfully, that half won. I finished my coffee and headed into the vast memorial grounds.

The first thing that hit me, once I'd been directed towards where The Wall was situated, was its sheer size and, with that, the enormity of what it represented. It stood in a giant L-shape, two enormous panels sunk into the ground, each one about ten feet tall where they joined – but tapering down to just a few inches at their furthest points. Running in horizontal lines were the names of every soul who fell, separated by either a small diamond – denoting "died in action" – or a small cross to indicate "missing" or "prisoner of war".

The sheer volume of names was overwhelming; there were too many, there was too much tragedy and loss to comprehend. It felt like every name in America was there. It was impossible to think about those numbers – over 58,000 – and then not think about the names beyond the names. The families and the friends and the colleagues who were all affected, in different ways, by the death of each and every one of those soldiers. If someone inscribed those on to The Wall as well, there'd be millions upon millions of names. It would be endless. When I killed, I never thought about the families left devastated by the lives I'd taken. But Kenpo had opened me to emotion and to thinking about loss and now, standing in front of The Wall, I realised what the true legacy of war really looked like.

I was with one of my top students, Kevin Mills, and we headed for a reception desk area so that we could be directed to the part where we would find Frank's name. As we approached, Kevin dropped back so that I could face this moment on my own, which is what I wanted. The photographs he subsequently took are the ones that went into my commemorative album.

Just seeing Frank's name was the hardest part. It was a strange sight to take in: on one hand, his stood out because it was the only name I knew and when I stared at it, all the other names seemed to dissolve until it seemed like he was the only soldier to die serving his country in Vietnam. Then, of course, my vision broadened out and all the other names came back into focus, their sheer numbers almost making his disappear. Together, they all merged into one awful tragedy. Alone – eternally carved into that Wall – they were individuals who had names and families and hopes and dreams, and the sacrifice they made was bigger than The Wall itself.

It was too much and I knew I had to leave. As I did, I saw the boy who'd tapped me on the shoulder, walking away with his father. In his right hand, hanging low to his side, I could see a tiny piece of greaseproof-style paper. Just like the one I was carrying in mine.

REMEMBRANCE

No matter how hard I tried, I couldn't entirely let go of the military. Some part of me still needed to feel attached, so I started buying and collecting Vietnam-era vehicles – I'd always loved driving the jeeps and trucks – and sometimes took them to military re-enactment shows. I even provided all the US army jeeps for the Hollywood blockbuster movie "Full Metal Jacket", which was shot entirely in England: the camp scenes in Canterbury barracks; the road scenes at Romney Marshes and combat scenes on the Isle of Dogs. I know this because I was there throughout the filming.

Inevitably, I needed somewhere to store all these vehicles. At the time, an American theme park – Spirit of the West – had opened in Cornwall; the owner heard about my collection and asked to meet because he was interested in setting up a Vietnam display there. In the end, that project never materialised but – through visiting the theme park near the tiny village of St Columb – Sheila and I stumbled upon a small bungalow that used to be part of an old petrol station and garage business. It was available, it had land, and it was perfect for storing my military vehicles – and for setting up a Kenpo studio in one of the many outbuildings. It's where Sheila and I still live today. We named it the wolf den, and for many years Kenpo students and instructors from across the world turned up on our doorstep – often unannounced – to quiz me. We often provided lodgings; many of them still visit today.

I must confess that I run the wolf den more like a military base than a home, mainly because I love and cherish it so much. I have to protect it, and if that means checking the perimeter fences, then so be it. Am I still at war? Possibly, yes. This is my castle, my territory, my HQ. Everything I care about is here: Sheila, our Kenpo studio, our two German Shepherds – even the remains of the seven other dogs we used to have, including a Great Dane, buried at the bottom of the garden.

I love the wolf den's isolation. I'm definitely not a socialite – I don't drink, I don't smoke, I'm not a party animal. Even in the old days, I'd be the last person you'd want at a party – unless you wanted it to kick off. The only times I like to see the wolf den packed with people is when they're in my Kenpo studio and we're training together. Then, everyone is focused and concentrated, and we're not trying to make small talk with one another.

There are parts of the wolf den that resemble a military museum – I have an enormous collection of memorabilia: medals and photographs and guns and knives. If anyone tries to break in, they'd certainly be taking their chances. I know exactly where every single weapon I have is placed in my house, and could reach for them blindfolded. I have one knife that's been with me ever since I was with the British army. It was given to me by a tracker in Borneo and it still has bloodstains that won't wipe clean. Trust me, it's razor-sharp.

In one room I have a line of tailors' dummies clad in full military uniform and I've also returned to my childhood fascination with toy soldiers, using them to build meticulously accurate reconstructions of famous battle scenes in some of the wolf den's outhouses. I also help run, voluntarily, the military museum in Bodmin – where one of my reconstructions is on display.

I cannot be ashamed of being a soldier. I'm still wearing a uniform – a karate suit; I still line up and I still drill, albeit in a Kenpo studio. In my mind, it feels like I'm still serving.

In fact, when I was 65 years old, I did something many might find incomprehensible. It was 2003, Britain had just invaded Iraq – and I tried to enrol once again, lying, of course, about my age. I nearly got away with it.

I'd heard that the TA medical corps in Plymouth was looking for volunteer ambulance drivers, so off I went to join. I wandered into a small recruiting office – bit like a Portakabin – and, inside, a sergeant was sat at a desk with a pile of forms. I took a seat alongside four or five other hopeful recruits. Eventually my turn came, so I stepped in front of the desk and tried my hardest to keep smiling so I might look younger than I really was. The Kenpo had kept my upper body firm and toned, so from where the sergeant was sitting, I would have looked reasonably strong and powerful at least.

The sergeant started to take down my details – name, address, occupation – and I was beginning to feel increasingly confident. He asked if I'd ever had any similar experience, so I trowelled on how much driving I'd done in Vietnam. I never mentioned the military police or the Legion; that might have made me seem suspiciously old. I sounded convincing, experienced, and the more I talked, the more I fancied my chances. He even seemed to be nodding as he wrote down my answers. Then came the killer question.

"Age?"

I looked him squarely in the face and replied: "Forty-one." He glanced up, fleetingly, then carried on writing. Just as I dared to believe I'd fooled him, his commanding officer suddenly marched in from an adjoining office, took one look at me – then another, more pronounced second glance, like he needed to be completely sure about something – and leaned over the desk sergeant to see what he was writing down.

"What's that age you've got there – does that say forty-one?" he asked. The sergeant nodded and the major turned and faced me once again. "I know you, don't I? You were in the military police in the '60s, stationed in Hong Kong, weren't you? I'd recognise your face anywhere."

I had no choice but to come clean. When I told him my real age, he smiled and said: "Go home, soldier. You've served your country once already, and that's quite enough."

I've thought long and hard about why I tried to enlist. The simplest answer is that I'll always be a soldier. I'm trapped, in a way, even though the combination of Frank's death, Kenpo and Sheila have made me think more and more about loss.

In fact, I am more affected by death than ever before, especially when Remembrance Sunday comes round. Each year, I place a commemorative wreath at a local cenotaph; on it, I pin a list with the names of all the people I've known who have died in battle or some similar atrocity. The worst truth is that my list keeps getting longer and longer as each year passes.

Frank's name is always at the top, closely followed by Rick Rescorla, who was born in Hale, Cornwall, but died in the 9/11 attack on the World Trade Centre as he tried to lead people out of the South Tower. Then, I've started to add the names of Kenpo students I've known who never made it back from conflicts like Afghanistan and Iraq, Northern Ireland and Kosovo. Names like Damion Mulvihill: I knew him when he was seven years old, coming to me because he was so excited to be learning Kenpo and staying with me all the way to black belt. He was one of the first to die in Afghanistan. Other names are Paul McLeish, Tony Loveys, Sam Bassett. Just names, but – just like the names on The Wall – names with lots of names behind them. Families, friends, wives, lovers, colleagues who all grieve each year for the space that suddenly opened in their lives and can never be filled.

MY SUCCESSOR

Inevitably, the wear and tear on my body has caught up with me. I've always been in pain ever since hitting the land mine in Algeria, but somehow I was able to fight that and even push it into the background. I've been less successful, however, in halting the march towards old age. Algeria left me with hairline fractures of the spine that never healed; my bottom two discs are mashed up like knotted string. I practically live off Co-codamol tablets and, in more recent years, I was diagnosed with type two diabetes after feeling increasingly tired, lethargic and short of breath. I never recovered from the motorbike display crash, either, and six years ago I was officially classed as disabled.

On Sunday, July 2, 2017, I even beat the Grim Reaper for a third time. I'd cheated death in Algeria, and then in 1993 when my angiogram went wrong – but this time I really thought my time was up. I had another heart attack, and I don't mind admitting I was genuinely scared. I was rushed into Truro hospital's A & E with severe chest pains and then transferred to a cardiology ward, where they told me I needed another angiogram. I was far from keen. There's only meant to be a one in three thousand chance of it going wrong – but I'd been the one back in '93, so I really didn't fancy my odds a second time round. In fact, I nearly did something I've never done before – I very nearly gave up.

For an hour and a half, I disappeared into the hospital and sat on my own in an empty room. I needed to connect with the spirit world; I needed to find the strength that had saved me twice before. I visualised the Blue again; I recalled a boy sitting alone in front of the Montana mountains and I saw Grey Wolf's face once more – strong, assured, unwavering. My resolve and confidence returned and I walked back into the ward, where I told the nurses: "Let's do it." Grey Wolf was back in the room.

Although sedated, I lay awake as the surgeons did the angiogram, telling me what they could see on their screen as they studied my veins and arteries. "There's a problem, and it's fairly serious," they said. "The original graft you had in '93 has worn and is now leaking. Do you want us to repair it right now?" I didn't even hesitate. "Yes, go for it." Three quarters of an hour later the problem was fixed, and I was back home the next day.

I have no doubt Grey Wolf keeps willing me back to fitness, although I'm now on so many tablets I'd rattle if you bumped into me. I can't perform all the moves I used to, so I've developed a form of chi kung and t'ai chi that is almost Kenpo in slow motion, designed to help with breathing and relaxation. My body simply can't cope with hard-core Kenpo combat any more, especially after the latest heart attack.

I'd already decided to ease off a little in 2012 and increasingly let Kevin Mills – who I'd taken to eighth dan and who'd come with me to The Wall – take control of the Kenpo. Not long afterwards, however, I began to hear complaints that students were being pushed excessively hard, and were even leaving the BKKU. I'm not saying who was to blame, but it was happening under Kevin's stewardship and it was a concern. I didn't realise it, but another split was just around the corner.

It all came to a head at a weekend seminar in Belgium, which Kevin attended with one of our best black belt students, Chris Canniford. I wasn't there but I was later told it had been a tough, bruising session. Kevin phoned me shortly afterwards to say – to my bewilderment – Chris was quitting the BKKU and that he'd removed his name from the website. "He wants to leave and do his own thing. It's done," he said. Alarmed, I rang Chris and he began to explain what had happened in Belgium. He'd barely started his side of the story when I said: "Stop, this is way too important, I'm coming round to see you right now so you can tell me face to face." So I drove the 90 miles to Honiton, where he lived, and he told me: "I can't carry on with Kevin in charge."

He continued: "I don't agree with his methods: he's been pushing students way too hard for weeks and weeks, in my opinion. I'm going to start my own 'street-wise kenpo' club here in Honiton."

Mr Parker had always impressed on me that individuality was at the heart of Kenpo. I had no problem with students branching off and wanting to set up and run their own clubs. Maybe it was time for our structure to reform and modernise so that new bodies and styles could be encouraged and embraced and we could keep in touch with young, fresh ideas. I called a meeting of all our senior instructors and students and said: "I propose that we form a new union and call it 'Integrated Kenpo Styles' (IKS). That way everyone is free do their own thing – all under one umbrella."

Kevin was vehemently opposed to the idea; we argued, and in the end were unable to reach an agreement. My mind was made up, though. "I founded the BKKU," I said, "and now I'm disbanding it."

There was uproar, but there was nothing Kevin could do. I simply formed the IKS, and the new organisation was recognised and accepted in America. To this day, all the diverse UK Kenpo clubs and styles come under the umbrella of my new organisation. I'm still heavily involved, although I simply can't teach any more at the same level I used to. I am proud to say, though, that I have found my natural successor and he is now holding the reins.

I'd known Damion Abbot since he was a young boy coming for his first Kenpo lessons. He rose through the gradings and reached sixth degree black belt after training, like me, in America with Larry Tatum. Three years ago, Damion launched a new weekend training event he labelled "The Calling" and I was invited to attend as a guest of honour. Damion took his seventh degree on that day in front of me and top US tutor Francisco Vigorux, an 8th Dan. It was the first time every dan grade had ever been represented at a Kenpo gathering – from first to 10th – and I have a cherished photograph of the historic moment when we all stood shoulder to shoulder. There was a similar event the following year and then, in July 2016, we held a competition in Exeter – attended by instructors and students from the US, Canada, Holland, Germany and all over the UK. I knew the time was right and so I officially handed the running of my organisation over to Damion. He's truly my natural successor and I know he will go all the way – in fact, I'll personally make sure he does.

ALWAYS A SOLDIER

Despite all the nightmares and all the loss, I remain a soldier at heart. It's all I was ever trained to be and nothing that I did, or witnessed, ever knocked the soldier out of me. I'm not a philosopher, I've never been educated or paid to think that way, and yet – ultimately – I'm left trying to answer deeply philosophical questions about the rights and wrongs of my life.

While I was learning Kenpo in America, I visited a Vietnam Veterans' Association in Los Angeles. I started listening to their stories, I told them about my experiences, and I realised I was beginning to open up about memories that I'd deliberately buried. I hadn't known what else to do with them. Those old soldiers spoke my language and I could see their souls were tormented just like mine. That's when I really became familiar with the expression post-traumatic stress disorder. I realised it was my problem.

I was also greatly affected by a chance meeting in Plymouth one afternoon. I fancied a cup of coffee so headed for the city's Barbican Centre, where there was a Greek café I liked.

I walked in, sat at one of the tables and looked around. There was only one other person there – a man, sitting alone. He was in a far corner, his hands circled round a mug, his head drooped towards his drink. It was a cold day and he looked like he was trying to stay warm; I could see his body tremble occasionally and at first I thought he was shivering. He was smartly dressed in a dark coat and shirt and tie but something about him suggested he was in a bad way.

I was intrigued. I wanted to see his face, which he hadn't raised once since I'd walked in. A few minutes passed until, finally, he looked up – I don't think he knew I was there – and it was clear, straightaway, that he was crying. His eyes were puffed and reddened and he reached over for a napkin to wipe away the tears. Instinctively, I got up and walked over to his table. "What's up mate?" I asked. "What's troubling you, then?"

I guessed he was in his 30s. Something about his physique, and the way he presented himself to the world, made me immediately suspect he was ex-military. He was reluctant to talk, after all I was a complete stranger, but nevertheless I heard him mutter: "Something happened to me in the Falklands."

That was the connection – I told him a bit about myself, and said: "Maybe we're in similar situations then. I was in Vietnam, and I'm still haunted by it all."

I had his attention from that point. He was ex-navy and had been serving as a chief petty officer on board a frigate that was sunk during the Falklands War. "I had to slam the hatch down on my own crew mates," he said. "I can't get their screams out of my head."

We spent the rest of the afternoon drinking coffee and chatting. I think I was the first person he had truly opened up to. It was only a fleeting moment in our lives, but it helped.

My PTSD still hasn't gone, I've just found ways of combating it. Kenpo is one. Talking to veterans – people who have actually been to war and experienced the horror – is another. Old soldiers have a whole language of their own; there are phrases and situations that seem abhorrent or exaggerated or unimaginable to the outside world, but they never need explaining to us because we've lived them. Banter is a crucially important factor in military relationships. Sometimes the banter can sound cruel and repulsive to civilians – but not to us. It bonds us.

I definitely peered into the pit of humanity, especially in Vietnam, but I'm not the first to have done so, and I certainly didn't discover it. The pit's been there for ever, and it's not going away. I can't work out if man is inherently good or evil. I can't even work out if I'm good or evil. When you're faced with the extremes, it doesn't take much for a human to become an animal. Which is worse – the savage animal or the savage human? In my experience it's the human, because he or she has the ability and potential to find another way and not choose death or devastation. Humans are capable of the bond Frank and I shared.

I don't sleep at night, I regularly dream that I'm being mortared and I regularly see the faces of people who died. Maybe I deserve all that.

It's a fact that I only fought in other people's wars. That might be part of my problem. It might have been easier for me if I was defending my country, the Queen, the flag. But I wasn't. The brutal truth is, I was a mercenary, and that word jars with me. I don't feel it reflects accurately the soldier I wanted to be. It hints at bloodlust and sport, as though I was killing for fun. One thing I do know, it was never for fun. Yes, I got an incredible adrenalin rush out of fighting for my life, or for doing my job professionally. But I didn't get a "high" out of the physical act of taking life. Quite the contrary: it left me cold, emotionless. That not-being-bothered bit bothers me a lot now. Why wasn't I bothered?

It was drilled into me by the Legion – and indirectly by watching the way my father conducted himself – that a good soldier executes an order, even if that means putting his own life on the line, and never questions why. The mantra "Ours is not to reason why, ours is but to do or die" embodied the soldier I strove to be.

Frank's death changed everything; for the first time in my life loss truly affected me, and instead of trying to rationalise why I was so affected, I reacted violently. It was the easiest option to take and it meant I didn't have to ask any difficult questions about myself and what made me a soldier. Instead I could kill without any restraint because I didn't give a damn if I got killed in the process. His death rendered all human life meaningless to me, including my own. The Blue taught me that: nothing I did would ever make a difference. None of it mattered.

I truly wanted to die at that time. I deliberately put myself in the firing line, hoping to get killed. I didn't have the courage to commit suicide, despite trying very hard to. The problem was, my plan didn't work and I survived.

Why did Frank matter so much to me? That's a question I am still grappling with. I've allowed him to be an endless and constant pain and I won't let go of that pain. Perhaps it's the only way I can feel pain for what I've done. Every day a voice inside me screams "You should have stopped him getting into the helicopter, he didn't need to be with you, it wasn't a Phoenix mission." But Frank was a true soldier, fighting for his country. Unlike me, he can be considered a hero.

Frank's death opened my eyes to killing and slaughter. The Legion had taught me to shrug it off and move on to the next target. Frank made me realise there were consequences. The Legion desensitised me to death; Frank's death plugged me back into the human race. In Algeria, I'd needed to feel pain to know I was still alive. I think it's the same with Frank – so long as I feel the pain of his loss, I know I'm still human.

Then came American Kenpo. How ironic: I stumbled upon a martial art that taught me even more ways to kill with my bare hands. What I never expected was the self-control and knowledge that came with it.

Until Kenpo, I'd relied on army discipline for control. The military allowed me to be a brutal killer, but only within the framework of orders and commands. I came back from Vietnam an extremely dangerous person – with no code of conduct, and nobody directing me. However, Kenpo kept me under control in a way I'd never foreseen – and it even made me start questioning the life I'd had and the stuff I'd done. I am absolutely certain that Grand Master Ed Parker – through his American Kenpo – saved my life.

Kenpo let me open the door on new emotions, ones I had deliberately drowned in alcohol in Algiers and Vietnam. The power of Kenpo to achieve that was – and is – phenomenal. The walls I had built around me were impregnable until then.

Thanks to Kenpo, I started to feel sensitivity and awareness towards people. Running the clubs, watching students struggle to learn new techniques then slowly conquer them and progress, hearing and learning about their own lives to the extent where I was actually genuinely interested in them – going to The Wall – this was totally uncharted territory for Bob Rose the soldier. I wasn't making myself do this, it was just happening to me as Kenpo took control of my life. I also began to see how Kenpo was a power of good for others as well: many of my students were like me, troubled individuals with their own demons. Slowly but surely, I'd see Kenpo bring calm and sanctity into their turbulent lives.

I truly began to see and understand and react to the world differently. I didn't have to put up a façade: I didn't have to do something awful and then walk away with an attitude of coldness – thinking that's what my commanding officers and comrades would want and expect to see. I could even let myself cry, and nobody judged me negatively. In fact, quite the reverse.

One thing I couldn't rid myself of, though, was the need for a disciplined structure. I will always need some code of conduct, some regime, regularity, guidelines. Thankfully, Kenpo gives me that as well. Kenpo discipline, though, is infinitely better than military discipline because it doesn't flirt with the extremes. I was ultimately professional in the military but, to be like that, I had to become immune to the horror I was confronting.

In a similar way, I've had to be ultimately professional in Kenpo. But the difference is this: Kenpo has left me with a far greater sense of achievement. It has made me a better person. I prefer that person. I'm even proud of him. I couldn't live with the other person. In fact, I needed to be permanently drunk to live with that person. That's why I will never go back to alcohol. I never want to see that other person again.

Confronting alcoholism was massively important; some part of me, it has to be the Grey Wolf part, chose to find a better way. I realise Grey Wolf is the warrior within me, a spirit that refuses to succumb, that has kept me alive despite incredible odds, and continues to help me in my daily battle against PTSD. Great-gran said to me "The spirit of the wolf is within you," and she was right. Grey Wolf helped me ditch alcohol; then Grey Wolf led me to Kenpo – just when I needed it most.

Like the military, Kenpo is brutal and violent, and based on principles of killing. Unlike the army, though, there is an inherent spirituality and beauty within it. I can block and retaliate and punch and they are devastating moves, but there is also grace and artistry – graceful violence. I don't have to become some icy-cold vessel of humanity to carry out commands. In fact, I don't follow orders at all. I am an individual within Kenpo. Here are my weapons: my empty hands.

The other salvation in my life has been my fourth wife, Sheila, and – of course – all my children and grandchildren. I have three children from my first marriage, two from the second, two more from my third, plus Sheila has two boys from her previous marriage. I even have an adopted daughter who lives in Israel. On top of that, I've got ten grandchildren and two great-grandchildren. I'm immensely proud of them all.

Sometimes I'm asked: "Would you let your own kids join the military?" I don't even hesitate – the answer is "Yes". If they want to join the best, then I'd even recommend the Legion. My eldest son, two grandsons and adopted daughter all serve in the forces. In fact, I lured one of my grandsons into joining. His mother had sent him to live with me because he'd got into bad ways. So, one day, I confronted him and said: "Right, what do you want to do with your life?"

"I want to join the army," he replied.

"You've no chance, you're not good enough, you're not fit enough, they wouldn't have you."

"Yes I am."

"Well, prove it to me." So I challenged him to do a five-mile run, and he agreed. Off he went, over some of the worst hills I could find, with me driving in my car alongside. I told him he could just walk fast where it was steep – but he didn't, he kept on running. I made him go out again the next morning – and, again, he managed it. On the third morning, he came out and said: "Where we running today?"

"We're not, you're coming with me in the car," I replied. And I drove him straight to the army recruitment office in Bodmin. "Get in there and sign up right now." He joined the Royal Artillery. I have no doubts or regrets about him, or any of them. That's the soldier bit in me that I can't get rid of.

It helped me enormously that Sheila needed and loved Kenpo as much as me and I'm eternally proud that she rose to 9th dan, becoming the highest-graded female in Western Europe – even though I had to ban her from training for six months first. She'd been sparring with one of my students – a policeman – and knocked him flat out when he got a technique wrong and caught her in the face with his elbow. She recoiled and instinctively responded with a lightning-fast upper cut that lifted him two or three inches off the floor!

I also encouraged Sheila to specialise in complementary medicine and she is now fully qualified in shiatsu, reflexology and acupuncture – as well as being an equine practitioner.

We've been together now over 40 years; every night I endure mortar attacks – and so does she, yet she's never been to war. Instead, she patiently steers me through the mine fields exploding in my mind, and I am eternally grateful.

She has encouraged me, too, to help counsel other post-traumatic stress victims returning from current war zones. I truly want to believe I am of some use to these soldiers. I never probe or interrogate, I wait for whenever they're ready to talk. As far as I'm concerned, they can take as long as they like because I'll always wait to listen. At least when I say to a PTSD sufferer "I know exactly how you're feeling", it's bloody true.

There remain, of course, bigger questions to ask, especially given my military experiences. Would we all be better off without armies? Would we have no wars and conflicts if we had no soldiers and weapons? In a fluffy, pink world, of course we'd all be better off and we could all hug and love each other and hold hands irrespective of race and religion.

Sadly, you and I will never see such a world. The awful terrorist attacks in Manchester and at London Bridge are testament to that; the nuclear uncertainty over North Korea another. The Middle East is a powder keg ready to erupt, and a nation without the ability to defend itself is clearly in an immensely vulnerable position.

So, the uncomfortable truth is that we do still need armies, which means we do need soldiers who are willing to put their lives on the line. The bigger problem is the politicians who decide how to use that resource. Do they always make the best decisions? Were President Bush and Tony Blair saviours of freedom, or a pair of power-crazed clowns? We want a world where democratically elected leaders make the big calls, because that's what our idea of civilisation is based upon. That means the military will always be under their ultimate command. But none of that matters one iota, unless there is a soldier down the line ready to fire a gun, or lay a mine, or push a button. A soldier who accepts: "Mine is not to reason why, mine is but to do or die".

So long as there is a universe, there will be a universal soldier. They'll all fight for the goodies, and they'll all fight for the baddies. Who knows, maybe I did both.

HOMECOMING

It may sound crazy, but I recently tried – without much success – to grow a scalp lock. I used to have one many years ago; the sides of my head were completely shaven but across the top was a long lock of hair that actually fell all the way down to the bottom of my back. I used to hide it underneath a hat so that nobody had a clue; they simply thought I was bald.

I wanted to regrow it because I am preparing for my inevitable journey into the spirit world. Should I have to fight there, the scalp lock would show that I am a warrior and I have the warrior spirit within me. I know this now with great certainty but, first, I needed Kenpo to show me what it actually meant.

Kenpo helped me define who I am and what my true nationality is. I was only a child when I lived on the Montana reservation, and while I was incapable of rationalising everything in my young mind, there was stuff that never left me. Like Grey Wolf. Like the sun dance and my own vision quest. I came away from the reservation believing in the Great Spirit, even though I was too young to properly comprehend that concept.

That belief and those memories never deserted me through my years in the Legion, the British Army and Vietnam, although I struggled to understand where I really fitted in and, more importantly, which race I belonged to. I felt split – between the white, Western world I was born in and went back to, and the Native American way of life I still remembered and cherished.

Part of me worried what Native Americans saw when they looked at me. Did they see a white man, or one of their own? The acclaimed Blackfoot Native American actor, Steve Reevis, talks about "wannabe" Indians, and there were moments when I worried that he was referring to the likes of me. Someone who romanticised about the Native Americans, about their cause, but who didn't truly belong. Was I just a white man who liked the idea of the Northern Cheyenne?

Deep down, I believed I was more than that. Deep down, the sense of family – the blood ties, the spirituality – they all felt way too powerful and profound. Yes, they were buried within me; I just needed something to bring them to the surface.

Kenpo did that for me. There are so many spiritual and lifestyle crossovers, shared core beliefs and values, that are common to the Native Americans and the Kenpo system. The very essence of Kenpo is that warrior spirit – ferocious on the outside but calm and tranquil within. Just like Grey Wolf. Just like I know my great, great-grandfather would have been at the Battle of the Little Bighorn.

There is a powerful connection, too, between the Native Americans and Mother Earth, a respect for her natural resources and how they can be used responsibly to survive and maintain life. The same is true of Kenpo; everything emanates from the ground. That's where the eight lines of attack are drawn that provide the entire foundation for all the techniques, forms and movements. Then, there is the respect for all forms of life – human and animal. Kenpo is violent but it teaches that life is precious and that attack is not the first and only option. Kenpo is a defence mechanism – not a form of assault. The same belief is basic to Native Americans: when I killed the deer,

I blessed it and thanked it for giving its life so that I could survive. When the Northern Cheyenne have killed in battle, it was to defend their lifestyle, their land, their property and their beliefs.

Bizarrely, the Western theme park that had been interested in my old Vietnam vehicles also played a part. It was fundamentally a Cornish tourist attraction based on a stereotypical reconstruction of an old Wild West town, complete with saloons and a sheriff's office.

The wolf den was next door, and I used to help out whenever the theme park did re-enactments of Wild West shootouts. I always ended up playing the Indian scout and it actually got me thinking more and more about my childhood memories on the reservation. Slowly, Sheila and I started to get involved in similar shows across the Southwest until we eventually met a couple who made replica Native American clothing and beadwork. I even kitted myself out completely with an authentic Northern Cheyenne traditional costume.

I started collecting Native American artefacts, too, and reading voraciously about Indian history. The more I learned, the more I empathised with their plight, and the way they had been – and remain – abandoned by mainstream America. I wanted to meet people who were as absorbed as I was becoming and, eventually, Sheila and I discovered AIM – the American Indian Movement – which campaigns and fights on their behalf.

I have become ashamed and appalled at the way Native Americans have been reduced to a level of Third-World poverty that shouldn't exist anywhere, never mind in the United States. They have been systematically stripped of their own land, left to rot on reservations where the earth is so impoverished that nothing can grow and cattle have no fodder. There are no jobs for them, no welfare systems, no legal rights and – unwanted and neglected – they have been reduced to insanely dangerous levels of alcoholism and substance abuse. There is nothing else left for them. It is now estimated that 25 per cent of all Native Americans live below the poverty line, and unemployment has reached 93 per cent on some reservations.

Native Americans have been murdered and raped and beaten up, yet the perpetrators have constantly escaped punishment or only been handed minimum sentences by a wider America that simply doesn't care. They've even been targeted by FBI infiltrators and, to this day, AIM leader Leonard Peltier remains imprisoned for the murder of an agent that all credible evidence proves he never committed. Sheila and I are committed AIM members and we both joined a protest in London outside the US Embassy to demand Peltier's release; sadly, former president Barack Obama didn't include him when he granted clemency to selected prisoners shortly before vacating the White House.

Only recently, President Donald Trump steamrollered through the Dakota Access Pipeline, ignoring protests from the Meskwaki and several Sioux tribal nations who feared it would pollute water supplies and cross sacred burial grounds. The brutal reality is that even today, Native Americans are vilified in their own country, which still sees them as the "baddies" in a cowboys and Indians movie; a sort of subhuman race incapable of humanity and feelings and therefore not entitled to normal constitutional rights.

Am I Native American? You're God-damned right I am. If I won the lottery tomorrow, I'd happily give my winnings to AIM. I no longer feel split. There is no ambiguity. In fact, I feel more Native American now than I've ever felt before.

When I die, I will enter the next world as a warrior, but in a spirit of peace. I will be re-united there with my mother and father and I will join all my forefathers. I have accepted death; death will be my homecoming. That is how certain I am that Bob Rose is a Native American.

OUT OF BODY

I open the door to my studio, walk in and immediately stand to attention, facing the giant mirror that covers the entire wall directly opposite me. For a few seconds I glimpse my reflection; I am wearing my black Kenpo uniform. I feel at home in this space. As the studio door closes behind me, I know I have entered another world, maybe another dimension, because I'm about to connect with something that saves my life every day.

Still standing to attention, I solemnly bow to a framed photograph of Senior Grand Master Ed Parker. Next, I bow to a photograph of his wife and then, finally, I bow to an image of the Great Spirit and offer, silently, the physical and mental pain I carry as a sacrifice to him. It is all I can give that truly belongs to me.

I then step forward into the middle of the room and stand directly in the centre, where the eight lines of attack converge on the floor, like a giant clock face. I sense my opponent is already waiting, his legs splayed apart in a familiar Horse Stance, knees slightly bent, upper body straight and ready for battle. We cannot speak; instead we bow respectfully to each other and I offer the Kenpo salutation of Hi Ken: graceful arm movements that tell him I am prepared to fight, my fist is my weapon, my open palm my shield.

I sense him edging towards me, his arms raised menacingly in front of his face, like a boxer, his bare fists clenched ready to unload punches. I can see the whites of his knuckles straining and bulging, and can imagine them smashing into my cheeks and jaws relentlessly. There is ferocity in his eyes and, as he moves closer, the space in front of me diminishes. He looms larger and larger with each approaching step. It's like I am watching my opponent through a rifle viewfinder all over again: I study his stance, his line of attack, how he's positioning his arms and elbows, and I brace myself.

Everything that follows is an explosion, everything happens in a choreographed whirlwind of arms and elbows and legs and fists. There is viciousness and yet immense grace in the way our hands cross each other in elegant-yet-deadly flourishes. His arms reach out menacingly and I am instantly thrown into a chain reaction. I know enough about the body to understand the domino effect – press one part and it will trigger movement elsewhere.

I block his left arm solidly, and execute a classic Crossing Tower movement: my flattened right palm smashes high across his mouth and nose, immediately followed by a rapid elbow straight to his chin and up through his face. Then my right hand takes a vice-like grip round his right arm and drags him down so he's bent double in front of me, his head staring straight to the floor. My left palm crosses the top of his head and my right knee rises to smash into his defenceless face.

He's tough, though, and he knows how to take the blows, breaking clear, re-aligning himself and then coming back for more. I retaliate with a Locked Wing, raising my left elbow over his head, turning myself so I can trap his right arm against the left side of my body. Now I can drag him round through 180 degrees and, as he stoops, I send my raised right knee smashing into his exposed mouth and nose.

He turns swiftly, his body behind me, so I pivot and unravel into a Throwing Wings, my bent right elbow pushing his down and then, in one uninterrupted movement, rising up so that my elbow rams into his face. So much of Kenpo is like this, so much of it one movement rapidly followed by the next and the next until the eye isn't enough to even see where the joins are.

The chain reaction is scientific now; everything is flowing and logical and precise. My movements are rhythmic combinations of circles and lines and angles that culminate in short yet lethal strikes. My body weight finds perfect symmetry within each deadly blow, my breathing stays delicately in tune with each of my violent manoeuvres.

A professor or a painter might see the beauty of it all, the circles within circles, the flow and the artistry within the science. Like I saw the paintings within the synchronised napalm attacks. We carry on, our bodies in opposition yet strangely in unison, our attacking sweeps and probes countered by textbook defences until together our offence and defence seems to blend in balanced fusions of blows and blocks. There are moments when the intensity and speed are almost too fast to comprehend and that's when our senses move into another dimension, when they anticipate and execute movements that are beyond sight and even sound.

We delve deeply into our memory banks for techniques that might make the difference. Instinctively, unprompted, my right elbow whips round in a semi-circular flow and twists so that I can glance a lightning hammer fist right across my opponent's exposed jaw. As I follow through, I am able to push and twist my thumb into his right eye socket. He cannot find the resources to counter and his neck is suddenly exposed for the next stage. My left hand pushes his chin back up violently and, as his head jolts back, my right fist smashes into his windpipe.

And then it happens. As my body executes more and more movements, my soul allows Kenpo to seize complete control and lifts away from my physical being. It's like I'm stepping out of my own frame so I can look back and watch myself twisting and turning, ebbing and flowing.

Only then, in that out-of-body moment, do I truly see how Kenpo directs and leads me. I see its extremes – its conflicting harmonies of beauty and brutality, artistry and attrition, savagery and spirituality. Kenpo has given me those balances – their equanimity has helped save me. Before, I had all the violent parts – but now I also have the counter: I have control. As I look back at myself, I see a human being I barely recognise. I see a strong, honed body that is still defying my advancing years. I see dedication and I see purpose. I see discipline and I see grace and balance and rhythm and belief. I see the spirit of Grey Wolf as I slowly arc from side to side, prowling, patiently sizing my opponent. Like Grey Wolf, my benign, hypnotic movements are just deceptions, camouflaging what lies within: a nuclear fusion of fury and speed and violence, waiting to explode with detonating ferocity. Just like Grey Wolf, Kenpo is beauty and brutality in one body; it can take life and it can save life.

With the spirit of Grey Wolf coursing through my blood and veins, my body and soul re-unite. My opponent and I have fought for over an hour now, exhausting the different forms and techniques within Kenpo until, ultimately, we have balanced each other out. Our duel is coming to an end and it is time to honour each other in the certain knowledge that we will return. So, we come to a standstill and adopt the meditation Horse Stance. Slowly, respectfully, we bow, each crossing a palm over a clenched fist to signify that we depart in peace, without aggression.

I walk back to the studio door and turn to face the mirror for a final time. My opponent has vanished and I smile. He was never there, he didn't exist, and yet I will see him again. I know him so well. He is there every day, in my mind, waiting for me to go through my Kenpo drill.

As I prepare to leave, I catch my reflection once again and pause. Staring back at me is a man prepared for the next life. Bob Rose, a proud Native American, a man who has found an eternal cause, one that will carry him into the spirit world so that he will see his forefathers once again.

Kenpo has made me understand the complete circle of my life.